WILEY

MW01670925

Accessing your Wiley Select CoursePack online

Thank you for purchasing a Wiley Select CoursePack. In addition to the material printed in this book, your CoursePack may contain material that is only available online. The directions below explain how to access the corresponding online version.

To access your CoursePack online:

1. Open a Web browser and go to www.xanedu.com.

2. **If you are a first-time XanEdu user:**
   You'll need to register and create a user name and password. Click the Register link under the "Students" login area. Click the button labeled 'Student Registration.' Complete the online registration form. Enter the 16-digit key shown below, including the hyphens, at the bottom of the form. Submit the form. Your My XanEdu page is displayed.

   If you are already a registered XanEdu user:
   Log in to go to your My XanEdu page. At the bottom of your My XanEdu page is a field labeled 'Do you have a key for a CoursePack.' Enter the 16-digit key shown below, including the hyphens, into this field and click 'Go.'

   The following key is unique. It can be used for only one registration:

   7322-6624-2038-9095

3. Select your CoursePack from the My CoursePacks list and click 'Go'.

Important things to know about the key and your online CoursePack

- You can enter the numeric key shown above only one time. If you have a problem or question, call XanEdu Customer Service at 800-218-5971, or send an email to cust.serv@xanedu.com.

- Access to your digital CoursePack cannot be resold. Once you enter the numeric key, only you can access the CoursePack.

- You will have unlimited access to your digital CoursePack until whichever comes first:
  - ♦ six months after the date of purchase,
  - ♦ or two months after the last day of your course (as specified by your instructor).

- To access your CoursePack at any time:
  1. Open a Web browser and go to www.xanedu.com.
  2. Log in with your user name/password combination.
  3. Select the CoursePack from the My CoursePacks list on your My XanEdu page.
  4. Click 'Go'.

OPIM 365: Management Information Systems

Sulin Ba - Spring 2006
University of Connecticut

ISBN 0471766771

WILEY Business Select

– In print copy only   – Online only

Unmarked items are available both in print and online

OPIM 365: Management Information Systems

Table of Contents

"Strategy and the Internet (HBR OnPoint Enhanced Edition)" by Porter, Michael E. 1

"The Real New Economy (HBR OnPoint Enhanced Edition)" by Farrell, Diana 23

"Chapter 2. The Big Picture: IT and Business" by Paul Gray 37

"The Worldwide Web and Internet Technology, Technology Note" by Austin, Robert D.; Rodd, Thomas 59

"Web and IT Hosting Facilities, Technology Note" by Austin, Robert D. 69

"Digital Certificates and Signatures: Microsoft Corp." by Farhoomand, Ali F.; Ho, Mary 77

"The iPremier Co.: Denial of Service Attack (A)" by Austin, Robert D.; Leibrock, Larry; Murray, Alan 81

"Your Next IT Strategy" by Hagel, John, III; Brown, John Seely 93

"Cisco Systems Architecture: ERP and Web–enabled IT" by Nolan, Richard L.; Porter, Kelley; Akers, Christina 105

"Chapter 4. Enterprise Requirements Planning" by Paul Gray 129

"Chapter 11. IS in Managing Business Operations: The Supply Chain" by Paul Gray 145

"Quantum Corp.: eSupplyChain Group" by McAfee, Andrew; Bounds, Gregory 161

"Monster.com: Success Beyond the Bubble" by Hallowell, Roger; Reavis, Cate 183

Bibliography 205

Harvard Business Review
OnPoint
ARTICLE

www.hbr.org

Strategy and the Internet

by Michael E. Porter

Included with this full-text *Harvard Business Review* article:

1 **Article Summary**
The Idea in Brief—*the core idea*
The Idea in Practice—*putting the idea to work*

3 **Strategy and the Internet**

21 **Further Reading**
A list of related materials, with annotations to guide further exploration of the article's ideas and applications

Product 6358

Harvard Business Review OnPoint

Strategy and the Internet

The Idea in Brief

Does the Internet render established rules about strategy obsolete? To the contrary, it makes them more vital than ever.

Why? The Internet weakens industries' profitability, as rivals compete on price alone. And it no longer provides proprietary advantages, as virtually all companies now use the Web.

The Internet is no more than a tool—albeit a powerful one—that can support or damage your firm's strategic positioning. The key to using it most effectively? *Integrate* Internet initiatives into your company's overall strategy and operations so that they 1) complement, rather than cannibalize, your established competitive approaches and 2) create systemic advantages that your competitors can't copy.

Integrating Internet initiatives enhances your company's ability to develop unique products, proprietary content, distinctive processes, and strong personal service—all the things that create true value, and that have always defined competitive advantage.

The Idea in Practice

THE INTERNET'S INFLUENCE

The Internet powerfully influences industry structure and sustainable competitive advantage.

Industry structure derives from the basic forces of competition: competitor rivalry; entry barriers for new competitors; the threat of substitute offerings; and the bargaining power of suppliers, channels, and buyers. How does the Internet affect these forces?

- It's an open system whose technological advances level most industries' playing fields—thus intensifying competitive rivalry and reducing entry barriers.
- It dramatically increases available information, shifting bargaining power to buyers.

Sustainable competitive advantage comes from operational effectiveness (doing what your competitors do, but better) or strategic positioning (delivering unique value to customers by doing things *differently* than your competitors).

Most companies define Internet competition in terms of operational effectiveness (speed, flexibility, efficiency). But because competitors can easily copy your firm's advances in these areas, strategic positioning becomes most important.

THE INTERNET AS STRATEGIC COMPLEMENT

Although the Internet makes it difficult to sustain operational effectiveness, it makes it easier to maintain strategic positioning. How?

- It lets you create a customized, common information technology platform for all your company's activities—resulting in unique, integrated systems that reinforce the strategic fit among your firm's many functions. Even better, competitors can't easily imitate these systems.
- Rather than cannibalizing your traditional ways of competing, it can complement them. For example, the Walgreens drugstore chain provides on-line prescription ordering. Because 90% of customers who order over the Web prefer to pick up their prescriptions at a store, Walgreens brick-and-mortar business benefits.
- By integrating virtual and physical activities to compensate for the Internet's performance limits (e.g., customers can't physically touch and test products), companies gain competitive advantage. For example, if you use your Web site to attract customers and draw them to flesh-and-blood salespeople who provide personalized advice and after-sales service, you reinforce connections—and strengthen sales.

The question isn't whether you should use the Internet or traditional methods to compete; it's how you can use *both* to your greatest strategic advantage.

Many have argued that the Internet renders strategy obsolete. In reality, the opposite is true. Because the Internet tends to weaken industry profitability without providing proprietary operational advantages, it is more important than ever for companies to distinguish themselves through strategy. The winners will be those that view the Internet as a complement to, not a cannibal of, traditional ways of competing.

Strategy and the Internet

by Michael E. Porter

The Internet is an extremely important new technology, and it is no surprise that it has received so much attention from entrepreneurs, executives, investors, and business observers. Caught up in the general fervor, many have assumed that the Internet changes everything, rendering all the old rules about companies and competition obsolete. That may be a natural reaction, but it is a dangerous one. It has led many companies, dot-coms and incumbents alike, to make bad decisions—decisions that have eroded the attractiveness of their industries and undermined their own competitive advantages. Some companies, for example, have used Internet technology to shift the basis of competition away from quality, features, and service and toward price, making it harder for anyone in their industries to turn a profit. Others have forfeited important proprietary advantages by rushing into misguided partnerships and outsourcing relationships. Until recently, the negative effects of these actions have been obscured by distorted signals from the marketplace. Now, however, the consequences are becoming evident.

The time has come to take a clearer view of the Internet. We need to move away from the rhetoric about "Internet industries," "e-business strategies," and a "new economy" and see the Internet for what it is: an enabling technology—a powerful set of tools that can be used, wisely or unwisely, in almost any industry and as part of almost any strategy. We need to ask fundamental questions: Who will capture the economic benefits that the Internet creates? Will all the value end up going to customers, or will companies be able to reap a share of it? What will be the Internet's impact on industry structure? Will it expand or shrink the pool of profits? And what will be its impact on strategy? Will the Internet bolster or erode the ability of companies to gain sustainable advantages over their competitors?

In addressing these questions, much of what we find is unsettling. I believe that the experiences companies have had with the Internet thus far must be largely discounted and that many of the lessons learned must be forgotten.

When seen with fresh eyes, it becomes clear that the Internet is not necessarily a blessing. It tends to alter industry structures in ways that dampen overall profitability, and it has a leveling effect on business practices, reducing the ability of any company to establish an operational advantage that can be sustained.

The key question is not whether to deploy Internet technology—companies have no choice if they want to stay competitive—but how to deploy it. Here, there is reason for optimism. Internet technology provides better opportunities for companies to establish distinctive strategic positionings than did previous generations of information technology. Gaining such a competitive advantage does not require a radically new approach to business. It requires building on the proven principles of effective strategy. The Internet per se will rarely be a competitive advantage. Many of the companies that succeed will be ones that use the Internet as a complement to traditional ways of competing, not those that set their Internet initiatives apart from their established operations. That is particularly good news for established companies, which are often in the best position to meld Internet and traditional approaches in ways that buttress existing advantages. But dot-coms can also be winners—if they understand the trade-offs between Internet and traditional approaches and can fashion truly distinctive strategies. Far from making strategy less important, as some have argued, the Internet actually makes strategy more essential than ever.

Distorted Market Signals

Companies that have deployed Internet technology have been confused by distorted market signals, often of their own creation. It is understandable, when confronted with a new business phenomenon, to look to marketplace outcomes for guidance. But in the early stages of the rollout of any important new technology, market signals can be unreliable. New technologies trigger rampant experimentation, by both companies and customers, and the experimentation is often economically unsustainable. As a result, market behavior is distorted and must be interpreted with caution.

That is certainly the case with the Internet. Consider the revenue side of the profit equation in industries in which Internet technology is widely used. Sales figures have been unreliable for three reasons. First, many companies have subsidized the purchase of their products and services in hopes of staking out a position on the Internet and attracting a base of customers. (Governments have also subsidized on-line shopping by exempting it from sales taxes.) Buyers have been able to purchase goods at heavy discounts, or even obtain them for free, rather than pay prices that reflect true costs. When prices are artificially low, unit demand becomes artificially high. Second, many buyers have been drawn to the Internet out of curiosity; they have been willing to conduct transactions on-line even when the benefits have been uncertain or limited. If Amazon.com offers an equal or lower price than a conventional bookstore and free or subsidized shipping, why not try it as an experiment? Sooner or later, though, some customers can be expected to return to more traditional modes of commerce, especially if subsidies end, making any assessment of customer loyalty based on conditions so far suspect. Finally, some "revenues" from on-line commerce have been received in the form of stock rather than cash. Much of the estimated $450 million in revenues that Amazon has recognized from its corporate partners, for example, has come as stock. The sustainability of such revenue is questionable, and its true value hinges on fluctuations in stock prices.

If revenue is an elusive concept on the Internet, cost is equally fuzzy. Many companies doing business on-line have enjoyed subsidized inputs. Their suppliers, eager to affiliate themselves with and learn from dot-com leaders, have provided products, services, and content at heavily discounted prices. Many content providers, for example, rushed to provide their information to Yahoo! for next to nothing in hopes of establishing a beachhead on one of the Internet's most visited sites. Some providers have even paid popular portals to distribute their content. Further masking true costs, many suppliers—not to mention employees—have agreed to accept equity, warrants, or stock options from Internet-related companies and ventures in payment for their services or products. Payment in equity does not appear on the income statement, but it is a real cost to shareholders. Such supplier practices have artificially depressed the costs of doing business on the Internet, making it appear more attractive than it really is. Finally, costs have been

Michael E. Porter is the Bishop William Lawrence University Professor at Harvard University; he is based at Harvard Business School in Boston. He has written many articles for HBR; the most recent, "Philanthropy's New Agenda: Creating Value," coauthored by Mark R. Kramer, appeared in the November–December 1999 issue. His book *Can Japan Compete?*, coauthored by Hirotaka Takeuchi and Mariko Sakakibara, was recently published in the United States by Perseus/Basic Books.

distorted by the systematic understatement of the need for capital. Company after company touted the low asset intensity of doing business on-line, only to find that inventory, warehouses, and other investments were necessary to provide value to customers.

Signals from the stock market have been even more unreliable. Responding to investor enthusiasm over the Internet's explosive growth, stock valuations became decoupled from business fundamentals. They no longer provided an accurate guide as to whether real economic value was being created. Any company that has made competitive decisions based on influencing near-term share price or responding to investor sentiments has put itself at risk.

Distorted revenues, costs, and share prices have been matched by the unreliability of the financial metrics that companies have adopted. The executives of companies conducting business over the Internet have, conveniently, downplayed traditional measures of profitability and economic value. Instead, they have emphasized expansive definitions of revenue, numbers of customers, or, even more suspect, measures that might someday correlate with revenue, such as numbers of unique users ("reach"), numbers of site visitors, or click-through rates. Creative accounting approaches have also multiplied. Indeed, the Internet has given rise to an array of new performance metrics that have only a loose relationship to economic value, such as pro forma measures of income that remove "nonrecurring" costs like acquisitions. The dubious connection between reported metrics and actual profitability has served only to amplify the confusing signals about what has been working in the marketplace. The fact that those metrics have been taken seriously by the stock market has muddied the waters even further. For all these reasons, the true financial performance of many Internet-related businesses is even worse than has been stated.

One might argue that the simple proliferation of dot-coms is a sign of the economic value of the Internet. Such a conclusion is premature at best. Dot-coms multiplied so rapidly for one major reason: they were able to raise capital without having to demonstrate viability. Rather than signaling a healthy business environment, the sheer number of dot-coms in many industries often revealed nothing more than the existence of low barriers to entry, always a danger sign.

A Return to Fundamentals

It is hard to come to any firm understanding of the impact of the Internet on business by looking at the results to date. But two broad conclusions can be drawn. First, many businesses active on the Internet are artificial businesses competing by artificial means and propped up by capital that until recently had been readily available. Second, in periods of transition such as the one we have been going through, it often appears as if there are new rules of competition. But as market forces play out, as they are now, the old rules regain their currency. The creation of true economic value once again becomes the final arbiter of business success.

Economic value for a company is nothing more than the gap between price and cost, and it is reliably measured only by sustained profitability. To generate revenues, reduce expenses, or simply do something useful by deploying Internet technology is not sufficient evidence that value has been created. Nor is a company's current stock price necessarily an indicator of economic value. Shareholder value is a reliable measure of economic value only over the long run.

In thinking about economic value, it is useful to draw a distinction between the uses of the Internet (such as operating digital marketplaces, selling toys, or trading securities) and Internet technologies (such as site-customization tools or real-time communications services), which can be deployed across many uses. Many have pointed to the success of technology providers as evidence of the Internet's economic value. But this thinking is faulty. It is the uses of the Internet that ultimately create economic value. Technology providers can prosper for a time irrespective of whether the uses of the Internet are profitable. In periods of heavy experimentation, even sellers of flawed technologies can thrive. But unless the uses generate sustainable revenues or savings in excess of their cost of deployment, the opportunity for technology providers will shrivel as companies realize that further investment is economically unsound.

So how can the Internet be used to create economic value? To find the answer, we need to look beyond the immediate market signals

Internet technology provides better opportunities for companies to establish distinctive strategic positionings than did previous generations of information technology.

to the two fundamental factors that determine profitability:

• *industry structure*, which determines the profitability of the average competitor; and

• *sustainable competitive advantage*, which allows a company to outperform the average competitor.

These two underlying drivers of profitability are universal; they transcend any technology or type of business. At the same time, they vary widely by industry and company. The broad, supra-industry classifications so common in Internet parlance, such as business-to-consumer (or "B2C") and business-to-business (or "B2B") prove meaningless with respect to profitability. Potential profitability can be understood only by looking at individual industries and individual companies.

The Internet and Industry Structure

The Internet has created some new industries, such as on-line auctions and digital marketplaces. However, its greatest impact has been to enable the reconfiguration of existing industries that had been constrained by high costs for communicating, gathering information, or accomplishing transactions. Distance learning, for example, has existed for decades, with about one million students enrolling in correspondence courses every year. The Internet has the potential to greatly expand distance learning, but it did not create the industry. Similarly, the Internet provides an efficient means to order products, but catalog retailers with toll-free numbers and automated fulfillment centers have been around for decades. The Internet only changes the front end of the process.

Whether an industry is new or old, its structural attractiveness is determined by five underlying forces of competition: the intensity of rivalry among existing competitors, the barriers to entry for new competitors, the threat of substitute products or services, the bargaining power of suppliers, and the bargaining power of buyers. In combination, these forces determine how the economic value created by any product, service, technology, or way of competing is divided between, on the one hand, companies in an industry and, on the other, customers, suppliers, distributors, substitutes, and potential new entrants. Although some have argued that today's rapid pace of technological change makes industry analysis less valuable, the opposite is true. Analyzing the forces illuminates an industry's fundamental attractiveness, exposes the underlying drivers of average industry profitability, and provides insight into how profitability will evolve in the future. The five competitive forces still determine profitability even if suppliers, channels, substitutes, or competitors change.

Because the strength of each of the five forces varies considerably from industry to industry, it would be a mistake to draw general conclusions about the impact of the Internet on long-term industry profitability; each industry is affected in different ways. Nevertheless, an examination of a wide range of industries in which the Internet is playing a role reveals some clear trends, as summarized in the exhibit "How the Internet Influences Industry Structure." Some of the trends are positive. For example, the Internet tends to dampen the bargaining power of channels by providing companies with new, more direct avenues to customers. The Internet can also boost an industry's efficiency in various ways, expanding the overall size of the market by improving its position relative to traditional substitutes.

But most of the trends are negative. Internet technology provides buyers with easier access to information about products and suppliers, thus bolstering buyer bargaining power. The Internet mitigates the need for such things as an established sales force or access to existing channels, reducing barriers to entry. By enabling new approaches to meeting needs and performing functions, it creates new substitutes. Because it is an open system, companies have more difficulty maintaining proprietary offerings, thus intensifying the rivalry among competitors. The use of the Internet also tends to expand the geographic market, bringing many more companies into competition with one another. And Internet technologies tend to reduce variable costs and tilt cost structures toward fixed cost, creating significantly greater pressure for companies to engage in destructive price competition.

While deploying the Internet can expand the market, then, doing so often comes at the expense of average profitability. The great paradox of the Internet is that its very benefits—making information widely available; reducing the difficulty of purchasing, marketing, and distribution; allowing buyers and sellers to find and transact business with one another more easily—also make it more difficult for companies to capture those benefits as profits.

We can see this dynamic at work in automobile retailing. The Internet allows customers to gather extensive information about products easily, from detailed specifications and repair records to wholesale prices for new cars and average values for used cars. Customers can also choose among many more options from which to buy, not just local dealers but also various types of Internet referral networks (such as Autoweb and AutoVantage) and on-line direct dealers (such as Autobytel.com, AutoNation, and CarsDirect.com). Because the Internet reduces the importance of location, at least for the initial sale, it widens the geographic market from local to regional or national. Virtually every dealer or dealer group becomes a potential competitor in the market. It is more difficult, moreover, for on-line dealers to differentiate themselves, as they lack potential points of distinction such as showrooms, personal selling, and service departments. With more competitors selling

How the Internet Influences Industry Structure

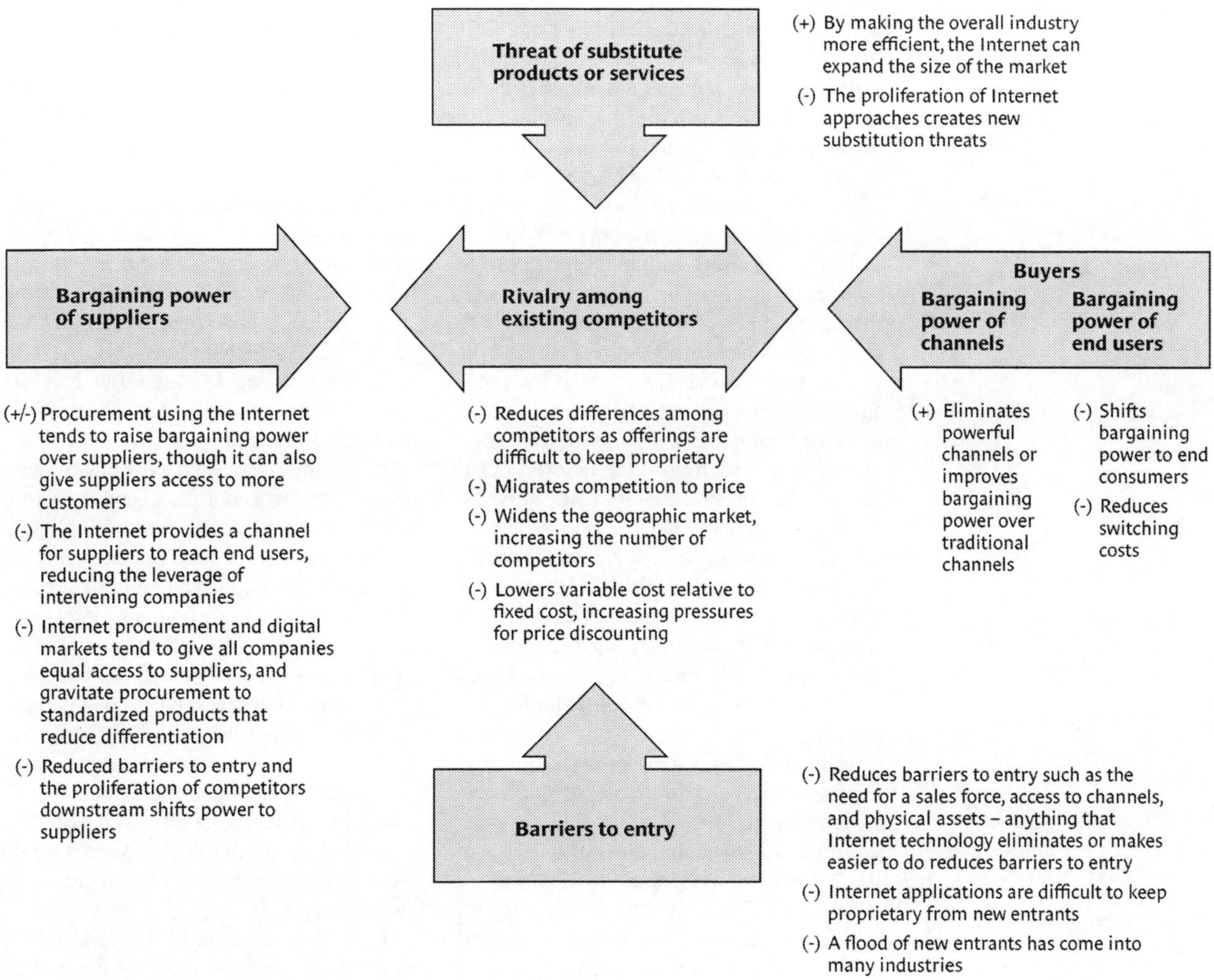

This discussion is drawn from the author's research with David Sutton.
For a fuller discussion, see M.E. Porter, *Competitive Strategy*, Free Press, 1980.

largely undifferentiated products, the basis for competition shifts ever more toward price. Clearly, the net effect on the industry's structure is negative.

That does not mean that every industry in which Internet technology is being applied will be unattractive. For a contrasting example, look at Internet auctions. Here, customers and suppliers are fragmented and thus have little power. Substitutes, such as classified ads and flea markets, have less reach and are less convenient to use. And though the barriers to entry are relatively modest, companies can build economies of scale, both in infrastructure and, even more important, in the aggregation of many buyers and sellers, that deter new competitors or place them at a disadvantage. Finally, rivalry in this industry has been defined, largely by eBay, the dominant competitor, in terms of providing an easy-to-use marketplace in which revenue comes from listing and sales fees, while customers pay the cost of shipping. When Amazon and other rivals entered the business, offering free auctions, eBay maintained its prices and pursued other ways to attract and retain customers. As a result, the destructive price competition characteristic of other on-line businesses has been avoided.

EBay's role in the auction business provides an important lesson: industry structure is not fixed but rather is shaped to a considerable degree by the choices made by competitors. EBay has acted in ways that strengthen the profitability of its industry. In stark contrast, Buy.com, a prominent Internet retailer, acted in ways that undermined its industry, not to mention its own potential for competitive advantage. Buy.com achieved $100 million in sales faster than any company in history, but it did so by defining competition solely on price. It sold products not only below full cost but at or below cost of goods sold, with the vain hope that it would make money in other ways. The company had no plan for being the low-cost provider; instead, it invested heavily in brand advertising and eschewed potential sources of differentiation by outsourcing all fulfillment and offering the bare minimum of customer service. It also gave up the opportunity to set itself apart from competitors by choosing not to focus on selling particular goods; it moved quickly beyond electronics, its initial category, into numerous other product categories in which it had no unique offering. Although the company has been trying desperately to reposition itself, its early moves have proven extremely difficult to reverse.

The Myth of the First Mover

Given the negative implications of the Internet for profitability, why was there such optimism, even euphoria, surrounding its adoption? One reason is that everyone tended to focus on what the Internet could do and how quickly its use was expanding rather than on how it was affecting industry structure. But the optimism can also be traced to a widespread belief that the Internet would unleash forces that would enhance industry profitability. Most notable was the general assumption that the deployment of the Internet would increase switching costs and create strong network effects, which would provide first movers with competitive advantages and robust profitability. First movers would reinforce these advantages by quickly establishing strong new-economy brands. The result would be an attractive industry for the victors. This thinking does not, however, hold up to close examination.

Consider switching costs. Switching costs encompass all the costs incurred by a customer in changing to a new supplier—everything from hashing out a new contract to reentering data to learning how to use a different product or service. As switching costs go up, customers' bargaining power falls and the barriers to entry into an industry rise. While switching costs are nothing new, some observers argued that the Internet would raise them substantially. A buyer would grow familiar with one company's user interface and would not want to bear the cost of finding, registering with, and learning to use a competitor's site, or, in the case of industrial customers, integrating a competitor's systems with its own. Moreover, since Internet commerce allows a company to accumulate knowledge of customers' buying behavior, the company would be able to provide more tailored offerings, better service, and greater purchasing convenience—all of which buyers would be loath to forfeit. When people talk about the "stickiness" of Web sites, what they are often talking about is high switching costs.

In reality, though, switching costs are likely to be lower, not higher, on the Internet than they are for traditional ways of doing business, including approaches using earlier generations of information systems such as EDI. On the Internet, buyers can often switch suppliers with just a few mouse clicks, and new Web technologies are systematically reducing switching costs even further. For example, companies like PayPal provide settlement services or Internet currency—so-called e-wallets—that enable customers to shop at different sites without having to enter personal information and credit card numbers. Content-consolidation tools such as OnePage allow users to avoid having to go back to sites over and over to retrieve information by enabling them to build customized Web pages that draw needed information dynamically from many sites. And the widespread adoption of XML standards will free companies from the need to reconfigure proprietary ordering systems and to create new procurement and logistical protocols when changing suppliers.

What about network effects, through which products or services become more valuable as more customers use them? A number of important Internet applications display network effects, including e-mail, instant messaging, auctions, and on-line message boards or chat rooms. Where such effects are significant, they can create demand-side economies of scale and raise barriers to entry. This, it has been widely argued, sets off a winner-take-all competition, leading to the eventual dominance of one or two companies.

But it is not enough for network effects to be present; to provide barriers to entry they also have to be proprietary to one company. The openness of the Internet, with its common standards and protocols and its ease of navigation, makes it difficult for a single company to capture the benefits of a network effect. (America Online, which has managed to maintain borders around its on-line community, is an exception, not the rule.) And even if a company is lucky enough to control a network effect, the effect often reaches a point of diminishing returns once there is a critical mass of customers. Moreover, network effects are subject to a self-limiting mechanism. A particular product or service first attracts the customers whose needs it best meets. As penetration grows, however, it will tend to become less effective in meeting the needs of the remaining customers in the market, providing an opening for competitors with different offerings. Finally, creating a network effect requires a large investment that may offset future benefits. The network effect is, in many respects, akin to the experience curve, which was also supposed to lead to market-share dominance—through cost advantages, in that case. The experience curve was an oversimplification, and the single-minded pursuit of experience curve advantages proved disastrous in many industries.

Internet brands have also proven difficult to build, perhaps because the lack of physical presence and direct human contact makes virtual businesses less tangible to customers than traditional businesses. Despite huge outlays on advertising, product discounts, and purchasing incentives, most dot-com brands have not approached the power of established brands, achieving only a modest impact on loyalty and barriers to entry.

Another myth that has generated unfounded enthusiasm for the Internet is that partnering is a win-win means to improve industry economics. While partnering is a well-established strategy, the use of Internet technology has made it much more widespread. Partnering takes two forms. The first involves complements: products that are used in tandem with another industry's product. Computer software, for example, is a complement to computer hardware. In Internet commerce, complements have proliferated as companies have sought to offer broader arrays of products, services, and information. Partnering to assemble complements, often with companies who are also competitors, has been seen as a way to speed industry growth and move away from narrow-minded, destructive competition.

Another myth that has generated unfounded enthusiasm for the Internet is that partnering is a win-win means to improve industry economics.

But this approach reveals an incomplete understanding of the role of complements in competition. Complements are frequently important to an industry's growth—spreadsheet applications, for example, accelerated the expansion of the personal computer industry—but they have no direct relationship to industry profitability. While a close substitute reduces potential profitability, for example, a close complement can exert either a positive or a negative influence. Complements affect industry profitability indirectly through their influence on the five competitive forces. If a complement raises switching costs for the combined product offering, it can raise profitability. But if a complement works to standardize the industry's product offering, as Microsoft's operating system has done in personal computers, it will increase rivalry and depress profitability.

With the Internet, widespread partnering with producers of complements is just as likely to exacerbate an industry's structural problems as mitigate them. As partnerships proliferate, companies tend to become more alike, which heats up rivalry. Instead of focusing on their own strategic goals, moreover, companies are forced to balance the many potentially conflicting objectives of their partners while also educating them about the business. Rivalry often becomes more unstable, and since producers of complements can be potential competitors, the threat of entry increases.

Another common form of partnering is outsourcing. Internet technologies have made it easier for companies to coordinate with their suppliers, giving widespread currency to the notion of the "virtual enterprise"—a business created largely out of purchased products, components, and services. While extensive outsourcing can reduce near-term costs and improve flexibility, it has a dark side when it comes to industry structure. As competitors turn to the same vendors, purchased inputs become more homogeneous, eroding company distinctiveness and increasing price competition. Outsourcing also usually lowers barriers to entry because a new entrant need only assemble purchased inputs rather than build its own capabilities. In addition, companies lose control over important elements of their business, and crucial experience in components, assembly, or services shifts to suppliers, enhancing their power in the long run.

The Future of Internet Competition

While each industry will evolve in unique ways, an examination of the forces influencing industry structure indicates that the deployment of Internet technology will likely continue to put pressure on the profitability of many industries. Consider the intensity of competition, for example. Many dot-coms are going out of business, which would seem to indicate that consolidation will take place and rivalry will be reduced. But while some consolidation among new players is inevitable, many established companies are now more familiar with Internet technology and are rapidly deploying on-line applications. With a combination of new and old companies and generally lower entry barriers, most industries will likely end up with a net increase in the number of competitors and fiercer rivalry than before the advent of the Internet.

The power of customers will also tend to rise. As buyers' initial curiosity with the Web wanes and subsidies end, companies offering products or services on-line will be forced to demonstrate that they provide real benefits. Already, customers appear to be losing interest in services like Priceline.com's reverse auctions because the savings they provide are often outweighed by the hassles involved. As customers become more familiar with the technology, their loyalty to their initial suppliers will also decline; they will realize that the cost of switching is low.

A similar shift will affect advertising-based strategies. Even now, advertisers are becoming more discriminating, and the rate of growth of Web advertising is slowing. Advertisers can be expected to continue to exercise their bargaining power to push down rates significantly, aided and abetted by new brokers of Internet advertising.

Not all the news is bad. Some technological advances will provide opportunities to enhance profitability. Improvements in streaming video and greater availability of low-cost bandwidth, for example, will make it easier for customer service representatives, or other company personnel, to speak directly to customers through their computers. Internet sellers will be able to better differentiate themselves and shift buyers' focus away from price. And services such as automatic bill paying by banks may modestly boost switching costs. In general, however, new Internet technologies will continue to erode profitability by shifting power to customers.

To understand the importance of thinking through the longer-term structural consequences of the Internet, consider the business of digital marketplaces. Such marketplaces automate corporate procurement by linking many buyers and suppliers electronically. The benefits to buyers include low transaction costs, easier access to price and product information, convenient purchase of associated services, and, sometimes, the ability to pool volume. The benefits to suppliers include lower selling costs, lower transaction costs, access to wider markets, and the avoidance of powerful channels.

From an industry structure standpoint, the attractiveness of digital marketplaces varies depending on the products involved. The most important determinant of a marketplace's profit potential is the intrinsic power of the buyers and sellers in the particular product area. If either side is concentrated or possesses differentiated products, it will gain bargaining power over the marketplace and capture most of the value generated. If buyers and sellers are fragmented, however, their bargaining power will be weak, and the marketplace will have a much better chance of being profitable. Another important determinant of industry structure is the threat of substitution. If it is relatively easy for buyers and sellers to transact business directly with one another, or to set up their own dedicated markets, independent marketplaces will be unlikely to sustain high levels of profit. Finally, the ability to create barriers to entry is critical. Today, with dozens of marketplaces competing in some industries and with buyers and sellers dividing their purchases or operating their own markets to prevent any one marketplace from gaining power, it is clear that modest entry barriers are a real challenge to profitability.

Competition among digital marketplaces is in transition, and industry structure is evolving. Much of the economic value created by marketplaces derives from the standards they establish, both in the underlying technology platform and in the protocols for connecting and exchanging information. But once these standards are put in place, the added value of the marketplace may be limited. Anything buyers or suppliers provide to a marketplace, such as information on order specifications or inventory availability, can be readily provided on their own proprietary sites. Suppliers and customers can begin to deal directly on-line without the need for an intermediary. And new technologies will undoubtedly make it easier for parties to search for and exchange goods and information with one another.

In some product areas, marketplaces should enjoy ongoing advantages and attractive profitability. In fragmented industries such as real estate and furniture, for example, they could prosper. And new kinds of value-added services may arise that only an independent marketplace could provide. But in many product areas, marketplaces may be superceded by direct dealing or by the unbundling of purchasing, information, financing, and logistical services; in other areas, they may be taken over by participants or industry associations as cost centers. In such cases, marketplaces will provide a valuable "public good" to participants but will not themselves be likely to reap any enduring benefits. Over the long haul, moreover, we may well see many buyers back away from open marketplaces. They may once again focus on building close, proprietary relationships with fewer suppliers, using Internet technologies to gain efficiency improvements in various aspects of those relationships.

The Internet and Competitive Advantage

If average profitability is under pressure in many industries influenced by the Internet, it becomes all the more important for individual companies to set themselves apart from the pack—to be more profitable than the average performer. The only way to do so is by achieving a sustainable competitive advantage—by operating at a lower cost, by commanding a premium price, or by doing both. Cost and price advantages can be achieved in two ways. One is operational effectiveness—doing the same things your competitors do but doing them better. Operational effectiveness advantages can take myriad forms, including better technologies, superior inputs, better-trained people, or a more effective management structure. The other way to achieve advantage is strategic positioning—doing things differently from competitors, in a way that delivers a unique type of value to customers. This can mean offering a different set of features, a different array of services, or different logistical arrangements. The Internet affects operational effectiveness and strategic positioning in very different ways. It makes it harder for companies to sustain operational advantages, but it opens new opportunities for achieving or strengthening a distinctive strategic positioning.

Operational Effectiveness. The Internet is arguably the most powerful tool available today for enhancing operational effectiveness. By easing and speeding the exchange of real-time information, it enables improvements throughout the entire value chain, across almost every company and industry. And because it is an open platform with common standards, companies can often tap into its benefits with much less investment than was required to capitalize on past generations of information technology.

But simply improving operational effectiveness does not provide a competitive advantage. Companies only gain advantages if they are able to achieve and sustain higher levels of operational effectiveness than competitors. That is an exceedingly difficult proposition even in the best of circumstances. Once a company establishes a new best practice, its rivals tend to copy it quickly. Best practice competition eventually leads to competitive convergence, with many companies doing the same things in the same ways. Customers end up making decisions based on price, undermining industry profitability.

The nature of Internet applications makes it more difficult to sustain operational advantages than ever. In previous generations of information technology, application development was often complex, arduous, time consuming, and hugely expensive. These traits made it harder to gain an IT advantage, but they also made it difficult for competitors to imitate information systems. The openness of the Internet, combined with advances in software architecture, development tools, and modularity, makes it much easier for companies to design and implement applications. The drugstore chain CVS, for example, was able to roll out a complex Internet-based procurement application in just 60 days. As the fixed costs of developing systems decline, the barriers to imitation fall as well.

Today, nearly every company is developing similar types of Internet applications, often drawing on generic packages offered by third-party developers. The resulting improvements in operational effectiveness will be broadly shared, as companies converge on the same applications with the same benefits. Very rarely will individual companies be able to gain durable advantages from the deployment of "best-of-breed" applications.

Strategic Positioning. As it becomes harder to sustain operational advantages, strategic positioning becomes all the more important. If a company cannot be more operationally effective than its rivals, the only way to generate higher levels of economic value is to gain a cost advantage or price premium by competing in a distinctive way. Ironically, companies today define competition involving the Internet almost entirely in terms of operational effectiveness. Believing that no sustainable advantages exist, they seek speed and agility, hoping to stay one step ahead of the competition. Of course, such an approach to competition becomes a self-fulfilling prophecy. Without a distinctive strategic direction, speed and flexibility lead nowhere. Either no unique competitive advantages are created, or improvements are generic and cannot be sustained.

Having a strategy is a matter of discipline. It requires a strong focus on profitability rather than just growth, an ability to define a unique value proposition, and a willingness to make tough trade-offs in choosing what not to do. A company must stay the course, even during times of upheaval, while constantly improving and extending its distinctive positioning. Strategy goes far beyond the pursuit of best practices. It involves the configuration of a tailored value chain—the series of activities required to produce and deliver a product or service—that enables a company to offer unique value. To be defensible, moreover, the value chain must be highly integrated. When a company's activities fit together as a self-reinforcing system, any competitor wishing to imitate a strategy must replicate the whole system rather than copy just one or two discrete product features or ways of performing particular activities. (See the sidebar "The Six Principles of Strategic Positioning.")

The Absence of Strategy

Many of the pioneers of Internet business, both dot-coms and established companies, have competed in ways that violate nearly every precept of good strategy. Rather than focus on profits, they have sought to maximize revenue and market share at all costs, pursuing customers indiscriminately through discounting, giveaways, promotions, channel incentives, and heavy advertising. Rather than concentrate on delivering real value that earns an attractive price from customers, they have pursued indirect revenues from sources such as advertising and click-through fees from Internet commerce partners. Rather than make trade-offs, they have rushed to offer every conceivable product, service, or type of information. Rather than tailor the value chain in a unique way, they have aped the activities of rivals. Rather than build and maintain control over proprietary assets and marketing channels, they have entered into a rash of partnerships and outsourcing relationships, further eroding their own distinctiveness. While it is true that some companies have avoided these mistakes, they are exceptions to the rule.

By ignoring strategy, many companies have undermined the structure of their industries, hastened competitive convergence, and reduced the likelihood that they or anyone else will gain a competitive advantage. A destructive, zero-sum form of competition has been set in motion that confuses the acquisition of customers with the building of profitability. Worse yet, price has been defined as the primary if not the sole competitive variable. Instead of emphasizing the Internet's ability to support convenience, service, specialization, customization, and other forms of value that justify attractive prices, companies have turned competition into a race to the bottom. Once competition is defined this way, it is very difficult to turn back. (See the sidebar "Words for the Unwise: The Internet's Destructive Lexicon.")

Even well-established, well-run companies have been thrown off track by the Internet. Forgetting what they stand for or what makes them unique, they have rushed to implement hot Internet applications and copy the offerings of dot-coms. Industry leaders have compromised their existing competitive advantages by entering market segments to which they bring little that is distinctive. Merrill Lynch's move to imitate the low-cost on-line offerings of its trading rivals, for example, risks undermining its most precious advantage—its skilled brokers. And many established companies, reacting to misguided investor enthusiasm, have hastily cobbled together Internet

The Six Principles of Strategic Positioning

To establish and maintain a distinctive strategic positioning, a company needs to follow six fundamental principles.

First, it must start with the *right goal*: superior long-term return on investment. Only by grounding strategy in sustained profitability will real economic value be generated. Economic value is created when customers are willing to pay a price for a product or service that exceeds the cost of producing it. When goals are defined in terms of volume or market share leadership, with profits assumed to follow, poor strategies often result. The same is true when strategies are set to respond to the perceived desires of investors.

Second, a company's strategy must enable it to deliver a *value proposition*, or set of benefits, different from those that competitors offer. Strategy, then, is neither a quest for the universally best way of competing nor an effort to be all things to every customer. It defines a way of competing that delivers unique value in a particular set of uses or for a particular set of customers.

Third, strategy needs to be reflected in a *distinctive value chain*. To establish a sustainable competitive advantage, a company must perform different activities than rivals or perform similar activities in different ways. A company must configure the way it conducts manufacturing, logistics, service delivery, marketing, human resource management, and so on differently from rivals and tailored to its unique value proposition. If a company focuses on adopting best practices, it will end up performing most activities similarly to competitors, making it hard to gain an advantage.

Fourth, robust strategies involve *trade-offs*. A company must abandon or forgo some product features, services, or activities in order to be unique at others. Such trade-offs, in the product and in the value chain, are what make a company truly distinctive. When improvements in the product or in the value chain do not require trade-offs, they often become new best practices that are imitated because competitors can do so with no sacrifice to their existing ways of competing. Trying to be all things to all customers almost guarantees that a company will lack any advantage.

Fifth, strategy defines how all the elements of what a company does *fit* together. A strategy involves making choices throughout the value chain that are interdependent; all a company's activities must be mutually reinforcing. A company's product design, for example, should reinforce its approach to the manufacturing process, and both should leverage the way it conducts after-sales service. Fit not only increases competitive advantage but also makes a strategy harder to imitate. Rivals can copy one activity or product feature fairly easily, but will have much more difficulty duplicating a whole system of competing. Without fit, discrete improvements in manufacturing, marketing, or distribution are quickly matched.

Finally, strategy involves *continuity* of direction. A company must define a distinctive value proposition that it will stand for, even if that means forgoing certain opportunities. Without continuity of direction, it is difficult for companies to develop unique skills and assets or build strong reputations with customers. Frequent corporate "reinvention," then, is usually a sign of poor strategic thinking and a route to mediocrity. Continuous improvement is a necessity, but it must always be guided by a strategic direction.

For a fuller description, see M.E. Porter, "What Is Strategy?" (HBR November–December 1996).

units in a mostly futile effort to boost their value in the stock market.

It did not have to be this way—and it does not have to be in the future. When it comes to reinforcing a distinctive strategy, tailoring activities, and enhancing fit, the Internet actually provides a better technological platform than previous generations of IT. Indeed, IT worked against strategy in the past. Packaged software applications were hard to customize, and companies were often forced to change the way they conducted activities in order to conform to the "best practices" embedded in the software. It was also extremely difficult to connect discrete applications to one another. Enterprise resource planning (ERP) systems linked activities, but again companies were forced to adapt their ways of doing things to the software. As a result, IT has been a force for standardizing activities and speeding competitive convergence.

Internet architecture, together with other improvements in software architecture and development tools, has turned IT into a far more powerful tool for strategy. It is much easier to customize packaged Internet applications to a company's unique strategic positioning. By providing a common IT delivery platform across the value chain, Internet architecture and standards also make it possible to build truly integrated and customized systems that reinforce the fit among activities. (See the sidebar "The Internet and the Value Chain.")

To gain these advantages, however, companies need to stop their rush to adopt generic, "out of the box" packaged applications and instead tailor their deployment of Internet technology to their particular strategies. Although it remains more difficult to customize packaged applications, the very difficulty of the task contributes to the sustainability of the resulting competitive advantage.

The Internet as Complement

To capitalize on the Internet's strategic potential, executives and entrepreneurs alike will need to change their points of view. It has been widely assumed that the Internet is cannibalistic, that it will replace all conventional ways of doing business and overturn all traditional advantages. That is a vast exaggeration. There is no doubt that real trade-offs can exist between Internet and traditional activities. In the record industry, for example, on-line music distribution may reduce the need for CD-manufacturing assets. Overall, however, the trade-offs are modest in most industries. While the Internet will replace certain elements of industry value chains, the complete cannibalization of the value chain will be exceedingly rare. Even in the music business, many traditional activities—such as finding and promoting talented new artists, producing and recording music, and securing airplay—will continue to be highly important.

The risk of channel conflict also appears to have been overstated. As on-line sales have become more common, traditional channels that were initially skeptical of the Internet have embraced it. Far from always cannibalizing those channels, Internet technology can expand opportunities for many of them. The threat of disintermediation of channels appears considerably lower than initially predicted.

Frequently, in fact, Internet applications address activities that, while necessary, are not decisive in competition, such as informing customers, processing transactions, and procuring inputs. Critical corporate assets—skilled personnel, proprietary product technology, efficient logistical systems—remain intact, and they are often strong enough to preserve existing competitive advantages.

Words for the Unwise: The Internet's Destructive Lexicon

The misguided approach to competition that characterizes business on the Internet has even been embedded in the language used to discuss it. Instead of talking in terms of strategy and competitive advantage, dot-coms and other Internet players talk about "business models." This seemingly innocuous shift in terminology speaks volumes. The definition of a business model is murky at best. Most often, it seems to refer to a loose conception of how a company does business and generates revenue. Yet simply having a business model is an exceedingly low bar to set for building a company. Generating revenue is a far cry from creating economic value, and no business model can be evaluated independently of industry structure. The business model approach to management becomes an invitation for faulty thinking and self-delusion.

Other words in the Internet lexicon also have unfortunate consequences. The terms "e-business" and "e-strategy" have been particularly problematic. By encouraging managers to view their Internet operations in isolation from the rest of the business, they can lead to simplistic approaches to competing using the Internet and increase the pressure for competitive imitation. Established companies fail to integrate the Internet into their proven strategies and thus never harness their most important advantages.

In many cases, the Internet complements, rather than cannibalizes, companies' traditional activities and ways of competing. Consider Walgreens, the most successful pharmacy chain in the United States. Walgreens introduced a Web site that provides customers with extensive information and allows them to order prescriptions on-line. Far from cannibalizing the company's stores, the Web site has underscored their value. Fully 90% of customers who place orders over the Web prefer to pick up their prescriptions at a nearby store rather than have them shipped to their homes. Walgreens has found that its extensive network of stores remains a potent advantage, even as some ordering shifts to the Internet.

Another good example is W.W. Grainger, a distributor of maintenance products and spare parts to companies. A middleman with stocking locations all over the United States, Grainger would seem to be a textbook case of an old-economy company set to be made obsolete by the Internet. But Grainger rejected the assumption that the Internet would undermine its strategy. Instead, it tightly coordinated its aggressive on-line efforts with its traditional business. The results so far are revealing. Customers who purchase on-line also continue to purchase through other means—Grainger estimates a 9% incremental growth in sales for customers who use the on-line channel above the normalized sales of customers who use only traditional means. Grainger, like Walgreens, has also found that Web ordering increases the value of its physical locations. Like the buyers of prescription drugs, the buyers of industrial supplies often need their orders immediately. It is faster and cheaper for them to pick up supplies at a local Grainger outlet than to wait for delivery. Tightly integrating the site and stocking locations not only increases the overall value to customers, it reduces Grainger's costs as well. It is inherently more efficient to take and pro-

The Internet and the Value Chain

The basic tool for understanding the influence of information technology on companies is the value chain—the set of activities through which a product or service is created and delivered to customers. When a company competes in any industry, it performs a number of discrete but interconnected value-creating activities, such as operating a sales force, fabricating a component, or delivering products, and these activities have points of connection with the activities of suppliers, channels, and customers. The value chain is a framework for identifying all these activities and analyzing how they affect both a company's costs and the value delivered to buyers.

Because every activity involves the creation, processing, and communication of information, information technology has a pervasive influence on the value chain. The special advantage of the Internet is the ability to link one activity with others and make real-time data created in one activity widely available, both within the company and with outside suppliers, channels, and customers. By incorporating a common, open set of communication protocols, Internet technology provides a standardized infrastructure, an intuitive browser interface for information access and delivery, bidirectional communication, and ease of connectivity—all at much lower cost than private networks and electronic data interchange, or EDI.

Many of the most prominent applications of the Internet in the value chain are shown in the figure on the next page. Some involve moving physical activities on-line, while others involve making physical activities more cost effective.

But for all its power, the Internet does not represent a break from the past; rather, it is the latest stage in the ongoing evolution of information technology.[1] Indeed, the technological possibilities available today derive not just from the Internet architecture but also from complementary technological advances such as scanning, object-oriented programming, relational databases, and wireless communications.

To see how these technological improvements will ultimately affect the value chain, some historical perspective is illuminating.[2] The evolution of information technology in business can be thought of in terms of five overlapping stages, each of which evolved out of constraints presented by the previous generation. The earliest IT systems automated discrete transactions such as order entry and accounting. The next stage involved the fuller automation and functional enhancement of individual activities such as human resource management, sales force operations, and product design. The third stage, which is being accelerated by the Internet, involves cross-activity integration, such as linking sales activities with order processing. Multiple activities are being linked together through such tools as customer relationship management (CRM), supply chain management (SCM), and enterprise resource planning (ERP) systems. The fourth stage, which is just beginning, enables the integration of the value chain and entire value system, that is, the set of value chains in an entire industry, encompassing those of tiers of suppliers, channels, and customers. SCM and CRM are starting to merge, as end-to-end applications involving customers, channels, and suppliers link orders to, for example, manufacturing, procurement, and service delivery. Soon to be integrated is product development, which has been largely separate. Complex product models will be exchanged among parties, and Internet procurement will move from standard commodities to engineered items.

In the upcoming fifth stage, information technology will be used not only to connect

the various activities and players in the value system but to optimize its workings in real time. Choices will be made based on information from multiple activities and corporate entities. Production decisions, for example, will automatically factor in the capacity available at multiple facilities and the inventory available at multiple suppliers. While early fifth-stage applications will involve relatively simple optimization of sourcing, production, logistical, and servicing transactions, the deeper levels of optimization will involve the product design itself. For example, product design will be optimized and customized based on input not only from factories and suppliers but also from customers.

The power of the Internet in the value chain, however, must be kept in perspective. While Internet applications have an important influence on the cost and quality of activities, they are neither the only nor the dominant influence. Conventional factors such as scale, the skills of personnel, product and process technology, and investments in physical assets also play prominent roles. The Internet is transformational in some respects, but many traditional sources of competitive advantage remain intact.

1. See M.E. Porter and V.E. Millar, "How Information Gives You Competitive Advantage," (HBR July–August 1985) for a framework that helps put the Internet's current influence in context.

2. This discussion is drawn from the author's research with Philip Bligh.

Prominent Applications of the Internet in the Value Chain

Firm Infrastructure
- Web-based, distributed financial and ERP systems
- On-line investor relations (e.g., information dissemination, broadcast conference calls)

Human Resource Management
- Self-service personnel and benefits administration
- Web-based training
- Internet-based sharing and dissemination of company information
- Electronic time and expense reporting

Technology Development
- Collaborative product design across locations and among multiple value-system participants
- Knowledge directories accessible from all parts of the organization
- Real-time access by R&D to on-line sales and service information

Procurement
- Internet-enabled demand planning; real-time available-to-promise/capable-to-promise and fulfillment
- Other linkage of purchase, inventory, and forecasting systems with suppliers
- Automated "requisition to pay"
- Direct and indirect procurement via marketplaces, exchanges, auctions, and buyer-seller matching

Inbound Logistics
- Real-time integrated scheduling, shipping, warehouse management, demand management and planning, and advanced planning and scheduling across the company and its suppliers
- Dissemination throughout the company of real-time inbound and in-progress inventory data

Operations
- Integrated information exchange, scheduling, and decision making in in-house plants, contract assemblers, and components suppliers
- Real-time available-to-promise and capable-to-promise information available to the sales force and channels

Outbound Logistics
- Real-time transaction of orders whether initiated by an end consumer, a sales person, or a channel partner
- Automated customer-specific agreements and contract terms
- Customer and channel access to product development and delivery status
- Collaborative integration with customer forecasting systems
- Integrated channel management including information exchange, warranty claims, and contract management (versioning, process control)

← • Web-distributed supply chain management →

Marketing and Sales
- On-line sales channels including Web sites and marketplaces
- Real-time inside and outside access to customer information, product catalogs, dynamic pricing, inventory availability, on-line submission of quotes, and order entry
- On-line product configurators
- Customer-tailored marketing via customer profiling
- Push advertising
- Tailored on-line access
- Real-time customer feedback through Web surveys, opt-in/opt-out marketing, and promotion response tracking

After-Sales Service
- On-line support of customer service representatives through e-mail response management, billing integration, co-browse, chat, "call me now," voice-over-IP, and other uses of video streaming
- Customer self-service via Web sites and intelligent service request processing including updates to billing and shipping profiles
- Real-time field service access to customer account review, schematic review, parts availability and ordering, work-order update, and service parts management

cess orders over the Web than to use traditional methods, but more efficient to make bulk deliveries to a local stocking location than to ship individual orders from a central warehouse.

Grainger has also found that its printed catalog bolsters its on-line operation. Many companies' first instinct is to eliminate printed catalogs once their content is replicated on-line. But Grainger continues to publish its catalog, and it has found that each time a new one is distributed, on-line orders surge. The catalog has proven to be a good tool for promoting the Web site while continuing to be a convenient way of packaging information for buyers.

In some industries, the use of the Internet represents only a modest shift from well-established practices. For catalog retailers like Lands' End, providers of electronic data interchange services like General Electric, direct marketers like Geico and Vanguard, and many other kinds of companies, Internet business looks much the same as traditional business. In these industries, established companies enjoy particularly important synergies between their on-line and traditional operations, which make it especially difficult for dot-coms to compete. Examining segments of industries with characteristics similar to those supporting on-line businesses—in which customers are willing to forgo personal service and immediate delivery in order to gain convenience or lower prices, for instance—can also provide an important reality check in estimating the size of the Internet opportunity. In the prescription drug business, for example, mail orders represented only about 13% of all purchases in the late 1990s. Even though on-line drugstores may draw more customers than the mail-order channel, it is unlikely that they will supplant their physical counterparts.

Virtual activities do not eliminate the need for physical activities, but often amplify their importance. The complementarity between Internet activities and traditional activities arises for a number of reasons. First, introducing Internet applications in one activity often places greater demands on physical activities elsewhere in the value chain. Direct ordering, for example, makes warehousing and shipping more important. Second, using the Internet in one activity can have systemic consequences, requiring new or enhanced physical activities that are often unanticipated. Internet-based job-posting services, for example, have greatly reduced the cost of reaching potential job applicants, but they have also flooded employers with electronic résumés. By making it easier for job seekers to distribute résumés, the Internet forces employers to sort through many more unsuitable candidates. The added back-end costs, often for physical activities, can end up outweighing the up-front savings. A similar dynamic often plays out in digital marketplaces. Suppliers are able to reduce the transactional cost of taking orders when they move on-line, but they often have to respond to many additional requests for information and quotes, which, again, places new strains on traditional activities. Such systemic effects underscore the fact that Internet applications are not stand-alone technologies; they must be integrated into the overall value chain.

Third, most Internet applications have some shortcomings in comparison with conventional methods. While Internet technology can do many useful things today and will surely improve in the future, it cannot do everything. Its limits include the following:

- Customers cannot physically examine, touch, and test products or get hands-on help in using or repairing them.
- Knowledge transfer is restricted to codified knowledge, sacrificing the spontaneity and judgment that can result from interaction with skilled personnel.
- The ability to learn about suppliers and customers (beyond their mere purchasing habits) is limited by the lack of face-to-face contact.
- The lack of human contact with the customer eliminates a powerful tool for encouraging purchases, trading off terms and conditions, providing advice and reassurance, and closing deals.
- Delays are involved in navigating sites and finding information and are introduced by the requirement for direct shipment.
- Extra logistical costs are required to assemble, pack, and move small shipments.
- Companies are unable to take advantage of low-cost, nontransactional functions performed by sales forces, distribution channels, and purchasing departments (such as performing limited service and maintenance functions at a customer site).
- The absence of physical facilities circumscribes some functions and reduces a means to reinforce image and establish performance.

• Attracting new customers is difficult given the sheer magnitude of the available information and buying options.

Traditional activities, often modified in some way, can compensate for these limits, just as the shortcomings of traditional methods—such as lack of real-time information, high cost of face-to-face interaction, and high cost of producing physical versions of information—can be offset by Internet methods. Frequently, in fact, an Internet application and a traditional method benefit each other. For example, many companies have found that Web sites that supply product information and support direct ordering make traditional sales forces more, not less, productive and valuable. The sales force can compensate for the limits of the site by providing personalized advice and after-sales service, for instance. And the site can make the sales force more productive by automating the exchange of routine information and serving as an efficient new conduit for leads. The fit between company activities, a cornerstone of strategic positioning, is in this way strengthened by the deployment of Internet technology.

Once managers begin to see the potential of the Internet as a complement rather than a cannibal, they will take a very different approach to organizing their on-line efforts. Many established companies, believing that the new economy operated under new rules, set up their Internet operations in stand-alone units. Fear of cannibalization, it was argued, would deter the mainstream organization from deploying the Internet aggressively. A separate unit was also helpful for investor relations, and it facilitated IPOs, tracking stocks, and spin-offs, enabling companies to tap into the market's appetite for Internet ventures and provide special incentives to attract Internet talent.

But organizational separation, while understandable, has often undermined companies' ability to gain competitive advantages. By creating separate Internet strategies instead of integrating the Internet into an overall strategy, companies failed to capitalize on their traditional assets, reinforced me-too competition, and accelerated competitive convergence. Barnes & Noble's decision to establish Barnesandnoble.com as a separate organization is a vivid

Strategic Imperatives for Dot-Coms and Established Companies

At this critical juncture in the evolution of Internet technology, dot-coms and established companies face different strategic imperatives. Dot-coms must develop real strategies that create economic value. They must recognize that current ways of competing are destructive and futile and benefit neither themselves nor, in the end, customers. Established companies, in turn, must stop deploying the Internet on a stand-alone basis and instead use it to enhance the distinctiveness of their strategies.

The most successful dot-coms will focus on creating benefits that customers will pay for, rather than pursuing advertising and click-through revenues from third parties. To be competitive, they will often need to widen their value chains to encompass other activities besides those conducted over the Internet and to develop other assets, including physical ones. Many are already doing so. Some on-line retailers, for example, distributed paper catalogs for the 2000 holiday season as an added convenience to their shoppers. Others are introducing proprietary products under their own brand names, which not only boosts margins but provides real differentiation. It is such new activities in the value chain, not minor differences in Web sites, that hold the key to whether dot-coms gain competitive advantages. AOL, the Internet pioneer, recognized these principles. It charged for its services even in the face of free competitors. And not resting on initial advantages gained from its Web site and Internet technologies (such as instant messaging), it moved early to develop or acquire proprietary content.

Yet dot-coms must not fall into the trap of imitating established companies. Simply adding conventional activities is a me-too strategy that will not provide a competitive advantage. Instead, dot-coms need to create strategies that involve new, hybrid value chains, bringing together virtual and physical activities in unique configurations. For example, E*Trade is planning to install stand-alone kiosks, which will not require full-time staffs, on the sites of some corporate customers. VirtualBank, an on-line bank, is cobranding with corporations to create in-house credit unions. Juniper, another on-line bank, allows customers to deposit checks at Mail Box Etc. locations. While none of these approaches is certain to be successful, the strategic thinking behind them is sound.

Another strategy for dot-coms is to seek out trade-offs, concentrating exclusively on segments where an Internet-only model offers real advantages. Instead of attempting to force the Internet model on the entire market, dot-coms can pursue customers that do not have a strong need for functions delivered outside the Internet—even if such customers represent only a modest portion of the overall industry. In such segments, the challenge will be to find a value proposition for the company that will distinguish it from other Internet rivals and address low entry barriers.

Successful dot-coms will share the following characteristics:

- Strong capabilities in Internet technology
- A distinctive strategy vis-à-vis established companies and other dot-coms, resting on a clear focus and meaningful advantages

example. It deterred the on-line store from capitalizing on the many advantages provided by the network of physical stores, thus playing into the hands of Amazon.

Rather than being isolated, Internet technology should be the responsibility of mainstream units in all parts of a company. With support from IT staff and outside consultants, companies should use the technology strategically to enhance service, increase efficiency, and leverage existing strengths. While separate units may be appropriate in some circumstances, everyone in the organization must have an incentive to share in the success of Internet deployment.

The End of the New Economy

The Internet, then, is often not disruptive to existing industries or established companies. It rarely nullifies the most important sources of competitive advantage in an industry; in many cases it actually makes those sources even more important. As all companies come to embrace Internet technology, moreover, the Internet itself will be neutralized as a source of advantage. Basic Internet applications will become table stakes—companies will not be able to survive without them, but they will not gain any advantage from them. The more robust competitive advantages will arise instead from traditional strengths such as unique products, proprietary content, distinctive physical activities, superior product knowledge, and strong personal service and relationships. Internet technology may be able to fortify those advantages, by tying a company's activities together in a more distinctive system, but it is unlikely to supplant them.

Ultimately, strategies that integrate the Internet and traditional competitive advantages and ways of competing should win in many industries. On the demand side, most buyers will value a combination of on-line services, personal services, and physical locations over stand-alone Web distribution. They will want a choice of channels, delivery options, and ways of dealing with companies. On the supply side, production and procurement will be more effective if they involve a combination of Internet and traditional methods, tailored to strategy. For example, customized, engineered

- Emphasis on creating customer value and charging for it directly, rather than relying on ancillary forms of revenue
- Distinctive ways of performing physical functions and assembling non-Internet assets that complement their strategic positions
- Deep industry knowledge to allow proprietary skills, information, and relationships to be established

Established companies, for the most part, need not be afraid of the Internet—the predictions of their demise at the hands of dot-coms were greatly exaggerated. Established companies possess traditional competitive advantages that will often continue to prevail; they also have inherent strengths in deploying Internet technology.

The greatest threat to an established company lies in either failing to deploy the Internet or failing to deploy it strategically. Every company needs an aggressive program to deploy the Internet throughout its value chain, using the technology to reinforce traditional competitive advantages and complement existing ways of competing. The key is not to imitate rivals but to tailor Internet applications to a company's overall strategy in ways that extend its competitive advantages and make them more sustainable. Schwab's expansion of its brick-and-mortar branches by one-third since it started on-line trading, for example, is extending its advantages over Internet-only competitors. The Internet, when used properly, can support greater strategic focus and a more tightly integrated activity system.

Edward Jones, a leading brokerage firm, is a good example of tailoring the Internet to strategy. Its strategy is to provide conservative, personalized advice to investors who value asset preservation and seek trusted, individualized guidance in investing. Target customers include retirees and small-business owners. Edward Jones does not offer commodities, futures, options, or other risky forms of investment. Instead, the company stresses a buy-and-hold approach to investing involving mutual funds, bonds, and blue-chip equities. Edward Jones operates a network of about 7,000 small offices, which are located conveniently to customers and are designed to encourage personal relationships with brokers.

Edward Jones has embraced the Internet for internal management functions, recruiting (25% of all job inquiries come via the Internet), and for providing account statements and other information to customers. However, it has no plan to offer on-line trading, as its competitors do. Self-directed, on-line trading does not fit Jones's strategy nor the value it aims to deliver to its customers. Jones, then, has tailored the use of the Internet to its strategy rather than imitated rivals. The company is thriving, outperforming rivals whose me-too Internet deployments have reduced their distinctiveness.

The established companies that will be most successful will be those that use Internet technology to make traditional activities better and those that find and implement new combinations of virtual and physical activities that were not previously possible.

inputs will be bought directly, facilitated by Internet tools. Commodity items may be purchased via digital markets, but purchasing experts, supplier sales forces, and stocking locations will often also provide useful, value-added services.

The value of integrating traditional and Internet methods creates potential advantages for established companies. It will be easier for them to adopt and integrate Internet methods than for dot-coms to adopt and integrate traditional ones. It is not enough, however, just to graft the Internet onto historical ways of competing in simplistic "clicks-and-mortar" configurations. Established companies will be most successful when they deploy Internet technology to reconfigure traditional activities or when they find new combinations of Internet and traditional approaches.

Dot-coms, first and foremost, must pursue their own distinctive strategies, rather than emulate one another or the positioning of established companies. They will have to break away from competing solely on price and instead focus on product selection, product design, service, image, and other areas in which they can differentiate themselves. Dot-coms can also drive the combination of Internet and traditional methods. Some will succeed by creating their own distinctive ways of doing so. Others will succeed by concentrating on market segments that exhibit real trade-offs between Internet and traditional methods—either those in which a pure Internet approach best meets the needs of a particular set of customers or those in which a particular product or service can be best delivered without the need for physical assets. (See the sidebar "Strategic Imperatives for Dot-Coms and Established Companies.")

These principles are already manifesting themselves in many industries, as traditional leaders reassert their strengths and dot-coms adopt more focused strategies. In the brokerage industry, Charles Schwab has gained a larger share (18% at the end of 1999) of on-line trading than E*Trade (15%). In commercial banking, established institutions like Wells Fargo, Citibank, and Fleet have many more on-line accounts than Internet banks do. Established companies are also gaining dominance over Internet activities in such areas as retailing, financial information, and digital marketplaces. The most promising dot-coms are leveraging their distinctive skills to provide real value to their customers. ECollege, for example, is a full-service provider that works with universities to put their courses on the Internet and operate the required delivery network for a fee. It is vastly more successful than competitors offering free sites to universities under their own brand names, hoping to collect advertising fees and other ancillary revenue.

When seen in this light, the "new economy" appears less like a new economy than like an old economy that has access to a new technology. Even the phrases "new economy" and "old economy" are rapidly losing their relevance, if they ever had any. The old economy of established companies and the new economy of dot-coms are merging, and it will soon be difficult to distinguish them. Retiring these phrases can only be healthy because it will reduce the confusion and muddy thinking that have been so destructive of economic value during the Internet's adolescent years.

In our quest to see how the Internet is different, we have failed to see how the Internet is the same. While a new means of conducting business has become available, the fundamentals of competition remain unchanged. The next stage of the Internet's evolution will involve a shift in thinking from e-business to business, from e-strategy to strategy. Only by integrating the Internet into overall strategy will this powerful new technology become an equally powerful force for competitive advantage.

The author is grateful to Jeffrey Rayport and to the Advanced Research Group at Inforte for their contributions to this article.

Reprint R0103D; *Harvard Business Review* OnPoint 6358
To order, see the next page
or call 800-988-0886 or 617-783-7500
or go to www.hbr.org

Strategy and the Internet

Further Reading

ARTICLES

What Is Strategy?
by Michael E. Porter
Harvard Business Review
November-December 1996
Product no. 4134

In this article, Porter sharpens the focus on the two components of sustainable competitive advantage discussed in "Strategy and the Internet": operational effectiveness and strategic positioning. He emphasizes that it's strategic positioning, not operational effectiveness, that lets a company most effectively distinguish itself from competitors. He then outlines three key principles behind strategic positioning: 1) creating a unique, valuable position through serving a few needs of many customers, broad needs of a few customers, or broad needs of many customers; 2) making trade-offs in competition (i.e., choosing what not to do); and—most relevant to his discussion of integration in "Strategy and the Internet"—3) improving "fit" among the company's activities so that they reinforce one another. As he explains, when a company's activities reinforce one another in a tightly interlocked system, competitors can't easily imitate that system.

Strategy as Simple Rules
by Kathleen M. Eisenhardt and Donald N. Sull
Harvard Business Review
November-December 1996
Product no. 5858

This article provides practical guidelines for strengthening your company's strategic positioning. Like Porter, Eisenhardt and Sull emphasize the importance of strategy in today's unpredictable, complex markets. They emphasize keeping strategy clear and simple by focusing on a unique set of strategic processes—e.g., product innovation, partnering, branding—that place your company where the flow of opportunities is swiftest and deepest, and then defining just a handful of simple rules to guide those processes. The authors outline five kinds of rules, including mandates for quickly ranking competing opportunities, deciding when to pull the plug on an opportunity, and distinctively executing your key processes.

BOOK

On Competition
by Michael E. Porter
Harvard Business School Press
1998
Product no. 7951

This book—a collection of Porter's articles from the *Harvard Business Review*, augmented by two new selections and an introduction—is a more expansive treatment of Porter's perspectives on the core concepts of competition and strategy, which he refers to in "Strategy and the Internet." He shows how crucial business activities, such as staking out and maintaining a distinctive competitive position and continually improving productivity, are intimately linked to strategic positioning.

To Order

For reprints, *Harvard Business Review* OnPoint orders, and subscriptions to *Harvard Business Review:*
Call 800-988-0886 or 617-783-7500.
Go to www.hbr.org

For customized and quantity orders of reprints and *Harvard Business Review* OnPoint products:
Call Frank Tamoshunas at
617-783-7626,
or e-mail him at
ftamoshunas@hbsp.harvard.edu

Harvard Business Review OnPoint

www.hbr.org

U.S. and Canada
800-988-0886
617-783-7500
617-783-7555 fax

ISBN 1-57851-635-8
90000
9 781578 516353

Harvard Business Review
OnPoint
ARTICLE

www.hbr.org

The *Real* New Economy

by Diana Farrell

Included with this full-text *Harvard Business Review* article:

1 **Article Summary**
The Idea in Brief—*the core idea*
The Idea in Practice—*putting the idea to work*

3 **The *Real* New Economy**

13 **Further Reading**
A list of related materials, with annotations to guide further exploration of the article's ideas and applications

Product 5127

Harvard Business Review
OnPoint

The *Real* New Economy

The Idea in Brief

Heated debate about information technology's strategic value continues unabated: What impact *does* information technology have on your company's ability to compete? *Did* IT really fuel the productivity surge of the 1990s—or were other factors as work?

Competition and innovation—much more than IT—led to that period's extraordinary productivity gains. Industries jockeying fiercely for customers and profits innovated aggressively. Those innovations—in technology *as well as* products and business processes—boosted productivity. As productivity rose, competition intensified further, bringing fresh waves of innovation. Result? A virtuous cycle of competition, innovation, and productivity growth.

IT enabled the innovation part of this cycle in three ways:

- It helped companies develop attractive new products and efficient new processes.
- It facilitated the rapid, industrywide diffusion of innovations.
- Its benefits multiplied quickly as its use expanded.

Industries dependent on intensive information processing gained the most from IT. Yet even in these industries, many firms failed to earn strong returns from their technology investments. Viewing IT as a panacea, they poured money into technology without understanding how the competition-innovation-productivity cycle worked in their businesses.

IT is not a silver bullet. But it *can* be a powerful competitive weapon—if you aim it accurately by applying four practices.

The Idea in Practice

TARGET THE PRODUCTIVITY LEVERS THAT MATTER.

Productivity levers vary across—and within—industries. General-purpose applications rarely influence productivity. And systems that pay off for one competitor may do little for you. Analyze your firm's economics, and concentrate your IT spending on the levers that will exert the *greatest* impact on productivity.

For example, in retail banking, customized IT applications that automate lending and credit-card operations have boosted productivity dramatically. In retailing, it's applications that streamline distribution, merchandise management, and store operations.

Even within an industry, levers vary. For instance, general-merchandise retailers such as Wal-Mart get the most benefit from tools, such as warehouse and transportation management systems, that tighten their links to suppliers and increase inventory turns for a given product. But specialty apparel retailers like the Gap benefit most from assortment and allocation planning tools to cut obsolescence and inventory-holding costs.

GET THE SEQUENCING RIGHT.

IT investments build on each other in complex ways. By carefully sequencing your investments you reap greater rewards.

▶ Example:
Wal-Mart first used IT to manage the flow and storage of products throughout its far-flung network of suppliers, warehouses, and distribution centers. Then it used IT to gain even greater efficiencies by coordinating operations more tightly with those of suppliers. Only then did it invest in technology to plan product mix and replenishment.

GET THE TIMING RIGHT, TOO.

Ask, "Should we lead or follow IT trends?" Rush an investment only when you're certain the technology will advance your firm's business goals and stave off imitation by rivals.

But watch for red flags indicating that an investment won't differentiate your firm—such as a rolling wave of competitors considering the same system. And know your company: its taste for risk, managers' confidence that they can merge IT with other advantages, your corporate track record in mobilizing people to effect change. Where indicators are weak, follow—don't lead—IT trends.

PURSUE MANAGERIAL AND TECHNOLOGICAL INNOVATIONS IN TANDEM.

Technological innovations have little value until managerial practices adapt to them. Wal-Mart, for instance, would have gained nothing from its investments in innovative information systems if it hadn't also redefined its relationships with suppliers and simplified its distribution centers' logistics.

CRM (customer relationship management software systems) in retail banking provides the cautionary tale. Despite massive spending on this technology, many banks' productivity has remained flat. Why? Banks' business units continue to be organized around specific products and customer segments, hindering the integrated management of overall customer relationships. And incentive structures for sales personnel undermine the cross-selling that CRM enables.

Yes, something big did happen in the 1990s. But it was less about technology and more about new forms of competition. The keys to success now? Aggressive innovation and highly targeted investments in IT.

The *Real* New Economy

A mythic aura surrounds the soar and swoon of the "new economy." The scale was breathtaking, illusions abounded, and the forces at work seemed at once powerful and elusive. As the bubble inflated, many felt that information technology, and the Internet in particular, would "change everything." Today, with the technology sector in shreds, more than a few believe that IT changed scarcely anything at all. The truth, of course, lies somewhere in between. But where? What became of all the innovation we thought we were seeing? What actually happened to productivity growth? What effect did IT really have on companies and their ability to compete? Most important, what can managers learn from it all?

For more than two years, the McKinsey Global Institute has been studying labor productivity in the United States, France, and Germany and its connection to corporate IT spending and use. My colleagues and I have examined a large body of statistical and experiential evidence and conducted in-depth case studies of 20 industries, eight in the United States and six apiece in Germany and France. The studies involved not only the collection and analysis of data on industry and company performance but also extensive interviews with executives in each sector.

We found that a new economy did indeed come into being in the 1990s, but that it is very different from the one that was widely promoted and discussed at the time. Rather than springing from the Internet, it emerged from intensifying business competition and a resulting surge in managerial innovation. Information technology's role in the new business world, we also discovered, is more complicated than has been assumed. IT is of great, but not primary, importance to the fate of industries and individual companies. By uncovering the true drivers of corporate success today, our research provides a clearer understanding of the recent upheavals in business and points the way to a more effective deployment of corporate IT investments and assets.

The Truth About Productivity

Something did change in the economy in the late 1990s, and it is visible in the productivity statistics. After growing at an anemic 1.4% annual rate from 1973 through 1994, U.S. labor productivity shot up 2.4% a year from 1995 through 1999. And productivity has remained fairly vigorous even during the recent economic downturn, rising at 2.9% in 2000, 1.1% in 2001, and 4.8% in 2002, according to the Bureau of Labor Statistics.

The late 1990s productivity surge coincided with a big increase in the money and attention U.S. companies devoted to information technology. In many industries, technology spending doubled as businesses wove computer and communications systems more deeply into the fabric of their operations. Overall, the percentage of the gross domestic product accounted for by technology goods rose sixfold, from 2% to 12%, during the decade.

Not surprisingly, many people looked at these numbers and concluded that the IT investments drove the productivity gains. But it's not that simple. When we examined the performance of different industries, we saw little correlation between productivity and IT investment. Although most industries significantly boosted their IT spending, their rates of productivity growth varied enormously. In fact, in the United States, productivity gains were concentrated in just six sectors: retailing, securities brokerage, wholesaling, semiconductors, computer assembly, and telecommunications. These sectors account for only 32% of the U.S. GDP, but they contributed 76% of the country's net productivity gain. Many other sectors, such as hotels and television broadcasting, invested heavily in IT but saw little or no productivity growth. (See the exhibit "America's Uneven Productivity Boom.")

If information technology wasn't the primary factor in the productivity surge, what was? The answer is clear: Intensifying competition led to productivity-boosting innovations in the six key sectors. Our research shows that managers in those industries were forced to innovate aggressively to protect their revenues and profits in the face of strong competition. It was those innovations—in products, business practices, and technology—that led to the gains in productivity. In fact, an important dynamic of the new economy—the *real* new economy—is the virtuous cycle of competition, innovation, and productivity growth. Fierce competition spurs innovation, in both technology and business processes. These innovations spread quickly, improving productivity across the sector. As productivity rises, competition intensifies further, bringing a fresh wave of innovation.

The crucial role played by competition can be seen clearly in the performance variations that were evident across countries and industries. In sectors where competition was promoted—through the dismantling of regulatory constraints, primarily—innovation flourished and productivity soared. But wherever regulation or other forces warped the competitive environment, competitive pressures eased, innovations failed to develop or to spread rapidly, and productivity growth slackened.

Look at the mobile-telecommunications industry. In the United States, the government's auction of additional spectrum in 1995 led to increased competition, with the average number of competitors in a local market jumping from two to almost five. Prices fell, usage increased, and the entire sector's productivity grew at an average annual rate of 15% during the decade. That's a very healthy rate, yet it pales in comparison with the 25% gains posted by the mobile-telecom sectors in France and Germany. The difference is that U.S. regulations created a fragmented and protected market with dozens of subscale regional providers and little national competition. Today, more than 50 providers serve fewer than 200,000 customers each in the United States. In France and Germany, by contrast, a handful of national providers serve an average of 10 million customers each. The strong rivalry among the big European providers, as well as their superior scale, led to the exceptional productivity gains.

Such differences between nations were evident in other sectors as well. Competition in retail banking, for example, is freer in the United States than in Germany, where small state-owned and cooperative banks have been unable to build sufficient scale yet remain shielded from the shareholder demands of capital markets. Our study showed that weaker competition kept German banking at a significant productivity disadvantage, even though the sector grew healthily as a result of higher customer demand and a wave of consolida-

Diana Farrell is the director of the McKinsey Global Institute in San Francisco.

tions. Retail banking productivity in Germany was only 74% of the U.S. level by the end of the 1990s.

In food retailing, France fell behind the United States in productivity gains. Again, the culprit was restrained competition. Zoning laws effectively shielded the dominant French hypermarkets from innovative competitors, and smaller, traditional merchants also enjoyed considerable governmental protection. The productivity of the French grocery sector actually fell at a 0.5% annual rate in the 1990s, while U.S. food retailers posted 1.6% annual gains.

Competition was not the only force driving productivity in the 1990s. Strong consumer confidence, for example, led customers to purchase more expensive goods, which also helped boost productivity. And buoyant capital markets contributed to gains in the securities sector. But our research clearly shows that wherever competitive intensity was greatest, innovative products and practices proliferated and productivity grew robustly. And wherever competition was constrained, innovation waned and productivity suffered.

The Role of Information Technology

When competition intensifies and companies face the possibility of lost customers and profits, managers have overwhelming incentives to pursue creative ways to cut the costs of their operations and increase the value they provide to buyers. The choice really is to innovate or die. There are many ways for managers to innovate, of course, but during the 1990s information technology proved to be a particularly powerful tool. We found three reasons why that was so. First, IT enabled the development of both attractive new products and efficient new business processes. Second, it facilitated the rapid industrywide diffusion of innovations. And third, it exhibited strong scale economies—its benefits multiplied rapidly as its use expanded.

IT's power to promote innovation was not felt equally in all industries, however. The sectors most dependent on intensive information processing—those with highly complex operating processes, heavy transaction loads, or technically sophisticated products, for example—reaped the lion's share of the gains. When an industry had such characteristics and exhibited intensifying competition, productivity boomed.

New Products and Processes. Some of the IT-based innovations of the last decade came in the form of new products and services (such as faster microprocessors or on-line securities trading). Others were enhancements to existing business processes (such as check imaging and centralized credit authorization in retail banking). In many cases, the new products and processes were tightly intertwined. In the semiconductor industry, for instance, the rapid increase in the complexity of chip designs required ever stricter process controls and diagnostics. That spurred the development of sophisticated new information systems for managing chip fabrication, which boosted productivity throughout the sector.

The six industries we identified as showing the greatest productivity gains during the 1990s all leveraged new IT capabilities to create products or refine processes. Sophisticated new IT systems were, for example, a godsend for retailing. Big retailers execute millions of relatively small transactions each day, creating

America's Uneven Productivity Boom

Most companies invested heavily in IT during the late 1990s, but only a few managed to reap the rewards of strong productivity growth. In fact, productivity gains were concentrated in just six sectors: retailing, securities brokerage, wholesaling, semiconductors, computer assembly, and telecommunications. These sectors account for only one-third of the United States' GDP, but they contributed more than three-quarters of the country's net productivity gain.

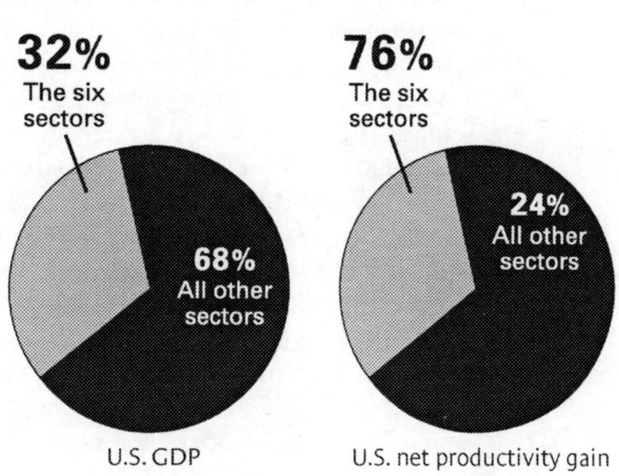

Fast diffusion is a double-edged sword. While it improves overall industry productivity, it can erode the competitive advantages of individual companies.

extraordinary operating complexity. IT helps them manage that complexity much more effectively. It not only automates routine functions such as inventory receiving and control, price scans, and checkout, it also optimizes many complicated processes, including supply chain management, merchandising, and customer relationship management.

Securities brokerage is another information-intensive industry that benefited greatly from new IT capabilities. Between 3 million and 4 million securities transactions, with an average size of $25,000, take place in the United States each day. With the spread of the Internet, innovators like Charles Schwab and E*Trade were able to incorporate highly efficient on-line trading into their already productive discount brokerage models. Our research reveals that, without on-line interfaces, these brokerages would have needed ten times more brokers or other customer service employees to handle the demand they encountered. The adoption of on-line interfaces has been remarkably swift. Almost no retail brokerage trades were executed on-line in 1995; by 2000, 40% were handled over the Internet. Interestingly, on-line trading was the only instance in which the Internet contributed significantly to the economy's overall productivity jump during the so-called dot-com boom.

In U.S. wholesaling, the use of IT in distribution centers significantly boosted productivity. By combining relatively simple hardware (like bar codes, scanners, and picking machines) with sophisticated software (warehouse management systems for inventory control and tracking, for example), wholesalers were able to partially automate the flow of goods and thereby reduce labor costs significantly.

Diffusion. As new technologies spread across a sector, they often had a striking impact on productivity. In the retail sector, for instance, many companies were quick to adopt warehouse management and automation systems, bar code scanners and readers, and ERP modules for human resources, payroll, and reporting. Those systems helped automate processes that traditionally required large staffs, leading to significant reductions in labor costs throughout the industry. In the U.S. trucking industry, major carriers rapidly embraced network optimization systems and bar coding and scanning technologies, driving productivity gains across the sector. French and German trucking firms, only recently exposed to strong competition through EU deregulation, lagged in their adoption of these new technologies. As a result, their productivity remained well below that of U.S. companies, with France at 85% and Germany at 83% of U.S. levels.

Technological innovations not only increased productivity in some sectors; IT itself also directly facilitated the diffusion of many business and technological innovations. Companies used more sophisticated corporate planning tools, improved communications systems, and continuous on-line monitoring to increase the speed with which they replicated the breakthroughs of their competitors. New technological capabilities played a particularly strong role in spreading innovations across distribution centers and stores in the retail sector and across banking and brokerage branches in the financial sector.

Fast diffusion is a double-edged sword, however. While it improves overall industry productivity, it can erode the competitive advantages of individual companies. Once rivals in a sector adopt an IT innovation, after all, it becomes just another cost of doing business. As a result, many companies that spent heavily on state-of-the-art technology in the 1990s failed to recoup their investments. On-line banking spread so rapidly, for example, that no individual bank was able to reap any competitive advantage—the benefits all went to customers. (In this case, the banks also had unrealistic expectations of changing consumer behavior. U.S. customers have adopted on-line banking so slowly that it has yet to have a major impact on sector productivity.)

The secret to retaining an edge from rapidly diffusing technologies, we found, is to couple them with other distinctive capabilities or processes in ways that are hard to replicate. J.P. Morgan Chase recently used IT to augment its strengths in the automotive finance market. In early 2001, the financial services giant had 9,000 dealers in its system and was a leader in the prime-lending segment. It then dramatically extended its distribution network—to 18,000 dealers—by rolling out its on-line DealerTrack system, which dealers use to help customers find and close loans electronically. Because DealerTrack supports J.P. Morgan Chase's existing advantages, its benefits cannot be easily copied by competitors—even if they install the same technology.

Scaling. The benefits of most IT innovations grow dramatically as scale increases. Once you install new software for transaction processing, for example, the marginal cost of processing additional transactions falls rapidly toward zero. Indeed, given the often high upfront costs of adopting a new technology, achieving scale is often crucial to reaping a return on an IT investment.

When technology innovations spread equally through countries, we found their impact on productivity could still vary widely depending on the extent of industry consolidation. IT innovations had their greatest impact in industries with a high degree of concentration or with a high volume output per customer. Retail banking is a good example. Retail banks in all three countries we studied have automated their back offices, enabling them to service a virtually unlimited number of transactions at negligible marginal cost. Yet U.S. banks have enjoyed the greatest productivity gains. That's because U.S. consumers typically carry two to three times more financial assets and loans than their French and German counterparts. U.S. banks simply process more transactions per customer.

German retailing is also illustrative. Weak corporate governance kept unproductive German retailers in business, leading to overcapacity and meager profits. That limited German retailers' ability to invest in the IT-enabled, long-term efficiency improvements that some French and most U.S. retailers were adopting.

A New Agenda for IT

Even in the six sectors that gained the most from IT, many companies failed to earn strong returns from their technology investments.

Working with the Productivity Equation

The productivity equation is simple: It is outputs divided by inputs. To improve productivity, you must raise the first, lower the second, or both. Smart managers look at all inputs (capital, materials, and labor) as well as outputs, and use IT creatively to improve productivity in the areas that matter. The chart below can help managers take a first cut at identifying the productivity levers best suited to their companies and industries.

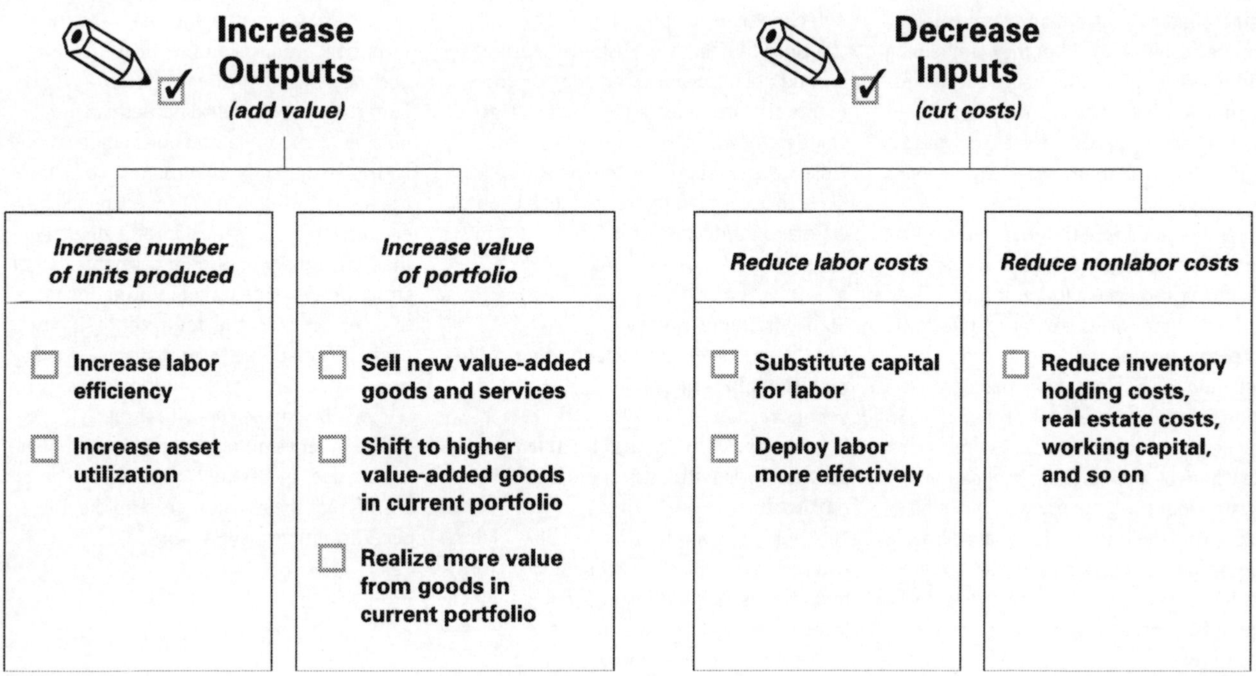

Some simply abandoned new systems when implementation difficulties arose or costs exceeded expectations. Others took a piecemeal approach, automating only parts of their business processes. Still others didn't invest in the areas with the biggest potential impact on productivity or invested too early in systems that competitors could easily copy.

Some of these errors seem surprisingly obvious. But in retrospect it's easy to see how some managers in the late 1990s got carried away with IT and spent money unwisely. As IT investment soared, so did productivity growth, economic growth, earnings, and stock market valuations. IT took on the appearance of a panacea, leading many managers to assume that "me-too" investments would pay off.

There's much to be learned from the companies that gained the most from their investments. Our research revealed, in particular, that three practices distinguish the companies that were most successful in their IT investments. First, such companies targeted their investments at the productivity levers that mattered most for their industries and themselves. Second, they carefully thought through the sequence and timing of their investments. Third, they didn't pursue IT in isolation but rather developed managerial innovations in tandem with technological ones. Let's look more closely at how these imperatives drive productivity. (For a discussion of the implications of these imperatives for technology companies, see the sidebar "The Challenge for IT Ven-

The Challenge for IT Vendors

Our research revealed three practices that distinguish the companies that gained the most from their IT investments. These imperatives for effective use of IT have important implications for vendors as well.

1

Managerial imperative

Target the productivity levers that matter.

Vendor response

Gain customer-specific know-how, and focus development and sales efforts on specific sectors and business models.

IT providers must learn more about how their technology can enhance each customer's business. Whether they are helping to improve retail supply chains, cut processing time for insurance claims, or reduce errors in hospital lab work, they must master the details necessary to raise their customers' productivity.

The shotgun approach—supplying all kinds of products to all kinds of customers—will almost surely be a losing strategy for vendors. Those with a panoply of offerings will become mired in the complexity of managing the business, and mediocre execution for all customers will likely ensue. So providers face hard choices. They must decide where to focus and, by implication, how to "right size" themselves. The good news is that the lessons of the past decade suggest that vendors can gain valuable benefits by addressing well-defined customer segments whose performance they can really improve.

2

Managerial imperative

Get the sequencing and timing right.

Vendor response

Help customers find value in sunken IT investments.

Many companies with apparently lifeless IT investments may be missing one final piece of technology. So IT vendors must develop solutions to help their customers turn around unsuccessful technology deployments and articulate and deliver a clear value proposition for future investments. Unless they do both, customers will be less likely to accept big up-front costs for software and hardware in the future.

3

Managerial imperative

Pursue managerial and technological innovations in tandem.

Vendor response

Innovate selectively, and form learning partnerships with customers and third parties.

Technology-driven innovation will remain vital, but as companies grasp the need for simultaneous managerial innovation, their IT investments will become much more selective. In this environment, partnering to learn is vital. Vendors in retail banking, for example, can build long-term partnerships with banks by working with them to identify and execute the business changes necessary to fully benefit from investments such as data warehouses, CRM, customer data integration, and on-line banking. Many customers made large infrastructure investments over the past five to eight years, and they want new products and services that leverage the assets they already have.

Partnering with third parties can also help vendors tie their technical innovations with managerial breakthroughs. To achieve the highest value from IT investments, buyers need to make critical improvements in their business processes and organizational structures. An integrated information system will achieve little, for instance, if business units continue to be managed in isolation without any cross-unit incentives or reviews. By partnering with firms that specialize in redesigning processes and managing change, successful IT vendors will help ensure that their customers reap the full benefits of their new systems.

dors.")

Target the productivity levers that matter. There are many ways to improve productivity, as the exhibit "Working with the Productivity Equation" illustrates. You can reduce labor or other factor costs. You can increase labor efficiency or asset utilization. Or you can sell new or higher value-added goods to your customers. IT can play a role in each of these areas. The trick is to concentrate your IT spending on those levers that will have the greatest effect on productivity. Many companies we looked at spent heavily on seemingly attractive new technologies, only to find that they had little effect on results.

The levers that matter vary from industry to industry. That explains why the IT applications with the greatest impact are often tailored to particular sectors. We found, in fact, that no general-purpose application had much effect on productivity. In retail banking, customized applications for automating lending, credit card operations, and back-office transactions provided the greatest boosts to productivity. In consumer retailing, the key applications focused on streamlining distribution and logistics, merchandise planning and management, and store operations. In the semiconductor industry, the greatest gains came from highly specialized tools for electronic design automation, process control, and yield optimization. CRM applications, on the other hand, generally purposed to increase revenue through better customer management, tended to yield mostly poor results.

Even within an industry, different productivity levers can have very different impacts. Consider retailing. General merchandise retailers like Wal-Mart are low-margin, high-turnover businesses selling a vast number of items, many of which are consumer staples. They get the most benefit from tools such as warehouse and transportation management systems that allow for a tighter link with suppliers and an increase in inventory turns for a given product. On the other hand, specialty-apparel retailers like the Gap handle many items with short shelf lives and therefore rely on assortment and allocation planning tools to cut obsolescence and inventory-holding costs. Among electronics retailers like Circuit City or Best Buy, store allocation and price optimization tools play a key role in reducing markdowns. Home improvement retailers, whose profits hinge on after-sales services such as warranties, home deliveries, and repairs rely on extended order management systems to ensure greater customer satisfaction.

As these examples show, simply following broad IT trends can backfire. The smartest companies analyze their economics carefully and spend aggressively on only those IT applications that will deliver outsized productivity gains. As for other necessary applications, they seek out the cheapest possible solutions. And they always remember that the system that pays off for one competitor may do little for another. Take supply chain management systems, for instance. Spending on these popular technologies has proven to be a boon to general merchandisers, but comparable investments by apparel companies have yielded very little.

Get the sequencing and timing right. IT investments build on one another, often in complex ways. Companies that install sophisticated (and expensive) new applications before they've done the necessary groundwork are almost always disappointed. They either fail to achieve the expected benefits, or they find themselves doing constant retrofitting. But companies that take a disciplined approach, sequencing their investments carefully, often reap great rewards.

Wal-Mart's "step change" approach to IT investment during the 1990s is a great example. First, the company installed software to manage the flow and storage of products through its far-flung network of suppliers, warehouses, and distribution centers. Once it had automated product flow, it focused on using IT to coordinate its operations more tightly with those of its suppliers, leveraging its greater efficiency. With that smoother coordination, Wal-Mart could invest effectively in technology to plan the mix and replenishment of its goods. Finally, after integrating all these capabilities, the company built a data warehouse that uses information pulled from a range of sources to handle complex queries.

KMart, by contrast, made a misstep in its IT investments that undermined their effectiveness. It invested in systems to improve promotions management before it had installed the supply chain systems necessary to handle fluctuations in sales volume. As a result, it was unable to capitalize on the more precisely targeted promotions. Many retail banks also made errors in sequencing. They invested in popular customer relationship management systems before they had built repositories of consistent and reliable customer data. Not surprisingly, the CRM investments fell well short of expectations.

Even with a sound plan for sequencing, firms have to consider the timing of their investments. They must ask themselves, in particular, one crucial question: Should we lead or follow IT trends? In making this decision, firms must understand that IT alone is almost never a true differentiator. As we saw with J.P. Morgan Chase's DealerTrack system, IT provides distinction only when coupled with other, less replicable advantages, such as scale or a strong brand.

A company should rush an investment, therefore, only when it's clear that the technology will advance the firm's business goals, enable true innovation that strengthens existing advantages, and be resistant to the leveling effect of imitation. In semiconductors, where superior chip design confers a major edge, Intel's investment in the development of the Pentium processor to replace the 486 proved essential to staying ahead of the competition. In semiconductor equipment, Applied Materials' aggressive investments in new manufacturing technologies also paid off, simply because its smaller rivals lacked the resources to rapidly imitate the advances.

Simply following broad IT trends can backfire. The system that pays off for one competitor may do little for another.

Of course, it's hard to foresee whether an investment will yield innovative results. At the critical moment of decision, managers must be alert for red flags indicating that the investment will not differentiate the firm, such as widespread hype about the IT opportunity or a rolling wave of competitors considering it. Such signals of broad awareness suggest that any added profitability from the innovation will quickly dissipate. Companies must also know themselves: their taste for risk, their confidence that they can merge IT with other advantages to stay ahead of the pack, and their corporate track record in mobilizing people and processes to effect change. Where the indicators are weak, the best course is usually to follow, not lead.

Pursue managerial and technological innovations in tandem. History shows that technological innovations are typically of little use until managerial practices adapt to them. That was certainly true in the 1990s, and it remains true today. Wal-Mart, for instance, would have gained little from its investments in innovative information systems if it hadn't also redefined its relationships with suppliers and dramatically simplified the logistics practices at its distribution centers. Best Buy and Target would not have become leaders in retailing if they hadn't combined advanced IT with collaborative purchasing systems and advances in warehouse automation, cross-docking, and inventory tracking. Intel's IT investments turbocharged its productivity because they accompanied breakthroughs in materials technology and manufacturing processes. In all these cases, business managers led the way, reshaping their companies' processes and practices so that the full benefits of new information systems could be realized.

CRM in retail banking provides the cautionary tale. Banks hoped that the new systems for gathering and sharing customer information would boost cross-selling rates, reduce customer attrition, attract new customers, and increase profitability per customer. Yet despite massive spending on CRM, the number of products held by an average household at its primary bank has remained flat over the past three years. One reason for this, as already noted, was poor sequencing—the required customer data was not yet in place when the CRM systems came on-line. But many bank managers also failed to make necessary changes to their sales and marketing processes. The banks' business units continued to be organized around specific products and customer segments, hindering the integrated management of overall customer relationships. In addition, incentive structures for sales personnel undermined the kind of cross-selling that CRM theoretically makes possible.

• • •

The success of IT investments hinges on the particular characteristics of different industries and the particular practices of different companies. That fact goes a long way toward explaining the lack of correlation between IT spending and productivity that we've seen in recent years. For IT to fulfill its promise, users and vendors must deploy it thoughtfully, tailoring it to individual sectors and businesses and merging it with other product and process innovations. The challenge will be to use existing systems effectively while at the same time making targeted new investments that maintain competitive parity and, when possible, strengthen differentiation and buttress advantage. IT is not a silver bullet. But if it is aimed correctly, it can be an important competitive weapon.

Reprint R0310G; *Harvard Business Review*
OnPoint 5127
To order, see the next page
or call 800-988-0886 or 617-783-7500
or go to www.hbr.org

The *Real* New Economy

Further Reading

ARTICLES

What Is Strategy?
by Michael E. Porter
Harvard Business Review
November-December 1996
Product no. 4134

Porter examines the leveling effect that IT and other tools for improving operational effectiveness eventually exert when all competitors in an industry adopt them. As adoption spreads, costs decrease and value improves within the industry—but not for individual competitors. Instead, companies become less distinguishable from one another and lose their edge.

To achieve *sustainable* competitive advantage, firms must preserve what's distinctive about them through their **strategic positioning**—performing *different* activities from rivals or *similar* activities in different ways.

Three principles underlie strategic positioning: 1) *Create a unique and valuable position* by serving few needs of many customers, broad needs of few customers, or broad needs of many customers. 2) *Make trade-offs in competing,* saying "No" to activities that give you gains in one area only at the expense of another area. 3) *Create a unique "fit" among your company's activities* so they reinforce one another and can't easily be copied by rivals.

Six IT Decisions Your IT People Shouldn't Make
by Jeanne W. Ross and Peter Weill
Harvard Business Review
November 2002
Product no. 2160

How to make your IT investments generate the best possible returns? Don't leave crucial information-technology decisions to IT executives—they'll likely make choices that inadvertently clash with your corporate strategy.

Instead, manage the following decisions yourself: 1) *How much to spend on IT.* Define crystal-clear IT goals, then set funding to achieve them. 2) *Which business processes should receive IT dollars.* Fund only those IT initiatives that will support your corporate strategy. 3) *Which IT capabilities should be firmwide.* Weigh trade-offs associated with centralizing IT capabilities—including saving money versus limiting business units' flexibility. 4) *How good your IT services need to be.* Don't buy "Cadillac" service when a "Buick" will do. 5) *Which security and privacy risks you'll accept.* Weigh trade-offs between privacy versus convenience. 6) *Whom to blame if an IT initiative fails.* The IT department is responsible for delivering systems on time and within budget. Your job is to make organizational changes that generate business value from those systems.

Harvard Business Review OnPoint

www.hbr.org

U.S. and Canada
800-988-0886
617-783-7500
617-783-7555 fax

ISBN 1-57851-512-7
90000
9 781578 515127

Chapter 2

The Big Picture: IT and Business

MANAGERIAL QUESTIONS

When does an information system become strategic?
How can I evaluate the strategic ability of the information systems I have?
What are examples of strategic use?
Is creating strategic advantage easy?
Why should I worry about business–IT alignment?
What are the economics of information technology?
Does information technology matter?
What kinds of information systems are there?
What are interorganizational systems and what can I do with them?
What are the key IT issues in the years ahead?

INTRODUCTION

Information systems are one of the many functions that make up a business. Like each of the other functions, it is vital to the modern business. To run even a small one or two person business requires some information technology, if only to keep records of transactions for tax purposes. Yet, unless IS is being used strategically or is intimately tied into a business process, many business people consider it a form of overhead cost that needs to be minimized.

In this chapter we consider the big questions in information systems. As described in the Managerial Questions above, they include the strategic use of IS, the alignment of IS with the business, the economics of information, the argument about whether IT matters at all in a business, and the key issues in the years ahead.

STRATEGIC ADVANTAGE VERSUS STRATEGIC NECESSITY

The strategic use of information systems can be divided into two groups: those that offer help with obtaining a strategic advantage and those that result from strategic necessity. Strategic advantage refers to obtaining a sustainable competitive edge over competitors. That is, the ability to obtain a greater than normal return on investment. A strategic necessity is a system that must be installed to remain competitive and, often, to stay in business.

Strategic advantage can be obtained from being the first (or dominant) mover to introduce an innovation. It can come from consolidating a first mover position by increasing the barriers to entry such as cost to enter or locking in such a large market share that the remaining market is too small to be worthwhile. It may result from seizing an opportunity from a discontinuity such as bank deregulation.[1]

Sustainable competitive advantage is difficult to achieve through information systems because they can be copied. Even with patent or trade secret protection, competitors can eventually achieve the same functionality. A strategic advantage does give a firm a period of time where it is ahead of the competition and thereby provides the opportunity to keep innovating to stay ahead. And innovating it must do to maintain the advantage.

Just as for other initiatives, competitive advantage does not necessarily go to the first mover for an information system. Although the first mover can usually obtain benefits such as higher market share and product prices, customer loyalty, retention through switching costs, enhanced reputation from being a leader, and many more, the first mover also faces some disadvantages. Disadvantages include development risk because product demand is not known, higher development costs, free rider effects by followers, emergence of a dominant design in the market, and shifts in technology. An example is the early PC makers who were eliminated when IBM entered the market.

Strategic advantage lasts for a finite amount of time because strategic advantages turn into strategic necessities. Classic examples of this change can be found in the following:

1. The automatic teller machine (ATM) which was introduced by the Citizens and Southern National Bank in Atlanta, Georgia,[2] in 1971 without connectivity to the bank's computer system. It rapidly added connectivity and then network capabilities (you can tap into your account from machines worldwide) and swept the world as banks introduced them in an effort to gain strategic advantage. However, once nearly all banks (and other stores such as groceries) had them, they became a bank's strategic necessity to stay in business.

EXAMPLE OF COMPETITIVE ADVANTAGE AND COMPETITIVE NECESSITY

The classic case of strategic advantage was American Airline's SABRE reservation system. An airline needs to know which seats are filled and which are still for sale. When an airplane takes off, all unsold seats are lost revenue. American's original automated system goes back to an installation in New York in 1945.[3] Over the years this system grew to cover the entire network, including information on all flights, not just its own. Moreover, American offered terminals connected to its flight information to travel agents, at a fee. SABRE eventually grew to where it was generating more profit than the operation of the airline that requires large capital investment in airplanes. Clearly, American achieved a major strategic advantage. However, this success was not immediate. It took many years for the system to grow to its full capabilities.

American's competitors were faced with a strategic necessity. They either had to license American's capability or build one of their own. For example, United Airlines built its Apollo system and began competing with American Airlines. Other systems (e.g., Galileo, Amadeus) arose. Today, SABRE is only the third largest reservation system for airlines. However, its many spin-offs (e.g., into railroad reservation systems) provide additional revenue.

The impact of American Airlines' competitive advantage from SABRE can be seen from the impact on European airlines. They were at a competitive disadvantage from, among other things, their lack of an automated reservation system.

[1] For example, Merrill Lynch's Cash Management Account, discussed below.

[2] Source: http://www.premiumatm.com/atm_history.html. Last consulted 10-12-03.

[3] H. H. Goode and R. E. Machol, Systems Engineering, p. 14, New York: McGraw-Hill, 1958.

2. Department stores used to close by 5:30 or 6 P.M. except once a week when they stayed open until 8:30 or 9 P.M. When one department store in a city went to daily 9 P.M. closing, all the others competed by going to late closing. The net effect was that late closing time became the norm rather than being an advantage.

Continual Improvement

To try to maintain strategic advantage, firms undertake continual improvement projects. They use the time gained by their initial advantage to stay ahead. This tactic implies that the strategic advantage can be improved over time. However, some innovations (such as ATMs) reach their limits early and cannot continue to be improved on.

It is important to be aware that the gains from continual improvement are not usually from making the information system more efficient. They come from leveraging other resources of the firm. Here are some examples of continuing improvement:

Merrill Lynch Cash Management Accounts. Information systems are incidental. Determinants are service quality, creating new products that use the accounts, and switching costs.

American Hospital Supply ASAP. Customizing the system to the needs of individual hospitals extended this system for customer ordering of hospital supplies.

McKesson and Robbins Economost. This order entry system for pharmacies moved from advantage to necessity because, like the ATM, it became the norm for the industry. Although it increased financial results, it did not achieve sustainable higher than average profitability. McKesson was not able to improve Economost at a sufficient rate to stay ahead.

Introducing Strategic Information Systems

Many strategic information systems come about almost accidentally. A firm creates a system to help it internally (e.g., American Airlines to record its seat inventory), finds additional uses for it, and then figures out that their system might be marketed to others and bring revenue. No unique answer, no magic formula exists to ensure successful introduction of a strategic information system. Some generalizations, however, evolved out of experience.

Before discussing these generalizations it is necessary to remember that strategic systems can be built around information or around information technology. Information technology is often the way these systems are tied together. For example, Denny's coffee shops used a standard hardware platform.

EXAMPLE: FEDEX

FedEx, a major package delivering service, started with an automated tracking system that recorded the location and delivery status of every package. Package tracking systems rapidly became a strategic necessity for its competitors.

EXAMPLE: OTISLINE

OTISLINE, a maintenance system introduced by Otis Elevator Company, is an example of continuous improvement. The seemingly innocuous system differentiated Otis from its competitors. It started out by recording the time between when a service call was received and when it was completed.[4] The data helped reduce the time the customer had to wait for service, thereby improving satisfaction. The company centralized its service data and added service performance, cost estimates, and elevator and building information. With this information it was able to determine frequency of breakdown by elevator type and even by elevator. By identifying weak and strong components, the spare parts inventory could be adjusted and incipient failures could be identified. Furthermore, elevator designers could improve failure-prone components both for new systems and for replacement parts.

Otis did not stop there. It expanded the system to give repair people handheld terminals that would bring up the history of the elevator, the building, and the elevator's previous repairs. They increased the priority of emergency calls from elevators stuck between floors.

The next step was to install a microprocessor with communications in every elevator; that is, create a remote elevator monitoring system, which logged performance and communicated elevator problems. Technicians were now dispatched before an elevator went out of service.

In creating a new strategic information system, the following are important:

1. ***The Vision.***
   Vision is not a synonym for creativity. Vision does not specify the solution to the problem. Many strategic systems are actually quite mundane.[5] However, both senior management and IS must buy into it.
2. ***The People Involved.***
   Not only must the CEO and the Chief Information Officer (CIO, see Chapter 12) buy into the vision, but so must the system's champion[6] and key end users whose work life will be affected.
3. ***Catalysts and Barriers to Overcome.***
   Depending on whether they are favorable or unfavorable, the same attributes can be a catalyst or a barrier. Examples are clarity of objectives, technical expertise in IS, the relations between the IS department and the rest of the organization, cost–benefit analysis, incentives (long-term vs. short-term), planning, organizational politics, organizational bureaucracy, and management support. Of particular importance is the alignment of IS with the business, a subject discussed later in this chapter.
4. ***Implementation.***
   Strategic information systems are generally large projects and hence quite visible. Implementing them is a major chore. Here are some things for IS in particular (but also the rest of the firm) to look out for:

---

[4] The total time from receiving the call to arrival was an hour and a quarter, and the average service time was also an hour and a quarter. These times are phenomenal, given that Otis operates less than 400 service locations in North America.

[5] For example, Bob Smith, the VP of Otis Elevator said: "When elevators are running well, people do not notice them.... Our objective is to go unnoticed."

[6] A champion is a senior, well-respected person in the organization who acts as the sponsor and advocate for the system, has sufficient "clout" that people respect his/her opinion, and controls some or all of the funds and resources involved. IS projects, particularly strategic ones, without a champion usually die.

- Measure the benefits anticipated in terms of the business objectives that the system supports.
- Make sure the technical infrastructure is integrated into the mainstream. Form partnerships among the departments involved.
- Support the champion just as the champion supports the system.
- Keep management on board. Strategic information systems typically are long-term projects rather than showing results every quarter.

Risks

The previous discussion described various aspects of strategic information systems without considering risk. Yet strategic systems, because of their complexity and their tendency to include innovation, are much riskier than most IS systems. Unfortunately, data on failed systems is difficult to find because no corporate PR group likes to brag about them as they do about the firm's successes.

All information systems, be they strategic or not, encounter intrinsic risks such as over budget, over promised time, failure to meet technical specifications, and scope creep. Strategic information systems add extrinsic risk, the risk of not meeting business objectives.

Among extrinsic risks are

- ***Being First.*** Although being the first mover with a new system can offer strategic advantage, competitors are given a model on which to improve (e.g., American Airlines' SABRE reservation system). They therefore do not incur as great a development cost. While American Airlines was first and enjoyed a lead for some time, it is only third today because competitors caught up.
- ***The Basis for Competition Changes.*** A strategic system gains an advantage for a period of time, usually by changing the basis for competition. Yet a change in competition is also a risk because, by technology improvements and new ideas, competitors can change the situation once again. Many firms, once they gain the advantage, tend to stay with their way of doing things while competitors are busy finding ways to change the marketplace. Creating a new information system is one way of changing the basis for competition.
- ***Lowering Customer Switching Costs.*** Although unintentional, customers may find it cheaper to switch when they need only to switch terminals. To counter this risk, American Hospital Supply kept improving its product to provide services before its competitors could.
- ***Legal Intervention.*** Given companies' tendency to sue and government antitrust actions, innovations are subject to lawsuits. Patent protection can help but outcomes are always uncertain.
- ***Lack of Customer Acceptance.*** Like dog foods that dogs won't eat, creating strategic information systems that customers do not buy (e.g., because added infrastructure is needed or they don't see the benefit) is a risk. Unfortunately, you don't find out about such risks until after you've made a large up-front investment.

BUSINESS–IT ALIGNMENT

In recent years, considerable attention has been given to the alignment of information systems with the rest of the business.[7] As information technologies evolve and business strategies change, it is easy for them to get out of alignment. But align they must if the business is to obtain maximum value from its information technology investments.

In thinking about proposed investments, the IS group needs to ask whether the investment makes sense in terms of the company's strategy. Similarly, management needs to examine new IS products and services to see where alignment can be improved. That is, both business appreciation of IT and IT awareness of the business are needed.

Alignment is multidimensional and involves six categories of maturity:

1. Communications
2. Competency/value measurement
3. Governance
4. Partnership
5. Technology scope
6. Skills

We discuss each of these six categories in turn.

- Communications maturity refers to the understanding between executives and IS. Automating ineffective processes or implementing technology for its own sake does not improve the organization's bottom line or improve the view of IS.
- Ways of measuring the contribution of IS should be in place and presented in terms that business people can understand.
- Governance implies a joint decision process between senior executives and IS. The principal shared decisions are project selection and setting priorities.
- Partnership means an equal role for IS with other functions in defining business processes and strategies. For example, IS capabilities determine whether and how processes can be improved.
- In technology, IS's role is to evaluate new technologies, provide and support a flexible infrastructure (Chapter 14), and create or obtain software solutions for the firm. For many companies (particularly in service industries) IS is the only group with technical skills in the firm. An atmosphere of trust must exist between IS and executives on technical matters.
- IS skills need to match the strategy requirements for the firm. For example, if a firm's strategy is to use its data resources in a data warehouse (Chapter 5) for competitive advantage, it needs people skilled in both data warehousing technology and in the analysis of the data produced. When an application innovation is introduced such as, say, customer relationship management (Chapter 6), individuals in IT should be provided a culture and a structure that supports the initiative.

---

[7] For detailed discussions of this topic see J. Luftman, "Assessing IT/Business Alignment" and other articles in a special issue of *Information Systems Management* 20(4): pp. 5-42, Fall 2003.

Assessing the Alignment Maturity Level

Since evaluating business alignment involves multiple criteria, it is inevitable that a firm will be at different levels of maturity on each of the criteria. The evaluation will inevitably be biased unless both business and IT executives evaluate each category. Typically, the evaluation process will produce divergent answers. It is this divergence that indicates where the alignment problems (and opportunities) are. However, after several iterations, the assessment should move toward convergence.

Table 1 shows the summary rating sheet proposed by Luftman.[8] Don't worry at this point if you don't understand all the terms used. Most of them will become clear as you proceed through this book. The important point is for you to see that it is possible to create numeric values for measuring alignment for each category. The numbers correspond to five levels of alignment:

Level	Alignment
1	No alignment
2	Beginning process
3	Establishing process
4	Improved process
5	Complete alignment

Assessment is a four-step process:

1. Form a team of IT and business executives. For large firms, between 10 and 30 people are involved.
2. Gather information either with all people in the same room or via a questionnaire.
3. Decide on individual scores. The purpose of this step is not the number but to understand where the firm stands. Average the scores in each category.
4. If you believe categories should not be weighted equally in your firm, get agreement on relative weights. Average the weighted scores.

ALIGNMENT CONSIDERATIONS

The overall alignment score serves two purposes:

- It is a benchmark that can be used to determine improvement over time.
- It can be used for comparison with other firms.

Fortune 1000 firms running this alignment assessment the first time tend to obtain an overall alignment at Level 2, although they score at Level 3 for a few alignment practices.

Alignment when Strategy Changes

Companies change their strategy from time to time. For example, emphasis may change from internal cost efficiency to providing superb customer service. Such strategy changes create IT alignment problems. The tighter the alignment, the more complex and costly it usually is to change IT so that

---

[8] J. Luftman, op. cit.

Table 1 SUMMARY RATING SHEET FOR MEASURING IT ALIGNMENT WITH BUSINESS STRATEGY

Practice Categories		Practices	Averaged Scores 1 1.5 2 2.5 3 3.5 4 4.5 5	Average Category Score
Communications	1	Understanding of business by IT		
	2	Understanding of IT by business		
	3	Organizational learning		
	4	Style and ease of access		
	5	Leveraging intellectual assets		
	6	IT–business liaison staff		
Competency/ value measurement	7	IT metrics value		
	8	Business metrics measurements		
	9	Link between IT and business metrics		
	10	Service level agreements		
	11	Benchmarking		
	12	Formally assess IT investments		
	13	Continuous improvement practices		
Governance	14	Formal business strategy planning		
	15	Formal IT strategy planning		
	16	Organizational structure		
	17	Reporting relationships		
	18	How IT is budgeted		
	19	Rationale for IT spending		
	20	Senior-level IT steering committee		
	21	How projects are prioritized		
Partnership	22	Business perception of IT		
	23	IT's role in strategic business planning		
	24	Shared risks and rewards		
	25	Managing the IT–business relationship		
	26	Relationship/trust style		
	27	Business sponsors/champions		
Technology scope	28	Primary systems		
	29	Standards		
	30	Architectural integration		
	31	How IT infrastructure is perceived		
Skills	32	Innovative, entrepreneurial environment		
	33	Key IT HR decisions made by:		
	34	Change readiness		
	35	Career crossover opportunities		
	36	Cross-functional training and job rotation		
	37	Social interaction		
	38	Attracting and retaining top talent		
			Your Alignment Score:________	

Source: J. Luftman, "Assessing IT/Business Alignment," *Information Systems Management,* p. 14, Exhibit 2 Tally Sheet, Boca Raton, FL: Taylor and Francis Group, LLC, Fall 2003. Used by permission.

it is in harmony with the new strategy, goals, and needs. In our example, a cost-efficient firm might minimize IT costs. Yet, when trying to please the customer, a customer relationship management (Chapter 6) software package may be needed that introduces major expense. Changing strategy implies considering the implication of the change on the IT function.

INFORMATION ECONOMICS

Some years ago, my Dean (the person for whom I worked) asked me: "Is IS a bottomless money pit?" I assured him that it was.

Information systems in organizations are beset by a multiplicity of issues:

1. Information systems are inherently not cheap nor can new systems be provided quickly.
2. Information systems people are well paid (because they possess special skills) but many of them are more interested in their technology than they are in their firm. Labor costs are a major portion of ongoing IT expense.
3. No matter how much IT service and capability is provided, people in other departments want more and they want the latest hardware and software. Of course, they assume that someone else would pay for acquisition, training, and maintenance.

The net effect is an economic love–hate relationship between the people in the firm and the information systems group.

The situation is no better at a macro level. In 1987, Nobel Prize MIT economist Robert Solow said, "We see the computer age everywhere except in the productivity statistics." This statement was enshrined as "the productivity paradox" and economists spent the next decade trying to obtain data to support or refute it. The outcome was that the so-called paradox was disproved, although as you will see below in the discussion of the Carr article, it does not go away. At the national level, Alan Greenspan, Chairman of the Federal Reserve Bank, hailed productivity growth and stated it was due to the use of computers in the economy.

The Search for Productivity

Information systems are installed to gain productivity, whether it is in manufacturing, services, or decision making. Initially (and often still yet), the computer is used to gain productivity by substituting for human labor.

Productivity, at the simplest level, is a measure of the output per worker per unit input of that worker. Although this definition sounds simple, it is difficult to determine, particularly because output is difficult to measure for knowledge workers who use computers.

Productivity is measured in two ways[9]:

1. labor productivity, which considers the output per man-hour,
2. total factor productivity (TFP) that takes into account how effectively both labor and capital are used.

To individuals, labor productivity matters because it determines their standard of living.[10] For economists, however, TFP growth is the key number because they see it as a costless way of

---

[9] Source: "Solving the Paradox," *The Economist,* September 21, 2000.

[10] It is reported that the productivity of U.S. workers increased by a factor of 7 during the twentieth century and that this productivity gain is reflected in the U.S. living standard.

increasing growth without increased use of scarce inputs. Faster TFP growth automatically increases labor productivity.

Labor productivity can be increased through IT in three ways:

1. by increasing the amount of capital invested per worker,
2. by speeding up the growth in TFP in industries that produce IT because of technical improvements, and
3. by speeding up the growth of TFP in sectors that use IT.

Clearly, the growth in the IT producing industry was large since 1980; however, that by itself was not sufficient to be reflected in the national productivity statistics.

Time Lag Effects[11]

Analysis of previous major technological changes, the steam engine and electricity, shows a 40 year lead time between the introduction of the technology into business and its major effects on productivity.[12] Computing, which was introduced into business in the 1960s, does not appear to be an exception.

Growth in productivity refers to the increase in output per worker per unit input. Using data from the U.S. government's Bureau of Labor Statistics, the annual growth in productivity in different periods was

- 2001–2003 4%/year
- 1996–2000 2.6%/year
- Prior to 1996 1.5%/year

The argument made is that the massive investment in computers in the 1990s started paying off in the last several years. The reason for the lag is that just installing equipment and software is not enough. People need to be trained; they need to learn how to use what they have, and over time find innovative ways to use their new capabilities.

The Micro Level

The data at the national economy level are made up of the experience of individual firms. Brynjolfssonn at MIT and Hitt at the Wharton School looked at 600 large U.S. firms in the 1987 to 1994 period and found that computers resulted in productivity gains.[13] On a TFP basis, computers boosted annual growth by 0.25% to 0.5%. Furthermore, the productivity gains increased in individual firms over time, confirming the lag effect. Firms that decentralized were able to achieve the greatest gains.

---

[11] The numbers are based on T. Hoffman, "The Lag Effect," *Computerworld,* p. 40, January 12, 2004.

[12] The leading analyst of this effect is Paul A. David an economist at Stanford University. See, for example, P. A. David, "The Dynamo and the Computer: A Historical Perspective on the Modern Productivity Paradox," *American Economic Review Papers and Proceedings* 1(2): pp. 355-361, 1990.

[13] E. Brynjolfsson, and L.Hitt, "Paradox Lost? Firm-Level Evidence on the Returns on Information Systems," *Management Science* 42(4): pp. 541-558, 1996.

Why Invest?[14]

In measuring productivity, the input and output numbers are obtained by counting—be it hours worked, number of circuit boards used, or the number of checks processed. These standard measures work well if a firm is trying to reduce cost to produce the same product. However, in many cases, managers want to invest for other purposes, for example, to improve service or product quality. In fact, the latter two reasons were found to rank consistently above cost reduction as the investment motive.

ATMs are an example of how conventional measurements can mislead. ATMs, being more convenient, reduced the number of checks written. Yet, for banks, the number of checks cleared was used as a surrogate for measuring productivity. Thus, ATMs could be seen to increase cost (for the machines) while at the same time decreasing output. Thus, when you can count the investment cost but find it difficult to assess benefits, particularly benefits that occur after a time lag, IT can look like a poor investment.

Firm-level data allows measuring some of the productivity intangibles associated with computers. When consumers will pay more for convenience and/or quality, then a firm's income will reflect the increase in intangibles. High-quality firms force low-quality firms to lower price to be competitive. The net effect can be that while the computer-using firms gain revenue, the industry as a whole can remain flat. Thus, industry data does not necessarily reflect the productivity gains being achieved. Firm-level studies consistently found that a dollar of IT capital results in a substantial increase in revenue each year. Of course, the value that IT brings to a company can vary substantially from firm to firm.

Organizational Change

It is unfair to make the simplistic statement that the entire long-term gain in productivity is the result only of the computer. The gain comes from integrating technology with organizational change that takes advantage of the technology. Generally, for every dollar invested in IT, several dollars need to be invested in organizational change to achieve the rise in productivity and value.

Peter Drucker,[15] the renowned management guru, argued as early as 1988 that technology-rich firms would change to a flatter form from hierarchical organizations. In such firms highly skilled knowledge workers would be more involved in making decisions. We are also seeing self-directed work systems, flexible production, and business process redesign. These organizational changes are only possible because of information technology and low cost communications. Are both high IT use and high decentralization needed to achieve the productivity gain? In an analysis of the relations between them,[16] it was found that high productivity and high decentralization are indeed correlated.

---

[14] E. Brynjolfsson and L. Hitt, 1996, op cit.

[15] P. F. Drucker, "The Coming of the New Organizations," *Harvard Business Review* 66(1): pp. 45-53, 1988.

[16] E. Brynjolfsson and L. Hitt, 1996, op. cit.

Some Practical Problems

Although the data show that computerization can lead to productivity gains, several practical problems need to be overcome. Examples abound of such problems. Here are two of them from a manufacturing context:

1. When a new system is installed, workers (often unconsciously) wind up resisting the change. They are not trying to sabotage the change, but they simply use their old habits. In conventional assembly line manufacturing, the main objective is to keep the machines running and to create long intervals between changes. When a flexible or a "cell" manufacturing system is introduced, the old habits make people try to use the new machines just like the old ones, thereby negating the hoped-for gain.

2. Although managers want to empower workers to make decisions, many are afraid to do so. They want to talk about last night's ball game, not improving quality control.

The lesson here is that simply introducing computerization is not enough. The cost of the equipment was the smaller part of the investment in the new manufacturing system. The bigger part was changing the organization and its work habits. Investment in the organizational costs needs to be included if the productivity gains are to be achieved. The organizational investments and the technology investments need to be in alignment.

DOES INFORMATION TECHNOLOGY MATTER?

In the May 2003 issue of the *Harvard Business Review*, Nicholas Carr, then editor at large of the magazine, wrote a lead article entitled "IT Doesn't Matter," a polemic, in which he argued that the days when IT offered strategic advantage are long since gone and that managers therefore should undertake a different approach to IT. The article, obviously, became notorious among people who make their living in information systems but was hailed by many who had experienced the love–hate relationship with IS. Even 2 years after it appeared, the article still stirs raw emotion among IS people. Viewpoints range from "How Dare He!" to "Right On!" Many, even people in the supposedly cloistered halls of academe, are engaged in the debate. Most of them, of course, take the former view.

Our objective in this section is to discuss Carr's arguments and the arguments for and against Carr's position.

Carr's Argument[17]

"What makes a resource ... the basis for a sustained competitive advantage—is not ubiquity but scarcity. You only gain an edge over rivals by having or doing something that they can't have or do.... The core functions of IT ... have become available to all. Their very power and presence have begun to transform them from potentially strategic resources into commodit(ies). They are ... costs of doing business ... paid by all but provide distinction to none."

Starting with this premise, Carr concludes that there is no advantage to be had from IT. Therefore, he argues, firms should spend as little as possible for IT both in people and in treasure since the primary objective for commodities is to minimize their cost.

---

[17] N. Carr, "IT Doesn't Matter," *Harvard Business Review* 85(5): pp. 41-49, May 2003.

Carr argues that in recent years, particularly during the dot.com era, too much money was being invested in IT with little to show for it. Therefore, he argues, it is time to call a halt. Enough is enough.

Carr doesn't actually say that IT doesn't matter. While he acknowledges that IT is essential for business operations, he makes the case that IT should be managed as a commodity input, squeezing cost out of IT budgets while at the same time ensuring that IT platforms deliver the necessary reliability and security to avoid business disruptions.[18]

The Response to Carr

The most cogent response to Carr is by Michael Schrage,[19] codirector of the MIT Media Lab eMarkets Initiative and a columnist for *CIO* magazine. Schrage argues that free and easy access to a commodity does not determine its strategic economic value to the company. Rather, management matters. That is, how the commodity is managed that determines its impact. He says: "The idea that companies can divorce their resources—no matter how cheap, powerful and ubiquitous—from the act of managing them is patently absurd."

This Book's Position

This book takes the position that Schrage is right: IT is a management problem. Further, it recognizes that few firms below the Fortune 500 (and even some of those) can afford all the IT tools that are now available. They must select which applications to undertake and must assign sufficient managerial effort and energy to obtain the benefits that can be achieved. Unless managers understand how they are (or are not) involving their company when they make a decision about information technology, they run the risk of making the wrong decision.

Before proceeding to discuss some of the issues involved, we devote the next several pages to considering the arguments for and against Carr's position. [20]

The Arguments for Carr

Until the mid-1990s, IT was unique for companies because most computer applications were either proprietary or highly modified from the basic computer packages that were on the market. Thus, Merrill Lynch with its Money Market accounts, American Airlines with its SABRE seat reservation system and its customer loyalty program, and American Hospital Supply with its online ordering were able to gain competitive advantage. These systems were strategic because they gained competitive advantage by moving computing from back-office operations (e.g., payroll, accounting) into customer-centric applications. Unfortunately, because the advantage came from computer programs, their general features could be copied and copied quickly. The competitive advantage did not last long. Innovators, in effect, had to keep inventing so that they would not be overtaken.

The early computer packages were generic and not tweaked for specific industries. Today's programs are industry specific, most "right out of the box." That is, they are commodities unless they are customized to distinguish the firm from its competitors. However, customizing is not cheap. Rarely can the return on investment (ROI) be justified. Worse, the application vendors continually

[18] J. Hegel and J. S. Brown, "IT Does Matter," http://www.johnhagel.com/blog20030515.html.

[19] M. Schrage, "Why IT Really Does Matter," *CIO* August 1, 2003.

[20] The discussion that follows is based on L. DeJarnett, R. L. Laskey, and H. E. Trainor, "From the CIO Point of View: The 'IT Doesn't Matter' Debate," *Communications of AIS* 13, p. 26, April 2004.

modify their programs, which implies that customizing must be repeated each time the program is upgraded. That's not a winning combination.

Another support for the Carr argument comes from IT itself. Many IT organizations lack people with user experience and perspective. Their people tend to be technocentric with internal rather than company goals. They seem to speak a strange language. The result is that they do not communicate well, if at all, with the rest of the enterprise. Furthermore, most firms experience some IT failures: systems that don't work, are delivered late, are over budget, or all of these three. Although each failure may be explainable and understandable, people in the rest of the organization only remember the outcome, the times they were burned by an IT venture. The net effect is that many IT organizations lack credibility within their own firm.

Carr's rules for firms that follow his viewpoint are

1. Spend less.
2. Follow, don't lead.
3. Focus on the risks of IT, not the opportunities.

These dicta are hard to argue with. Companies that spend the most on IT do not necessarily do the best financially. Following rather than leading reduces risk. Vulnerabilities from technical glitches, outages, and security breaches are threats. These arguments make sense to a CEO or CFO.

Note that if a company gives up on IT as its strategic advantage, then it needs to find some other means of distinguishing itself in the marketplace, for example, patents, branding, or superb service.

The Arguments against Carr's Position

The Carr article triggered a series of letters to the *Harvard Business Review* to rebut Carr's position. Here are some excerpts[21]:

> *IT adds great first mover value: "With standards in place, the IT staff can finally concentrate on ... applications that reflect the firm's distinctive characteristics and allow it to share information easily with customers and suppliers." IT is not a commodity because, "Even the most tightly controlled generic application suite ... can deliver completely different results for look-alike firms."*
>
> Paul Strassman, former CIO for the department of Defense and for Xerox Corporation

> *While there are no innovative ways of using other infrastructure commodities like electricity, adding the human element to IT proves that more is going on here than meets Carr's eye. It's actually business practice innovation plus IT innovation that results in success: "The differentiation is not in IT itself but in the new practices it enables. IT does indeed matter," citing Wal-Mart and Dell as companies that used IT to help build and sustain strategic advantage.*
>
> *"It has never been true that IT matters in isolation. It only matters in the context of a concerted effort to innovate based on new possibilities and opportunities offered by the technology. Then it matters—and will continue to—a lot."*
>
> John Seeley Brown, former Chief Scientist at Xerox and John Hagel III, management consultant

[21] These comments are based on the letters to *Harvard Business Review* responding to the Carr article. They were organized by Line 56.com http://www.line56.com/articles/default.asp? NewsID=4650.

Carr asks why lead in IT when being first follower is easy, timely, and involves less risk? "The fast follower is up against less risk but also has to recover lost ground," they noted, offering Charles Schwab versus Merrill Lynch, and Walgreens versus CVS as examples. American Airlines' SABRE reservation system, an IT innovation, is responsible for the very existence of "an otherwise doomed" organization.

Warren McFarlan and Richard L. Nolan, Harvard Business School professors

Carr's point that "simple possession of infrastructure technology" is in itself a misguided premise, because it is actually the integration of innovative processes with technology (as in the case of Wal-Mart and Dell) that leads to real IT benefits.

Marianne Broadbent, Mark McDonald, and Richard Hunter of Gartner Group

"Information systems can be embedded in a company's ... processes and combined inextricably with other capabilities and assets to produce superior performance."

Vladimir Zwass, professor Fairleigh-Dickinson University and editor of the *Journal of Management Information Systems*

John Hegel III and John Seeley Brown (whose letter is cited above) also wrote:[22]

Extracting business value from IT requires innovations in business practices. *In many respects, we believe Carr attacks a red herring—few people would argue that IT alone provides any significant business value or strategic advantage.*

The economic impact from IT comes from incremental innovations, rather than "big bang" initiatives. *A process of rapid incrementalism enhances learning potential and creates opportunities for further innovations.*

The strategic impact of IT investment comes from the cumulative effect of sustained initiatives to innovate business practices in the near-term. *The strategic differentiation emerges over time, based less on any one specific innovation in business practice and much more on the capability to innovate continually around the evolving capabilities of IT.*

TYPES OF INFORMATION SYSTEMS

Computer-based information systems are usually classified into three broad categories:

- Transaction processing systems
- Management information systems
- Decision support systems

Transaction Processing Systems

Transaction processing systems are the workhorses that create much of the productivity gains from computerization. In retail establishments, the day of the clerk laboriously entering every sale, payment, and return by hand and ringing up the cash register are long gone. Rather, clerks scan a bar code and punch a keyboard or swipe a credit card, and see the transaction recorded on a screen. Sitting underneath this activity is a computer (often one bought long ago and now called a legacy) and its software that records the transaction and keeps track of simple quantities such as the total sales and returns by register.

---

[22] Published in John Hegel III's weblog: http://www.johnhagel.com/perspectives.html May 15, 2003.

Management Information Systems

Although transaction systems do well at keeping track of individual events as they occur and can create some totals, they do not give a picture to managers of how well or poorly a business is doing. That's the next step up. Here, for example, the information system aggregates the transactions in various ways: by department, by store, by line of business, by sales person, and more. The core of management information system is the standard and ad hoc reports it produces. These reports allow first-level, mid-level, and senior managers to keep track of where their organization stands.

In more formal terms, a management information system (MIS) provides previous, current, and forecast information needed for planning, organizing, and controlling business operations. Management information systems deal with structured problems; that is, problems which are repetitive and well understood.

Decision Support Systems

Decision support systems (DSS) deal with semistructured problems. Such problems arise when managers are faced with decisions where some but not all aspects of a procedure or task are known. To solve these problems and use the results for decision making requires judgment of the person using the system. Typically, such systems include models, data manipulation tools, and the ability to handle risk and uncertainty. Thus, for example, decision support systems can include the ability to do what-if analysis to look at the impact of changes in assumptions, goal seeking to find the value of the inputs needed to reach specified objectives (e.g., profit level, return on investment), and simulation capabilities to show the potential distribution of outcomes. Models may include standard financial models or more complex management science models.

A simple form of decision support system is a spreadsheet. It can be used for what-if analysis, for goal seeking, and, with add-in software, for simulation.

A sophisticated form is a group decision support system (GDSS). The idea is to use the computer to support groups of people involved in a decision. Although the early efforts in GDSSs were designed to help people in a conference, the present technology focuses on Web-based systems, such as Lotus Notes and Domino from IBM and NetMeeting from Microsoft , that help people dispersed in time and space.

Knowledge-Based and Other Systems

In recent years, a number of large-scale specialized computer-based systems were developed that don't fit neatly into the three categories of transaction systems, MIS, and DSS. We will discuss a number of them in the following chapters of this book. As indicated in Chapter 1, these specialized systems include (in alphabetic order) business and competitive intelligence, customer relationship management (CRM), data mining, enterprise requirements planning (ERP), knowledge management, and supply chain management.

INTERORGANIZATIONAL COMPUTING

Interorganizational computing is the last step in an evolution of business computing:

1960s	Stand-alone applications for a single business or SBU
1970s	Online and integrated applications that support multiple applications

1980s	Enterprisewide computing where data are a computer resource across multiple computer systems
1990s forward	Leverage data and information technology across firms.

As implied by the list, interorganizational computing refers to sharing computer information (and systems) between two or more firms. An example is the national networks for ATMs that allow you to use almost any bank's ATM machine to access your account at another bank. Sharing can also be the result of the greater interdependence of firms as they rely on one another as parts of the supply chain (Chapter 11).

Interorganizational computing does not imply the need for major new hardware and software. The technology that is used for enterprisewide computing is applied to allow access to people outside the organization. These systems also require communications access, but that is often handled through the World Wide Web. The systems need to know (e.g., by creating lists) which outside firms are to be given access to which data. Access is a matter of security (Chapter 15) about what is critical to the firm. For example, a firm may be willing to share information about anticipated demand to their supplier (so that supply can be adjusted to anticipated production) but not pricing and certainly not customer lists.

A common way to think about interorganizational systems is in terms of four questions[23]:

- ***Why?*** Is there a business purpose? Can you leverage the existing business or enter a new business?
- ***Who?*** Who participates (customers, dealers, suppliers, competitors)?
- ***What?*** What information capabilities are given to participants? Do these capabilities include entering, storing, and manipulating data? The specific capabilities depend on the way the firms cooperate.
- ***How?*** How do participants improve the way they work together?

In the "what" question, three ways of cooperating can be defined. The simplest is a boundary transaction where one firm enters an order or scans a catalog. More complex is where a firm's database is shared among participants, such as the FedEx tracking system for packages. The greatest complexity occurs when the firm helps its clients perform their internal functions, for example, maintaining inventory in a drugstore.

Interorganizational systems, working between separate legal entities, can introduce legal problems. For example, when does an e-mail become an order or an order cancellation?

Replacing Intermediation through Electronic Markets

Interorganizational systems started with electronic data interchange where two or more business partners exchanged orders according to a rigid format to gain operational efficiencies. These systems are now expanded to where a firm can scan the price and availability lists of its vendors to find the best vendor with whom to place an order.

Electronic markets reduce the need for intermediation, since they are themselves intermediaries. Whether it is Reuters for currency exchange or NASDAQ for brokering stocks, the communications link replaces the intermediary. Disintermediation is also the case in air travel, where the share of bookings by travel agents (the intermediaries) declined significantly as travel schedules and prices became available online and electronic tickets replaced physical tickets.

---

[23] Neumann, op. cit., p. 58.

KEY ISSUES

For over 25 years, periodic surveys sponsored by the Society for Information Management (SIM)[24] were made to determine the key issues in information systems. This section describes the most recent of these surveys, taken in 2003.

The results are based on 253 responses from SIM members and 48 from the Conference Board.[25] The top 10 managerial concerns are listed in Table 2 and then described individually.

Table 2 TOP 10 MANAGERIAL CONCERNS ABOUT IT

1. IT and business alignment	6. Measuring performance of IT organizations
2. IT and strategic planning	7. Creating an IT architecture
3. Security and privacy	8. Avoiding complexity
4. The supply of IT professionals	9. Speed and agility
5. Measuring the value of IT investments	10. IT governance

Source: J. Luftman and E. R. McLean, "Key Issues for IT Executives," *MISQ Executive* 3(2): p. 91, June 2004, copyright by the University of Minnesota. Used by permission.

1. ***IT and Business Alignment.***

Alignment of the IT organization, discussed earlier in this chapter, implies that IT is applied appropriately and in a timely way. Thus, IT should be in harmony with business strategies. Re-alignment may be needed when corporate strategy changes.

2. ***IT Strategic Planning.***

Strategic planning differs from strategic use of IT (Chapter 1). It is closely related to IT and business alignment.

3. ***Security and Privacy.***

The vulnerability of IT to terrorists, hackers, viruses, and other ills as well as the loss of privacy and the threat of identity theft are included here. Security and privacy (Chapter 15) also relate to homeland security.

4. ***The Supply of IT Professionals.***

Despite the recession of the early 2000s and the offshoring of jobs (Chapter 9) that led to extensive layoffs, firms believe that attracting, developing, and retaining IT professionals is a serious problem. The fewer people studying IT in the universities and the shortage of people who can manage the new global sources are particularly worrying.

5. ***Measuring the Value of IT Investments.***

As discussed earlier in this chapter, there is a division of opinion, based on interpreting the IT productivity statistics and represented by articles such as Carr's, on whether IT makes a difference

---

[24] The Society for Information Management (SIM), located in Chicago, Illinois, is an international professional association of about 3000 senior people in information systems, most of who are IS executives and Chief Information Officers. Established in 1968, SIM is a community of thought leaders who share experiences and intellectual capital, and who explore future IT direction. The data in this survey is presented in J. Luftman and E. R. McLean, "Key Issues for IT Executives," *MIS Quarterly Executive* 3(2): June 2004, on which this discussion is based.

[25] http://www.conference-board.org.

in the firm's bottom line. Part of the problem is that it is difficult to measure the contribution of particular IT projects or of IT as a whole to the business. Simply saying that a firm would close down without its IT capabilities is not enough.

6. ***Measuring the Performance of IT Organizations.***

Just as it is difficult to measure the economic impacts of IT at both the national and firm level, it is difficult to determine how well a particular IT organization is doing. Is the IT organization developing applications cost-effectively? Is it doing a good job compared to IT organizations in similar firms? Only a few firms try to use quantitative measurements to measure performance.

7. ***Creating an Information Architecture.***

Architecture is usually thought of in terms of the plans and aesthetics of a building. In IT, "architecture" describes how the firm's infrastructure (its processors, its PCs, its networks, its software, and other components) works together. Over time, the architecture of a firm becomes more complex and the need to integrate the pieces (Chapter 10) becomes greater. Some equipment and software become legacies in that they come from an earlier era and must work with later acquisitions. Integration is a difficult task and never seems finished. Outsourcing (Chapter 9) becomes an appealing alternative if integration becomes too difficult to do well.

8. ***Reducing Complexity.***

Complexity is linked to architecture. If a firm streamlines its information architecture by creating common IT platforms and standard configurations, it reduces complexity. Complexity is also an issue with respect to the IT hardware, software, and services that a firm buys. Vendors continually offer upgrades and additional features, many of which do not serve a business purpose but which incur training and conversion costs.

9. ***Speed and Agility.***

As the business pace quickens, the time available for activities and changes moves from years to months or weeks. IT must be able to deal with this time compression if the firm is to lead rather than follow. IT, like other parts of the business, is moving into a "sense and respond" mode and must attain as much if not more speed and agility than other functions.

10. ***IT Governance.***

Governance refers to how IT is organized and run. Some firms use an IT steering committee, consisting of executives from the other functions and the Chief Information Officer, to provide policy and governance oversight. The steering committee also sets priorities for the order in which projects should be accomplished when the number of desirable projects exceeds the funds and manpower available. In this approach, the CIO doesn't become the one who determines whose job gets done next. Others argue that no other function in a business has a steering committee (e.g., a marketing steering committee? an accounting steering committee?) and that therefore IT should not be singled out.

Although issues moved up and down over the years, most of them were in the top 10 on many of the previous lists. Therefore it is reasonable to expect that the current issues will still be there in the years ahead. Note that, over time, the emphasis shifted from the top five concerns, including two or three technology issues, to the 2003 survey where the top five issues were all business related.

Table 3 shows the issues ranked from 11 to 20.

Some of the issues in Table 3 such as managing outsourcing relationships (15), Sarbanes–Oxley (17), and societal impacts (20) can well be expected to become more important in the future.

Table 3 ISSUES RANKED 11 TO 20

11. Business process reengineering	16. Leveraging the legacy investment
12. Introducing rapid business solutions	17. Sarbanes–Oxley Act of 2002
13. The evolving role of the CIO	18. Globalization
14. IT asset management	19. Impact of offshore outsourcing on IT careers
15. Managing outsourcing relationships	20. Societal implications of IT

Source: J. Luftman and E. R. McLean, "Key Issues for IT Executives," *MISQ Executive* 3(2): p. 91, June 2004, copyright by the University of Minnesota. Used by permission.

Application and Technology Developments

In addition to looking at the managerial concerns, this survey also ranked application and technology developments. The 13 areas identified are listed in Table 4.

Unlike the key issues for management described above, where many issues reappeared year after year, only infrastructure development (which appeared in 1994 as issue 1) reappeared in 2003. The reason is that all the other technologies are effectively new since 1994.[26]

The top application, business intelligence (Chapter 8), combines many other applications and technologies, including data warehousing and data mining (Chapter 5), CRM (Chapter 6), and knowledge management (Chapter 7) so that firms can leverage information about their own business and their competitors and make improved decisions. Business intelligence, in particular, makes use of large data bases to help managers assess the firm's performance better and improve its operational productivity.

On the other hand, e-business strategies (Chapter 3), which was first or near first in many recent surveys, slipped to sixth, indicating that we are beginning to understand e-business better and are able to make it just another way of delivering products.

Table 4 RANKING OF APPLICATION AND TECHNOLOGY DEVELOPMENTS

1. Business intelligence	8. Customer relationship management (CRM)
2. Infrastructure development	9. Enterprise resource planning (ERP)
3. Enterprise application integration	10. Employee portals
4. Web services	11. Mobile and wireless applications
5. Knowledge management	12. Supply chain management
6. E-business strategies	13. Supplier portals
7. Customer portals[27]	

Source: J. Luftman and E. R. McLean, "Key Issues for IT Executives," *MISQ Executive* 3(2): p. 96, June 2004, copyright by the University of Minnesota. Used by permission.

[26] Although there were precursors and early versions in 1994 for some of the technologies and applications (such as ERP) listed in Table 3, they all rose to prominence in the years since then.

[27] Portals, discussed briefly in Chapter 1, refer to gateways to websites, which may be public (e.g., Yahoo or Google) or private (e.g., to a corporate website). A customer portal, for example, is designed to lead prospective buyers through the various wares offered by vendors such as Dell or an auction house such as eBay. Employee portals are available only to people who work in a firm. They can include, for example, human relations information (e.g., work rules or forms to be filled out), parts lists, or company private knowledge bases.

ANSWERS TO MANAGERIAL QUESTIONS

When does an information system become strategic?

An information system becomes strategic when it helps a firm increase its return on investment above the normal level in an industry. Strategic advantage tends to be transient because the functions and outputs of strategic information systems can be copied.

How can I evaluate the strategic ability of the information systems I have?

Most strategic systems were developed for other purposes. They became strategic when they were modified to perform functions that had not been done before and management understood that the new product or service would change the terms of competition in their industry.

What are some examples of strategic use?

Airline reservation systems, online customer ordering systems, Merrill Lynch's Cash Management account, and Otis Elevator's maintenance system.

Is creating strategic advantage easy?

No, definitely not. It requires vision, strong implementation, dealing with risks, and more.

Why should I worry about business–IT alignment?

Business–IT alignment measures how well the objectives and actions of the information systems group coordinate with and support the objectives of the firm as a whole. If they are not aligned, the firm is wasting resources.

What are interorganizational systems and what can I do with them?

In simplest terms, interorganizational systems allow sharing computer information (and systems) between two or more firms.

What are the economics of information technology?

The large, continuing investment by firms in information technology is designed to improve productivity in the office and the factory. Whether the productivity gains pay for the investment was long a subject of dispute. As we moved into the twenty-first century, it became clear from data at both the national and the firm level that the desired productivity gains are being achieved and that they can be expected to continue into the future.

However, just spending money on IT is not enough. IT changes the way people work. Thus, it is necessary to introduce organizational changes to take advantage of the technology. Simply making a new system act like an old system is not sufficient.

Investments in information technology are also designed to improve customer service and product quality, which turn out also to increase productivity.

Does information technology matter?

Critics of IT argue that information technology no longer distinguishes firms from one another. That is, since everyone can buy and use the same equipment and software, IT is a commodity. Therefore, IT costs should be minimized. The counterargument to this view is that firms that are clever in the way they use IT can, in fact, outcompete others in their industry. IT advocates argue that free and easy access to a commodity does not determine its strategic economic value to a company. Rather, management matters. That is, how the commodity is managed determines its impact. Schrage, for example, says, "The idea that companies can divorce their resources—no matter how cheap, powerful, and ubiquitous—from the act of managing them is patently absurd."

What kinds of information systems are there?

Information systems are characterized by what they do. They range from transaction processing systems (TPS) that keep track of events as they occur, to management information systems (MIS) that aggregate events and provide the data managers need to keep the business running, to decision support systems that combine data and models to help solve semistructured problems. In addition, specialized systems are used for such tasks as enterprise requirements planning, managing knowledge, business and competitive intelligence, customer relationship management, and supply chain management.

What are the key IT issues in the years ahead?

The three top management issues are

- Business–IT alignment
- IT strategic planning
- Security and privacy

The three top application and technology developments are

- Business intelligence
- Infrastructure development
- Enterprise application integration

Complete lists are provided in the Key Issues section of this chapter.

PROBLEMS

1. STRATEGIC INFORMATION SYSTEMS

   Consider your own industry (or one with which you are familiar). Describe the strategic advantages that have been gained by your firm and by your competitors through information technology. Indicate which of these are still competitive advantages and which have become strategic necessities. Indicate the time periods for both advantages and necessities. In addition to listing the changes that occurred, pick one and describe its history in detail.

2. DOES IT MATTER?

   Examine the original Carr article in *Harvard Business Review*, the responses to the article, if possible Carr's book on *IT Doesn't Matter*, and the *Communications of AIS* article (http://cais.isworld.org/contents.asp Volume 13, Article 26, April 2004). Consider Carr's main arguments and discuss why you agree or disagree with each of them. Give examples from your own firm if possible.

3. BUSINESS–IT ALIGNMENT

   Consider a firm where business and IT are finally aligned. Suppose something occurs in the business (e.g., a change in profitability, a new technology by a competitor, a new CEO with a different approach) that causes the firm to change direction or change its way of doing business. At this point, the work on alignment has to be done over to face the new realities. Describe some of the things that can be done by IT (and/or the business) to realign. Use specific examples of situations and responses. Consider the costs and benefits involved.

4. INFORMATION ECONOMICS

   The key argument made for investment in information systems is that IT increases productivity. Such arguments are relatively straightforward when transaction processing systems are considered. However, it is not as clear that they apply when other types of information systems, such as decision support systems are involved. Present arguments (pro or con) on why the other types of systems considered in this chapter lead to productivity improvements for the firm.

5. WEB-BASED SYSTEMS

   The 1990s were the era of client-server hardware systems. The idea was that rather than doing all the computing at centrally located mainframes, the computer at a worker's desk would perform the calculations needed to create the interface and other functions. A countertrend was the thin client, where all computing was done centrally and the terminals are given little or no computer capability. A third way, an evolution in the twenty-first century, is the use of web-based (e.g., Internet) computing where users need only use the browser on their machines. Discuss the advantages and disadvantages of the three ways of organizing computing.

9-198-020
REV: FEBRUARY 13, 2003

ROBERT D. AUSTIN

The Worldwide Web and Internet Technology

Introduction

The information resource known as the World Wide Web has grown rapidly in recent years. Private households, universities, and corporations in every geographic region of the world have invested in technology that supports Web use. Web technology enables users to access an immense and growing body of information that resides on hundreds of millions of computers linked to a vast network known as the Internet.

A person connects to the Internet using a Personal Computer (PC), some PC software, and previously arranged connection services provided by a third party or employer. Once connected, PC software known as a browser provides an interface which allows the computer to access Web content.

Ways of Connecting to the Internet

Phone	PC connects to phone line
Cable	PC connects to cable TV line
Satellite	PC connects to satellite dish
LAN	PC has direct network access

This Technology Note is intended to provide background on the evolution of the Internet and the Web, on characteristics of the supporting technology, and on current issues surrounding use of the technology. Designed for nontechnical readers, this Note aims to provide a general overview of what makes Internet and Web technology different from other information technologies and why those differences matter to individuals and businesses who are using the technology.

Types of Connection Services

Internet Connection Provider (e.g., "ISP" or cable company)	Basic connection services
Proprietary Content Provider (e.g., AOL)	Connection services plus subscriber-only content

A Brief History of the Internet

The Internet evolved from U.S. Department of Defense (DOD) communications infrastructure initiatives in the 1960s. To ensure continuous military communication in the event of an attack on the United States, the DOD sought to develop a system that did not rely on critical communication lines that might be targeted by an enemy. This survivability requirement led to the development of an

Research Associate Thomas Rodd prepared this note under the supervision of Professor Robert D. Austin, with assistance from Doctoral Student Mark Cotteleer and Jose Royo (MBA, 1998), as the basis for class discussion.

intelligent process for dividing information into individually addressed "packets" which could then be "routed" via any of a large number of paths to their destination. Routing of information packets along many paths remains a distinguishing characteristic of Internet technology.

The Internet began as a single network in 1969, called ARPANET, managed by DOD's Advanced Research Projects Agency (ARPA). Initially, the network linked researchers with remote computer centers, enabling hardware and software resources to be shared by many users. During the 1970s, access to the ARPANET was restricted to the military, defense contractors, and universities conducting defense research. In the early 1980s, the system was split into two networks, ARPANET and Milnet, and connections were made between the two in order to maintain communication. Users began to refer to the interaction between these two networks as "the Internet."

The birth of the Internet as it exists today came with the development of the National Science Foundation Network (NSFNET) in 1986. This network used five supercomputers to link researchers from around the country. NSFNET quickly expanded to include mid-level and statewide academic networks that already existed to connect universities and research institutions. Having been superceded by a large and expanding network, ARPANET was officially dismantled in 1990.

Internet Characteristics

Internet technology possesses characteristics that distinguish it from other information technologies. These characteristics make the technology easy to use, extremely powerful, and economically attractive. Consider:

The Internet is based on open standards and "protocols." Because the Internet is comprised of many different computer networks and many different systems, a common language standard must be used for interconnection. "TCP/IP" ("Transmission Control Protocol/ Internet Protocol") is the adopted common language of the Internet. TCP/IP standards define how computers send and receive data packets. The standard was developed for DOD's ARPANET using public funds and, therefore, exists as a public resource. The fact that TCP/IP is a free resource helps make the Internet largely independent from reliance on proprietary solutions that are developed and marketed by private companies. Insistence on open standards and solutions has become part of the ethos of the Internet's community of administrators and developers.

> *What happens to information when it is sent?*
>
> The information is first divided into packets. A "header" is attached to each packet that contains a "sequence number" and the packet's origin and destination "IP addresses"—four numbers from 0 to 255, separated by decimal points (19.67.89.134, for example). Packets are then transmitted via a "router"—a computer that tracks addresses—across an available link to other computers in the direction of the destination address. The process is repeated until a packet finds its way to its destination. A packet waits at its destination for arrival of the other information packets that were sent with it. When all packets in a group arrive, the sent information is reconstructed using the sequence numbers in packet headers. If a packet has not arrived after a certain period of time, a request to resend it is issued to the origin address found in the headers of other packets in its group.

The Internet is "asynchronous." Communication of information via the Internet does not rely on dedicated, bi-directional connections between sender and receiver, as with a telephone call, for example. Rather, packets are fired off toward their destination without any prior coordination between the sender and receiver. Internet services like the Web that involve exchanges of information within small time intervals (e.g., a few seconds), *do* require that sender and receiver be simultaneously connected to the Internet. But Web communication is still asynchronous in that no dedicated link is established. For other services, such as email, the receiver's computer need not even be switched on at the time the message is sent. Email messages are addressed and sent over the Internet much as physical mail is sent via a postal service. As with postal mail, a recipient has a mailbox where mail can accumulate until it is accessed. Unlike regular mail though, email messages can be sent around the globe almost instantaneously.

What is bandwidth?

The bandwidth of a communication link is the maximum rate at which information can be transmitted along the link. The smallest unit of information handled by computers is called a "bit." Bandwidth is measured in bits per second, or bps. Bandwidths associated with today's technologies are usually referenced in terms of their orders of magnitude:

- kbps kilobits per second (thousands)
- mbps megabits per second (millions)
- gbps gigabits per second (billions)

The Internet has "inherent latency." The computers that make up the Internet are connected by links of varying size or "bandwidth." As packets carry information along different paths toward a common destination, some packets flow quickly through wide links while others move more slowly through narrow links. Packets that together comprise a single message do not arrive at the destination in the same moment. Thus, there is variable wait time between the sending of a message and the arrival at destination of the last packet in a message. Because traffic volume is somewhat unpredictable, wait time can be difficult to predict. Although much can be done to make it likely that latency—wait time—will be within certain tolerances, latency is inherent in the design of the Internet.

Technology Bandwidths and Common Users

Communication Technology	Bandwidth*	User Type
Telephone Modem	56 kbps	Individuals and small businesses
Cable Modem	128 kbps – 512 kbps	Individuals and small businesses
Digital Subscriber Line (DSL)	128 kps – 1.5 mbps	Individuals and small businesses
Ethernet LAN	10 mbps–100 mbps	Most medium to large businesses and organizations
Leased Lines (T1, T3)	1.544 mbps, 45 mbps	Government, universities, and large corporations
Asynchronous Transfer Mode (ATM)/ Gigabit Ethernet	155 mbps–25.6 gbps	Government, universities, and large corporations

* Some of these technologies are theoretically capable of higher bandwidths. Also, some technologies perform at different speeds upstream and downstream.

The Internet is distributed. There is no central traffic control point within the Internet. Computers that are connected to the Internet do not need to be "defined" to a central control authority, as with some older networking technologies. There is also no central authority which oversees or governs the development or administration of this system (except for one that assigns TCP/IP addresses). As a result, individuals and organizations are responsible for managing their own Internet facilities in a way that does not hinder operation of the larger network.

The Internet is "scalable." Because the Internet communication is intelligently routed along multiple paths, adding to the Internet is as simple as connecting to a machine already connected. Just as the Internet is not significantly affected when a link is removed (packets simply get routed a different way), it is also not significantly affected when another link is added. Additional links can be added in parallel with overworked links, to provide more paths along which packets can be routed. Furthermore, Internet technology allows relatively easy reorganization of sub-networks; if a network segment has become overloaded, the network can be split up into more manageable sub-networks. In general, Internet technology allows more gracefully expansion than many of its network technology predecessors.

System Architectures

The large-scale computer networks of today are relatively new features of the computing landscape. Today's "Internetworking" world evolved from earlier centralized and client-server computing paradigms.

The Mainframe Computing Era: 1960s–1970s

Computers have been used by people and organizations to manage and disseminate information since the 1950s. Until the 1980s, a centralized computing architecture was prevalent, based on a central "mainframe" computer and "dumb" terminals. The mainframe provided computational and storage capabilities, while terminals were used as simple input/output devices. It was not until organizations began to share information and services among mainframes that computer networks were developed. Early networking technologies were proprietary and relatively simple, since they needed to handle traffic between a small number of large mainframe computers.

> ***An Internet Analogy***
>
> Imagine a complex highway system on which millions of cars are always moving. There are groups of cars that belong to the same travel party heading to the same place. But individual drivers only know the address where they are heading. They have no maps and no sense of direction. Members of groups make no attempt to stay together. At junctures along the highway network, there are routing stations where cars stop, show their destination addresses, and are told "try going that way." A single routing station may send cars heading for the same destination in different directions. Eventually, though, a car arrives at its destination. It waits for other members of the travel party to arrive, and then they all do something useful together. This is an overly simple, but fairly accurate depiction of how the Internet works.

Distributed and Client-Server Computing: 1980s

With the introduction of PCs in 1981, individuals could install significant computing power on their own desktops. Much of the processing and data storage that had occurred on a central mainframe could, therefore, be distributed throughout the organization. Coordination of this much more distributed processing necessitated the development of much more sophisticated and robust networking technologies.

The "client-server" computing model was the eventual result of distributing computer processing. Client-server divides the work done on computing facilities into front and back ends. Client programs are installed on the user's local workstation (usually a PC) and allow the user to interact over a network with back-end computers, called "servers." User interface and some processing duties are handled by the local workstation. Tasks requiring more power or access to information stored elsewhere are sent across the network to powerful servers, which send back results when they are finished. Sharing processing in this way can more efficiently distribute work, eliminate bottlenecks, and improve performance.

Internetwork Computing

Internetwork computing is an extension of client-server computing characterized by the linkage of an ever larger number of diverse computers into a global network. Internetwork computing presumes the existence of a publicly accessible common technology platform – the Internet – that can be leveraged by individuals and companies to productive ends. In effect, the Internet becomes an extension of the computing capabilities of connected individuals and companies, enhancing capabilities in a way that in earlier times would only have been possible (if at all) via each company's individual investments in private, proprietary technologies.

> *LAN, WAN, and MAN?*
>
> A Local Area Network (LAN) is a relatively small computer network that tends to use one type of transmission medium and covers an area usually within a building. A Wide Area Network (WAN) links LANs to form a larger network. A router defines the boundary between LAN and WAN. A Metropolitan Area Network (MAN) is a hybrid term sometimes used to refer to a WAN geographically contained (within a city, for example).

A corollary trend that continues with the spread of Internetwork computing is the migration of data storage and processing capabilities to back-end servers, which leaves clients operating increasingly as standardized input/output devices. In large companies, for example, processing systems may be designed to operate on centralized servers housed in a corporate data center. Or, back-end servers might migrate outside the company entirely, to vendor companies where they are accessed across Internet linkages. As network bandwidth grows, the need to locate processors close to users of processed information diminishes.

The ability to access processing and software functionality across a network allows new kinds of outsourcing and centralization strategies. Outsourcing companies and infrastructure providers support many customers and are thereby able, in the long run, to realize economies of scale that lower costs and increase service reliability. Because functionality and data storage is centralized, computing is equally accessible from every geographical location where an Internet connection is available, and there is rarely a need to move data from one client machine to another. In addition, because processing is handled primarily on servers, changes that would have previously required physically visiting each client machine can be distributed automatically from a central point.[1]

Internet vs. Web: A Distinction

Although the words are often used interchangeably, the "Web" and the "Internet" are not the same thing. Simply put, the Internet is the network upon which the service known as the World Wide Web runs. The Internet supports a wide variety of non-Web services also.

[1] For more information on these new models of outsourcing, see "Jamcracker" (Harvard Business School case number 602-007), which describes a sophisticated service delivery model; also, the "Selecting a Hosting Provider" exercise (Harvard Business School case number 601-171) and the "Web and IT Hosting Facilities" Technology Note (Harvard Business School case number 601-134) describe the economic and operational characteristics of outsourced infrastructure management options.

The Web is the assemblage of content documents in browser-accessible formats dispersed throughout the Internet. These documents contain text, data, and sometimes embedded graphics, video, and audio. They are identified by addresses (a.k.a. "URLs") such as "www.hbs.edu." "Hyperlinks" on document pages connect documents to other documents. Those documents can be any other place on the network. The tangled and complex nature of these hyperlink connections amounts to a "Web" of information connections—hence the name.

> *Some Non-Web Internet Services*
>
> Electronic Mail (Email): Allows individuals to send and receive electronic messages.
>
> File Transfer Protocol (FTP): Supports copying a file from one Internet location to another.
>
> Telnet: Enables remote access of an Internet connected computer.

Creating and Accessing Web Content

"Web content" is the substantive material stored on the Internet and gives this medium its energy and life. Content is created using standard presentation languages, the most prevalent of which is the "Hypertext Markup Language" (HTML). Using text editors or more sophisticated authoring tools, content designers lay out pages in a browser-readable format.

Maneuvering around the Web to access information is often called "browsing" or "surfing the web." Browser software, installed on a user's workstation, employs a graphical user interface (GUI) to guide the user so content files can be located and accessed quickly. The browser is essentially a navigational tool—a web "surfboard"—used to access and display files.

Users can locate files of interest by typing in a known address (e.g., www.hbs.edu) or they can use "search engines" to look up information by keyword or combinations of keywords. Search engines such as Google and Yahoo are web sites where a user can stop and ask for directions. They have functionality embedded in the page that permits a user to, for example, find all sites related to "Kansas City Barbecue." Search technologies vary and not all search engines provide equivalent results. But the technology is very useful and it is getting better all the time.

> *Some Sample HTML*
>
> **How it looks in the HTML document...**
>
> ```
> <HTML>
> <HEAD>
>       <TITLE>Text placed in browser title bar</TITLE>
> </HEAD>
> <BODY>
>       <I>This is how text is italicized,</I>
>       <B>and this is how it is bolded.</B>
> </BODY>
> </HTML>
> ```
>
> **How it looks through your browser...**
>
> **Text placed in browser title bar**
>
> *This is how text is italicized,* **and this is how it is bolded.**

Internet Security

Security is a primary concern for most people who are considering business uses of the Internet. The same open standards and protocols that make the Internet a powerful communication medium also create a need to govern who has access to what. Unlike mainframe-era systems to which access was denied unless explicitly enabled, Internet access is enabled unless explicitly denied. Information exchanged on the Internet can be passively intercepted in the same way telephone lines can be tapped. Internet links can be entry points for "hackers" who intend harm to an organization's computer systems. Malicious hackers can employ attack techniques aimed at disabling a web-connected computer without actually gaining access into it. These threats are real, but security measures are increasingly available to protect Internetwork-based computer systems.

Encryption and Digital Certificates

Software vendors and financial institutions have collaborated to develop sophisticated "encryption" techniques, as well as "digital certificates" to ensure information can be sent safely across the Internet. Encryption uses mathematical algorithms to alter information so it is unrecognizable to electronic eavesdroppers or other unauthorized individuals. An encrypted document looks nothing like the original and cannot be interpreted without a digital key both the user and sender possess for the purpose of decryption. More advanced techniques that use multiple keys are becoming more prevalent.

Digital certificates work in conjunction with encryption techniques. The certification process uses a trusted third party to assure the identity of an individual who transmits information. In order to obtain a digital certificate, the user must first generate an encrypted key and provide this to the issuing authority. Once the legal status of the organization and the contact names associated with the key have been verified, a certificate is issued which is installed on the user's Web server. This digital certificate is then used to ensure others of the user's authenticity and that the connection is secure.

Firewalls

While encryption and digital certificates are designed to protect transmissions sent across a network from eavesdropping, a "firewall" is a system used to prevent unauthorized access to an organization's internal systems. The firewall effectively blocks message traffic along certain paths, or allows it only after authentication. A firewall is commonly placed between the company's private internal network and the public Internet. The idea is to provide services and access for members of the organization while at the same time making it impossible for unauthorized users to access the private network from outside the company.

Denial of Service (DoS) Attacks

Over a period of a few days in early February of 2000, several prominent web sites were overwhelmed by floods of traffic designed to shut down all transactions at the sites. This attack technique, wherein automated programs direct huge amounts of apparently legitimate traffic to a target web site, sometimes from many locations at once, has become increasingly prevalent. Defense techniques include installing traffic monitoring software that recognizes the pattern of an attack and instructs the web site to ignore traffic from the attacker. Attackers continue to innovate in their patterns of attack, however; technology improvements continue, but there is no completely reliable defense against DoS attacks.[2]

Organizational Uses of Internet Technologies

Internet technology and the Web are rapidly being deployed inside organizations and between partner organizations, replacing older technologies in areas ranging from order processing to electronic data interchange (EDI). Internal and external uses of Web technology are sometimes described in terms of "Intranets" and "Extranets."

---

[2] For more information on DoS attacks and Internet security management, see "The iPremier Company: Denial of Service Attack (A, B, C)" case series (Harvard Business School case numbers 601-114, 601-115, and 601-116).

Intranets

An "Intranet" is an Internet technology-based network used within the boundaries of an organization. Intranets need not be connected to the public Internet, but most are. Those that are Internet-connected are protected by firewalls from outside intrusion.

An Intranet provides a cost-efficient way for an organization to exchange corporate data and files. The most common use of Intranets is to electronically publish company documents, such as employee manuals, product catalogs, brochures, 401(k) information, or engineering drawings. Documents published in this way can be accessed and used by employees around the office or, depending on the size of the organization, around the world.

Intranets are also capable of supporting business and technical computing applications that include all of the functionality that can be produced using older technologies. Organizations are increasingly moving more and more of their transaction-based day-to-day communications to their Intranets.[3]

Extranets

An Extranet extends an organization's Intranet to include outside companies it interacts with regularly. Extranets enable organizations to have direct interaction with suppliers, dealers, and customers, while maintaining security through the use of a firewall. Authorized personnel from partner companies can exchange information such as proposals, cost estimates, and product specification. This can be accomplished regardless of whether the physical separation between the two locations is across town or across the country. Technology now emerging will permit Extranets (and Intranets) to be acquired from service providers as a turn-key purchased service. Aggressive use of Extranets in areas such as Purchasing and Supply Chain Management have resulted in substantial cost reductions and cycle time improvements.[4]

When companies exchange data between diverse systems, the need to standardize moves beyond the common "languages" required to assure accurate transmission of information (achieved by TCP/IP) and to assure consistent display of information (achieved, more or less, by HTML). Business partners sharing data must also be sure they have common definitions for transmitted data, so data received gets stored, displayed, used, and interpreted correctly. For example, if one company transmits a "part number," the company that receives it must have a way of realizing what it has received is a part number. A standard, called eXtensible Markup Language (XML), is increasingly used for this purpose. Like HTML, XML uses "tags" attached to data items to provide information on how the data should be "handled" (e.g., in HTML <B> and </B> turn bold on and off). Unlike HTML, though, XML tags describe what is in a document rather than how it should be displayed. XML uses meaningful tags such as <EMPLOYEE>, <SSNUMBER>, and <DOB>, to describe content rather than its formatting. Standardized content labels make it possible to assure information received from a partner will be stored in the correct place in a database, for example, and that it will be used correctly in formula calculations.

---

3 For more information on Intranets, see "Ford Motor Company: Maximizing the Business Value of Web Technologies" (Harvard Business School case number 198-006) and "Sun Microsystems: Realizing the Potential of Web Technologies" (Harvard Business School case number 198-007).

4 For more information on Extranets and their uses, see "Ford Motor Company: Supply Chain Strategy" (Harvard Business School case number 699-198) and several Cisco cases such as "Cisco Systems: Implementing ERP" (Harvard Business School case number 699-022), "Cisco Systems Architecture: ERP and Web-Enabled IT" (Harvard Business School case number 301-099), and "Cisco Systems: Web-Enablement" (Harvard Business School case number 301-056).

The Need for Speed

The Internet is a voracious consumer of network bandwidth. Bandwidth is consumed almost as quickly as it is made available, by evermore bandwidth-hungry Internet applications. New technologies that permit order-of-magnitude higher transmission speeds are, therefore, of great interest in Internet circles. New high-bandwidth technologies are generally implemented first on the heavy traffic paths along the "backbone" of the Internet, then spread to connect individual machines to the backbone as the costs of the technology come down.

"Asynchronous Transfer Mode" (ATM), a high-bandwidth technology in common use along backbones, incorporates aspects of circuit switching, typical of telephone calls, where a direct, temporary connection is established between two parties. This "virtual circuit," established before information is sent, remains in place for the length of time the transmission requires. The main advantage of such dedicated circuits is that they support transfer of information within (very small) guaranteed time intervals. Hence ATM can be guaranteed to be fast enough to support real-time applications like video teleconferencing.[5] Internet technologies, with their inherent latency, can offer probabilistic assurances (e.g., "the transaction will arrive within one second of being sent with 99.95% probability"), but not guarantees.

Also in common use are "Gigabit Ethernet" and other technologies that are faster versions of existing Internet-related technologies. To support real-time video and other time-sensitive applications, enhanced Internet technologies must, because of their inherent latency, develop reliable schemes for giving time-sensitive messages priority as they traverse a network and for assuring a transmission path will always be available for high-priority messages. As these technologies improve, they are able to make "near guarantees" close to the guarantees ATM provides.

High-bandwidth technologies currently being deployed for connecting end users to the Internet (the so-called "last mile" of the connection) include satellite technologies, broadband cable (such as provides cable TV services), DSL (Digital Subscriber Line) and other variations on wireless and telephone technologies. Each of these technologies has advantages and disadvantages, and each fits most naturally with a subset of the communication challenge.

Conclusions

The Internet and the Web are changing the way organizations and individuals work, communicate, and obtain information. The technology is different in at least three important ways from its predecessors.

First, its reliance on open technologies facilitates economic efficiencies that could not be realized using older technologies. Historically, technologies from different companies did not work easily together. Choosing a computer hardware or software vendor locked the purchaser into that company's offerings even in areas where its products were not the best. Computer companies embraced this strategy of locking in clients to proprietary architectures. The Internet has changed the game somewhat by making open technology a priority. Companies that once would have resisted modifying their products to work with others' products now must do it routinely or risk market censure. For users of the technology, this means more product and vendor choices. It also means

[5] Robert S. Borsi, "Asynchronous Transfer Mode (ATM)—Technology Note." *Harvard Business School Publishing,* October 1996. Reprint No. 397-014.

systems that have not worked well together can be consolidated around the common TCP/IP standard, thus saving the costs of operating and maintaining redundant networks and systems.

Second, because of the scalability and openness of Internet technology, it has become very pervasive in a short period of time. The Internet is, literally, everywhere. Information providers are racing to make their information available via the TCP/IP language. Never in history has there been a comparable race to make information accessible via the same widespread medium.

Third, Internet technology is inherently attractive to a broad cross-section of people. Unlike many technologies implemented in the past, Internet services (especially email and the Web) have been demanded by their prospective users with vehemence even before they could be installed. While "user acceptance" has always been a concern of those who implement new technologies, there is a real sense in which Internet services were accepted before they appeared. People *want* to use this technology. They use it at home as well as at work, and they carry their expertise from home use with them into work.

Increasingly, the distinction between Intranets, Extranets, and the Internet blurs. There is one global network; everyone has access to some places and not other places. Geographically dispersed organizations work better together. The world is now smaller, in no small part because of Internet and Web technology.

HARVARD | BUSINESS | SCHOOL

9-601-134
REV: MARCH 4, 2003

ROBERT D. AUSTIN

Web and IT Hosting Facilities

Technology Note

The emergence of the commercial Web has accelerated creation of a worldwide computer network capable of transmitting large volumes of data reliably across vast geographic distances. As the network grows in capacity and reliability, companies gain more options for delivering IT services to end users, whether they are customers or employees. Managers are faced with new decisions about how underlying IT infrastructure should be designed and managed. Making the wrong decision can have severe impact on a business that relies on IT services to operate. Unsatisfied customers, unplanned outages, or security breaches that shatter customer confidence are among the disasters that can readily result from poor infrastructure design or management.

This technology note focuses on decisions about where to physically locate a company's computer systems. More specifically, this note introduces readers to emerging Web and IT hosting technologies which make it possible to move computer systems outside a company's own walls and into data centers belonging to companies that specialize in data center management. Outsourcing mission critical systems in this way generates new management challenges, not least of which is assuring that IT services are available and perform well enough to satisfy end users.

Hosting facilities physically house Web, application, and database servers, storage devices, and networking equipment in a robust environment that enables network based computer systems to function in a secure and reliable manner. These facilities are designed to provide space, power, and Internet connectivity, as well as a range of supporting services that varies across hosting providers. Although hosting centers are often referred to as data centers, they should not be confused with the mainframe data centers built by many enterprises during the last three decades to house their own computer applications. Enterprise data centers were typically designed around a different set of platforms (mainframes) and performance expectations; they are usually only partially able to meet the requirements of a modern hosting facility.

Proponents of hosting based infrastructures describe a future in which companies routinely obtain much of the IT functionality they need for day-to-day business "over the Net" from a variety of service providers. Services accessed in this way, they suggest, will replace many services that have traditionally been provided by internal IT departments. Hosting companies play a vital role in this picture, by owning and managing the facilities to house computers that provide over-the-Net services.

Professor Robert D. Austin prepared this note from published sources as the basis for class discussion.

The Hosting Value Proposition

Using a hosting provider to house and manage computer applications can potentially help companies meet several important challenges as they seek to maximize the return on IT investments. These challenges include:

The shortage of skilled IT workers

According to the US government, there will be 4 million unfilled IT jobs in the US by 2003. By outsourcing management of computer system infrastructure to hosting providers, companies can potentially reduce their need for IT staff, or at least reduce the number of very skilled employees that they must hire. Such benefits are especially important to the small and medium sized businesses that have the most difficulty attracting and retaining IT talent. Hosting companies can also realize savings, which can be passed on to customers, from economies of scale in the use of IT staff. For example: according to IT Centrix, the number of gigabytes of storage that an IT manager can manage ramps rapidly as the storage infrastructure becomes more centralized and shared.[1]

The need for 24x7 operation

Unlike traditional business operations, Web based businesses are expected to operate around the clock. Businesses seeking efficiencies from the Web derive them partly from the real-time and "always on" nature of the Web. But most companies lack in-house infrastructure capable of assuring 24x7 operation. Some enterprises have their own data centers, but many of those facilities were designed for different computing platforms (mainframes) and different performance and availability expectations. In contrast, hosting company data centers are designed for modern (server based) computing architectures and high availability. Because their facilities are shared across many customers, hosting companies can justify larger investments in performance and availability than their customers can individually.

The drive to reduce costs throughout the IT service supply chain

Hosted services offer cost saving benefits to hosting customers as well as to numerous other service providers. In addition to the staffing economies of scale that have already been mentioned, cost savings can also be generated by sharing computing infrastructure across customers. Hosting based models reduce the cost of making changes in a client company's software because fixes or upgrades only need to be applied to platforms within the hosting facility. Packaged software vendors favor the hosting service model because it reduces the potential for software piracy by keeping most software resident inside secure hosting facilities even while it is being used. Distributors of software can benefit from the reduced need to transport physical media for software (e.g., CD-ROM) and the smaller inventory of packaged software "boxes" that need to be managed. Studies have shown that moving applications to hosting providers lowers costs. Morgan Stanley Dean Witter estimates that costs can be reduced by as much as 80%-90%.[2]

---

[1] "The Internet Hosting Report." Jeff Camp, April Henry, Jaime Gomezjurado, Kristen Olsavsky. Morgan Stanley Dean Witter. November 2000.

[2] Camp, et al., ibid.

The need to reduce time-to-market

In recent years, businesses have increased their emphasis on using IT to enhance revenues by creating new business models, products, services, and industries. Revenue-side opportunities often offer significant early mover advantages. Seizing these opportunities depends on getting functionality up and running quickly. Here hosting helps by providing an immediately available physical facility to house new applications. Hosting companies also partner with Web systems integrators to offer standardized quick start packages.

The unfavorable cash-flow profile of IT investments

IT investments have traditionally required large up-front cash outlays and yielded only eventual and uncertain (because of high IT project failure rates) benefits. Hosted services typically require relatively small up-front setup fees and allow for subscription-based payment for specific IT services. Furthermore, hosting customers can decide to add additional services in relatively small increments and relatively quickly. Adding a new service or increasing the level of an existing service can happen in hours or days.

The need to make applications globally accessible

Hosted IT services are designed to make geography relatively unimportant to service delivery capability so that centralized data centers can serve large geographic areas. A side benefit of this design is that services can easily be available from any computer with a Web browser and the ability to authenticate. Traveling employees can access the same virtual "workspace" regardless of where they are physically in the world. The IT overhead associated with moving a worker from one location to another is eliminated because the IT infrastructure is geography neutral.

Inside a Hosting Facility

Although there is much variation in what are sometimes called hosting facilities, there are well-defined data center features to which providers aspire and that constitute a de facto standard. Particular facilities may fall short on one or more "standard features," but in the mainstream of the hosting industry providers tend to offer at least the following on a 24x7 basis:

Uninterruptible electric power delivery

Facility design typically allows for redundant power delivery to each piece of computing equipment housed in the facility (i.e., two power cables for each computer—high availability computing equipment often accepts two power inputs). Power distribution inside the walls of the facility avoids single points of failure and includes uninterruptible power supplies (UPSs) to maintain power to computing equipment even in the event of a sudden loss of power to the facility. Connections to external sources of primary power are also redundant; typical facilities can access two power grids. Redundant diesel generators are available for backup power generation with on-site fuel tanks containing fuel for a day or more of operation. There is usually a plan for high priority access to additional fuel in the event of a prolonged primary power outage. All components in the facility that are critical to continuing service delivery have at least one redundant stand-by unit.

Physical security

Security guards are posted in protected ("bulletproof") enclaves at all points of entry and exit, and they patrol the facility regularly. Closed-circuit TV monitors all critical infrastructure at all times and can provide immediate visibility into any area of the facility from a central security desk that is constantly attended. Access to internal areas of the facility requires picture ID and must be pre-arranged (i.e., there is a list of people authorized to enter the facility that is checked against the picture ID). Anyone entering the facility must cross through a "mantrap" buffer zone that can be locked down. Items (e.g., boxes, equipment) brought into the facility are opened and inspected. The building that physically houses the data center is dedicated to that use and is not shared with other aspects of the hosting company's businesses.

Climate control and fire suppression

Facilities typically contain redundant heating, ventilating, and air conditioning (HVAC) equipment capable of maintaining temperatures in ranges suitable for computing and network equipment in all areas of the facility that house computing and network equipment. Mobile cooling units are often used to alleviate "hot spots." Integrated fire suppression systems include smoke detection, alarming, and gas-based (i.e., no equipment damaging water-based) fire suppression.

Network connectivity

External connections to Internet backbone providers[3] are redundant, involving at least two backbone providers, and typically connect into the building through two physically separate points of entry. Hosting companies have agreements with private peering partners that permit significant percentages (say, 50%) of network traffic to travel from origin to destination without having to traverse often-congested public Internet junctions. There is a 24x7 network operations center (NOC) staffed with network engineers who monitor the connectivity infrastructure of the facility; a redundant or mirrored NOC on another site is usually capable of providing most of the services provided by the primary NOC.

Help desk

Customers are able to contact facility staff for assistance at any time. The facility has procedures for responding to unplanned incidents that can be invoked regardless of the time of day or night. Automated trouble ticketing systems are integrated with similar systems at service delivery partners so that complex problems involving interactions between multiple service providers can be quickly tracked down and alleviated.

Additional Hosting Facility Features

In addition to de facto standard features, some facilities provide further measures of protection. As hosting providers add these enhancements, the de facto standard seems to be rising. It appears likely that some of these additional features will become de facto standards in the not-too-distant future:

---

[3] "Backbone providers" own the very large data transmission lines via which large quantities of data are moved long distances.

Hardened physical structure

Facility structure is hardened against external explosions, earthquakes, and other disasters. Entry into facilities is through multiple, single-person capacity ("hostage proof") mantraps with integrated metal and explosive detection. Access to zones within the facility is controlled by biometric scanning technologies.[4] Internal private rooms and high security vaults are available to house the most sensitive equipment. Motion sensors supplement video monitoring. Perimeter fencing surrounds the facility.

Enhanced network infrastructure

This may include one or more of the following: mirrored NOCs, greater capacity for private peering traffic (up to 90%), three or more Internet backbone providers, placement of all mission-critical network components in segregated enclosures.

Enhanced power delivery infrastructure

This could include primary power generation by an independent power plant with first level of backup power from local utility power grids and redundant diesel generators for second level backup. UPSs might employ battery-less, flywheel-based technologies.

A Note Concerning Redundancy and Availability

The level of redundancy of mission-critical components that is commonly implemented today within a hosting facility is designated "N+1." This means that for each type of critical component, there should be at least one extra component of that type standing by. For example, if a facility requires four diesel generators to meet its power demands in the event of a primary power outage, N+1 redundancy would require that the facility have five such generators in total (four to operate, one to stand-by). Obviously, N+1 redundancy provides a higher level of availability if the underlying number of components (the N in the N+1) is small.

Increasingly hosting companies are aspiring to a higher level of redundancy, designated "N+N." This level of redundancy requires that there are twice as many mission-critical components as are necessary to run the facility at any one time. For example, a facility that requires four diesel generators to meet its power demands in the event of a primary power outage would need eight such generators on-site to achieve N+N redundancy. Where N+1 facilities are typically able to commit to service levels in the 99.9% availability range, N+N facilities can ensure availability levels in the 99.999% level. Not surprisingly, this very high level of availability is very costly. Forrester Research estimates that increasing the availability of a Web site from 99% to 99.999% — that is, reducing downtime from 90 hours per year to less than 5 minutes per year — will require additional initial spending of $3.7 million and additional annual fees of $1.8 million.[5] Morgan Stanley Dean Witter estimates that the cost of building a 99.999% availability data center is in the $400 to $550 per square

---

[4] "Biometric" technologies identify people by their biological characteristics; examples include retina scanners, palm readers, and technologies that recognize individual voices.

[5] "The Best of Retail Site Design," Randy K. Souza with Harley Manning, Hollie Goldman and Joyce Tong, October 2000.

foot range. For comparison, a data center capable of 99-99.9% uptime costs about $150 per square foot to build.[6]

Hosting facilities are often categorized according to the level of uptime they are able to support. Level 1 data center infrastructure is available 99-99.9% of the time. Level 2 is commonly equated to 99.9-99.99%. Level 3 ensures uptime in the 99.99-99.999% range. Level 4, the highest level of availability in current common usage, equates to 99.999-99.9999% uptime. A Level 4 facility experiences downtime at that is unnoticeable by most end users, literally seconds per year.

Managed Services

Guarantees of power, connectivity, climate control and security do not in themselves guarantee reliable and secure operation of a computer system within a hosting facility. An e-commerce application, for example, will not necessarily run well just because it is housed within a state-of-the-art data center. Rather, a computer application requires ongoing administration and tuning of the software, databases, and other elements of the computing infrastructure. Table 1 shows the layers of services that can be provided to a customer to support a computer application.

Table 1 Levels and Descriptions of Services

Level of Service	Description of Service
Business operating services[a]	Administering and operating an application.
Application support services[a]	Support for software above the operating system level; application support; application performance monitoring and tuning; design of applications for scalability, reliability, security.
Platform services[a]	Support for hardware, operating system; reboot services; data backup and disaster recovery services; URL monitoring.
Network services	Connectivity within the facility and externally to the public Internet and to private peering networks; monitoring of network traffic at the transport layer; service level assurances at the packet loss and network availability layer; network security.
Real estate services (lowest level)	Suitable floor space and physical facilities; maintenance of the space and facilities

[a] "Managed Services" - Business operating, Application support and Platform services

Notice that previously discussed hosting facility features are all at the network or real estate services level. This fact prompts a question: who should provide higher-level services? Customers can of course, provide platform, application and business operating services for themselves, but some may wish to outsource these services as well. Hosting companies are arguably well positioned to provide some of these "managed services" along with their facilities related offerings. Because high value-add managed services offer potentially high margins, hosting companies aggressively pursue this lucrative revenue source.

[6] Camp, et al., ibid.

Hosting Models

Hosting companies design their facilities based on one of three hosting models: shared, dedicated, and co-location. Each model assumes different levels of customer involvement in managing the computer systems housed in the facility. The hosting model also directly influences the degree of operational robustness that can be supported and the cost to the customer of the hosting service.

Shared Hosting

In shared hosting, servers are owned and operated by the hosting provider and customers purchase space on servers. Multiple customers share a single physical server. Some providers use sophisticated clustering technologies to achieve highly secure and reliable performance. But this model is usually considered best suited to non-mission critical hosting for small companies or individuals for whom low cost is an important requirement. Large customers are often wary of the degree of sharing implicit in this model, because of its perceived negative implications for security and reliability. Shared hosting typically provides entry-level Web site hosting for companies that want to post static content or mount basic applications, such as functionality to support basic e-commerce transactions.

Dedicated Hosting

As with shared hosting, servers are owned and operated by the hosting provider. Unlike the shared model, however, there is no sharing of servers between customers; servers are "dedicated" to individual customers. Other infrastructure components that provide network, storage, and some other services are shared across customers. Dedicated hosting providers usually offer a complete managed services package that includes everything needed to run the customer's systems at the required level of security and availability. Dedicated servers are able to support very high levels of security and availability. Hence, this model is suited to hosting the mission-critical application of large and medium-sized customers.

IDC separates the dedicated hosting category into three sub-categories called simple, complex, and custom dedicated hosting, defined as follows[7]:

Simple dedicated hosting This option relies on Web server appliances to deliver a narrow menu of highly standardized functionality, such as basic kinds of Web hosting. Web server appliances do not require complex configuration and are very simple and inexpensive to operate. In this dedicated hosting model, server appliances are typically allocated one per customer. Simple dedicated hosting is inexpensive but limited.

Complex dedicated hosting This option relies on two or more servers with different functions (e.g., Web, application, database) to meet a single customer's business needs. The offering supports a wider range of functionality than does simple dedicated hosting, but there is still an emphasis on standardized hardware and software configurations. The hosting company partners with manufacturers and developers of components that comprise the hoster's standard offerings; the hosting provider's staff becomes vendor-certified to support these components. By focusing on standard configurations that are more complex than those in simple dedicated hosting, this model facilitates reliable and economical operation of larger, but still somewhat limited, computer systems.

---

[7] "Web Hosting Service: US Web Hosting Market Forecast, 1999-2004," Melanie A. Posey and Courtney Munroe, December 2000.

Custom dedicated hosting As the name suggests, hosting offerings in this category are designed specifically to support custom functionality. Custom architectures usually involve multiple servers of types that go beyond the hosting company's established standards. To reliably design, build, and operate custom functionality, hosting providers often team with systems integrators, MSPs, and other professional service providers, who work and bill on a one-time, project basis to design and deploy custom infrastructure.

Co-location Hosting

Co-location hosting companies provide no-frills access to a facility and its infrastructure. Customers rent floor space, connectivity, and power inside a facility. Everything beyond these basics is provided à la carte and not necessarily by the hosting provider. Customer space is usually enclosed inside floor-to-ceiling cages, and the customer owns and retains responsibility for all servers and equipment inside the cages. The hosting company often knows very little about what is running inside customer cages. Needless to say, this model requires that the customer has (or acquires from a third party) the IT expertise to design, maintain, and operate the equipment inside the cages. This model supports a wide range of architectural possibilities and is generally capable of offering high availability. Large and medium-sized businesses are typical users of services in this category.

亞洲商業案例中心
Centre for Asian Business Cases
School of Business, The University of Hong Kong

Digital Certificates and Signatures: Microsoft Corporation

On 22 March, 2001, the Microsoft Corporation warned computer users that an individual posing electronically as a company representative had fooled VeriSign Inc., the leading digital certificate authority, into issuing two fraudulent electronic certificates in Microsoft's name. The certificates were issued on 29 January and 30 January, 2001. Despite the discovery of the fraud and the follow-up investigation by the FBI, the identity of the person who had registered the certificates remained unknown. The flawed certificates in the Microsoft case were used to prove the origin and authenticity of software programmes and data on the Internet, a key requirement for users who downloaded patches or software updates. Similar certificates issued by companies such as VeriSign were also used in creating secure Internet transactions with commercial Websites, sending secure and authentic e-mail, and in related applications.

The accident posed a great risk to computer users and could have affected all users of Microsoft's operating systems, ranging from Windows 95 to Windows 2000. An attacker armed with such certificates could produce digitally signed code and appear to be an official representative of Microsoft Corporation. In this scenario, the party could potentially host a malicious programme on a Website and then try to deceive users into installing and running the software. This meant that unsuspecting users who thought they were downloading an update of Internet Explorer or some other Microsoft software – from a site not affiliated with Microsoft – could end up with a destructive programme that could trash their hard drive or give hackers access to their entire network. The attacker could also choose to package the malicious code as an ActiveX control (an Office document with macros or other executable content) and send it to users by e-mail.

The Microsoft case was the world's first reported case of digital certificate fraud.[1] It raised serious questions about CA's practices in issuing digital certificates. Class 3 certificates, the kind that were given out to software publishers and developers, were supposed to be issued only after the most stringent measures had been applied to ensure that the identity of the applicant was valid.[2] Obviously, something had broken down in VeriSign's technical control and screening procedures.

[1] Palfreyman, J., "How to ensure e-security for e-biz", *The Business Times Singapore*, 6 August, 2001.

[2] Certificate Authorities usually offer a range of digital certificates, graded according to the level of inquiry used to confirm the identity of the subject of the certificate.

Mary Ho prepared this case under the supervision of Dr. Ali Farhoomand for class discussion. This case is not intended to show effective or ineffective handling of decision or business processes.

This case is part of a project funded by a teaching development grant from the University Grants Committee (UGC) of Hong Kong.

Ref. 02/139C 12 July, 2002

Officials of VeriSign took responsibility for issuing the certificates via an automatic Internet-based system. Mahi deSilva, Vice President and General Manger of the company, blamed the accident on human error and claimed the company's automated and manual process for examining certificate applications and identifying individuals who submitted them had held up. VeriSign cancelled the certificates on 9 March and 12 March, 2002, but could not be certain as to whether the false certificates had been used. Whilst details of the revoked certificates were included in VeriSign's Certification Revocation List, the list could not be downloaded automatically by web browsers. This forced Microsoft to develop an operating system update with information about revoked certificates.

The incident highlighted the tricky nature of ensuring trust on the Internet and the sophistication of digital certificates. Consumers did not know, when they were trusting Microsoft, that they were in fact relying on VeriSign's certification policies and procedures. Yet digital certificates issued by VeriSign could not provide absolute proof of identity. This means that similar e-business transactions that are conducted and secured by electronic certificates are also vulnerable to such a security flaw [see **Example 1**].

Example 1

Company A entered into an on-line business arrangement whereby it performed a service for a company that held a digital certificate of Company B. The digital certificate that Company A relied on was an erroneous certificate but the certificate authority failed to detect it. When Company A later attempted to enforce its electronic contract and collect from the real Company B, it found that it had become a victim of fraud. Should the certificate authority be liable in contract for its acts and omissions? Given that the certificate authority did not have a contract with Company A, what remedies were available to Company A?

The situation could be further complicated if the participants lived in different jurisdictions, as it would often be unclear which jurisdiction's laws would apply. Under the Utah Act, a digital certificate subscriber defrauded by a criminal could be liable for the loss caused by a forgery [see **Example 2**].[3]

Example 2

LCA, a licensed certification authority, duly issued a certificate to Kenny. LCA published the certificate in a recognised repository. Kenny's private key, which corresponded to the public key in the certificate, was kept on his computer's hard disk. Bob, a computer hacker, released a computer virus on the Internet that allowed Bob to gain access into Kenny's computer. Subsequently, when Kenny used his private key, the virus programme sent a copy of Kenny's private key to Bob. Bob immediately used the private key to cash an electronic check drawn upon Kenny's account payable to an anonymous account in a state having rigorous bank secrecy laws. Bob disappeared and could not be found. As soon as Kenny discovered the fraud, he revoked his certificate.

Under the Utah Digital Signature Act, Kenny would be liable for the loss caused by the forgery if he failed to exercise reasonable care in protecting his private key. Thus Kenny would have to obtain the services of an attorney and go to court. He would have to overcome the presumption that the electronic check signed with his digital signature was valid and binding upon him, and he would have to prove that in fact he did not affix the digital signature in question. Furthermore, he would have to show that he did not breach his duty of care in allowing Bob, the criminal, to obtain his private key. Under this Act, a digital certificate subscriber might have to bear an immense amount of risk.

[3] Biddle, C. B., Misplaced Priorities: The Utah Digital Signature Act and Liability Allocation in a Public Key Infrastructure, 18 October, 1996.

How could Microsoft and general subscribers protect themselves against the potential threat posed by these fraudulently acquired certificates or signatures? What possible remedies were available to those who relied on them in electronic transactions? What action could CAs take and how could legislators regulate the conduct of CAs, subscribers and relying parties?

HARVARD | BUSINESS | SCHOOL

9-601-114
REV: OCTOBER 17, 2003

ROBERT D. AUSTIN

The iPremier Company (A): Denial of Service Attack

January 12, 2003, 4:31 AM

Somewhere a telephone was chirping. Bob Turley, CIO of the iPremier Company, turned beneath the bed sheets, wishing the sound would go away. It didn't. Lifting his head, he tried to make sense of his surroundings. Where was he?

The Westin in Times Square. New York City. That's right. He was there to meet with Wall Street analysts. He'd gotten in late. By the time his head had hit the pillow it was nearly 1:30 AM. Now the digital display on the nearby clock made no sense. Who would be calling at this hour? Why would the hotel operator put a call through?

He reached for the phone at bedside and placed it against his ear. Dial tone. Huh? The chirping was coming from his cell phone. Hanging up the hotel phone, he staggered out of bed. No sooner had his feet met the floor than his pager went off. Almost simultaneously, the hotel phone erupted, as if protesting being placed back in its cradle. Fumbling in his briefcase, he located the cell phone and hit "answer" on the tiny keypad.

"This is Bob Turley."

"Mr. Turley?" There was panic in the voice at the other end of the line. "I'm sorry to wake you, Joanne told me to call you."

The pager was still sounding. He found it in his briefcase and silenced it. The hotel phone stopped ringing as suddenly as it had started.

"Who is this?"

"It's Leon. Leon Ledbetter. I'm in Ops. We met last week. I'm new. I mean I was new, last month."

Professor Robert D. Austin, Dr. Larry Leibrock, Chief Technology Officer, McCombs School of Business, University of Texas at Austin, and Alan Murray, Chief Scientist, Novell Service Provider Network prepared this case. HBS cases are developed solely as the basis for class discussion. Cases are not intended to serve as endorsements, sources of primary data, or illustrations of effective or ineffective management. The situation described in this case is based on real accounts of denial of service attacks directed against several companies during 2000 and 2001. Company names, product/service offerings, and the names of all individuals in the case are not real, however. Any resemblance to actual companies, offerings, or individuals is accidental.

"Why are you calling me at 4:30 in the morning, Leon?"

"I'm really sorry about that Mr. Turley, Joanne said—"

"No, I mean what's wrong? Why are you calling?"

"It's our web site, sir. It's completely locked up. I've tried accessing it from three different computers and nothing's happening. Our customers can't access it either; the help desk is getting support calls."

"What's causing it?"

"Joanne thinks—if we could only—well, someone might have hacked us. Someone else might be controlling our site. Support has been getting these emails—We thought it was just the web server, but I can't even telnet[1] to anything over there. Joanne is on her way to the colo.[2] She said to call you. These weird emails, they're coming in about one per second."

"What do the emails say?"

"They say 'ha.'"

"Ha?"

"Yes, sir. Each one of them has one word in the subject line, 'ha.' It's like 'ha, ha, ha, ha.' Coming from an anonymous source. That's why we're thinking—."

"When you say they might have hacked us—could they be stealing customer information? Credit cards?"

"Well, I guess no firewall[3]—Joanne says—actually we're using a firewall service we purchase from the colo, so—."

"Can you call someone at the colo? We pay them for monitoring 24x7, don't we?"

"Joanne is calling them. I'm pretty sure. Is there anything you want me to do?"

"Does Joanne have her cell?"

"Yes sir, she's on her way to the colo. I just talked to her."

"Call me back if anything else happens."

"Yes sir."

Turley stood up, realizing only then that he had been sitting on the floor. His eyes were bleary but adrenaline was now cranking in his bloodstream. Steadying himself against a chair, he felt a vague wave of nausea. This was no way to wake up.

---

[1] "Telnet" is a network service that permits access to a computer from a remote location.

[2] "Colo" is short for "colocation facility," where Internet companies often house their vital computing hardware. Colocation facilities are sometimes called "Internet Data Centers" or simply "hosting facilities." They provide floor space, redundant power supplies, high-speed connectivity to the Internet, and a variety of other services to their customers.

[3] A "firewall" is a combination hardware/software platform that is designed to protect a local network and the computers that reside on it against unauthorized access.

He made his way to the bathroom and splashed water on his face. This trip to New York was a great assignment for someone who had been with the company such a short time. It demonstrated the great confidence CEO Jack Samuelson had in him as the new CIO. For a moment Turley savored a memory of the meeting in which Samuelson had told him he would be the one to go to New York. As that memory passed another emerged, this one from an earlier session with the CEO. Samuelson was worried that the company might eventually suffer from "a deficit in operating procedures." "Make it one of your top priorities," he had said. "We need to run things professionally. I've hired you to take us to the next level."

Looking himself over in the mirror, seeing his hair tussled and his face wet, Turley lodged a protest with no one in particular: "But I've barely been here three months."

The iPremier Company

Founded in 1994 by two students at Swarthmore College, the iPremier Company had evolved into one of the few success stories of web-based commerce. From its humble beginnings, it had risen to become one of the top two retail businesses selling luxury, rare, and vintage goods on the web. It was also one of the few profitable entities in the so-called "new economy." Based in Seattle, Washington, the firm had grown at a rapid rate and held its own against incursions into its space from a number of well-funded challengers. For the fiscal year 2001, profits were $2.1 million on sales of $32 million. Sales had grown at more than an 50% annual rate for more than three years, and profits had begun to trend favorably.

Immediately following its Initial Public Offering in late 1998, the company's stock price had nearly tripled. It had continued up from there amid the euphoria of the 1999 markets, eventually tripling again. A follow-on offering had left the company in a strong cash position. During the NASDAQ bloodbath of 2000, the stock had fallen dramatically but it had eventually stabilized and even climbed again, although not to pre-2000 levels. In the treacherous Business-to-Consumer (B2C) segment, the iPremier Company was one of a very few survivors.

Most of the company's products were priced between fifty and a few hundred dollars, but there were a small number of items priced in the thousands of dollars. Customers paid for items on-line using their credit cards. The company had flexible return policies, intended to allow customers to thoroughly examine products before deciding whether to keep them. The iPremier Company's customer base was high-end, so much so that credit limits on charge cards were rarely an issue, even for the highest-priced products.

Management and Culture

The management team at the iPremier Company was a mix of talented young people who had been with the company for some time and more experienced managers who were gradually being hired as the firm grew. Recruitment had focused on well-educated technical and business professionals with reputations for high performance. Getting hired into a senior management position required excelling in an intense series of three-on-one interviews. The CEO interviewed every prospective manager at the director level and above. The reward, for those who made the grade, was base compensation above the average of managers at similar firms, and variable compensation that could be a significant multiple of the base. All employees had options based on the company stock price, and managers received particularly lucrative incentives. When the share price had fallen off in 2000, senior management had gone to the company's board of directors twice to reorganize the option plans and maintain strong employee incentives. All employees were subject to quarterly performance reviews that were tied directly to their compensation. Unsuccessful managers did not last long.

Most managers at the iPremier Company described the environment as "intense." The company formally stated its governing values in terms of "discipline, professionalism, commitment to delivering results, and partnership for achieving profits." Unlike many Internet companies, the iPremier Company had emphasized a balanced approach to growth and profitability, although growth had tended to rule the day. Throughout the company, there was a strong orientation toward doing "whatever it takes" to get projects done on schedule, especially when it came to system features that would benefit customers. The software development team was proud of its record of consistently launching new features and programs a few months ahead of major competitor MarketTop. Value statements aside, it was well-understood by senior managers that their compensation and future prospects with the company depended primarily on executing to plan. Managers pursued "the numbers" with almost obsessive zeal.

Technical Architecture

The company had historically tended to outsource management of its technical architecture and had a long-standing relationship with Qdata, a company that hosted most of the iPremier Company's computer equipment and provided connectivity to the Internet. Qdata was an early entrant into the Internet hosting and "colocation" business, but it had lost any prospect of market leadership. The facility was close to the corporate offices of the iPremier Company, but some felt there was little else to recommend it. Qdata was a steady provider of basic floor space, power, connectivity, environmental control, and physical security, and it offered some higher-level "management services," such as monitoring of web sites for customers at its Network Operations Center (NOC) and some Internet security services (such as the firewall service used by the iPremier Company). But Qdata had not been quick to invest in advanced technology and had experienced difficulty in retaining staff.

The iPremier Company had a long-standing initiative aimed at eventually moving its computing to another facility, but several factors had conspired to keep this from happening. First, and most significant, the iPremier Company had been very busy growing; hence the move to a better facility had never quite made it to the top of the priority list. Second, the cost of more modern facilities was considerably higher—two-to-three times as expensive on a per-square-foot basis. iPremier Company computers occupied a good deal of space, so a move to another facility would have increased costs significantly enough to affect the slender but increasing profit trend the company was eager to maintain. Third, there was a perception—not necessarily supported by fact, according to the operations staff—that a move might risk service interruption to customers. The operations staff maintained that with appropriate modernization of the computing infrastructure, growth could be accomplished by adding installations in other facilities, rather than by expanding floor space in the existing facility. The work of planning how this might be carried out had never been done, though. Finally, one of the founders of the iPremier Company felt a personal commitment to the owners of Qdata because the latter company had been willing to renegotiate their contract at a particularly difficult time in iPremier's early days.

Exhibit 1 provides a diagram of the iPremier Company's technical architecture.

4:39 AM

Turley situated himself at the desk in his hotel room and began paging through the digital phonebook on his cell phone. Before he could find the number for Joanne Ripley—his technical operations team leader—the phone began to chirp. The incoming call was from Ripley. Turley tapped the answer key.

"Hello, Joanne. How are you this morning?"

A cautious laugh came from the other end of the circuit. "About the same as you, I'm guessing. I assume Leon reached you."

"He did, but he doesn't know anything. What's going on?"

"I don't know much either, yet. I'm in the car, on my way to the colo."

"You can't do anything from home?"

"Well—no. Leon can't telnet into any of the boxes behind the firewall via the T1 line at the office,[4] so something is screwy with our connectivity to the colo. Sounds like a problem outside the perimeter of our architecture. I called Qdata, but they assure me that there is no problem with connectivity into or out of the building. They're looking into it further, but their night shift is on duty. I don't know where they get those bozos. I haven't talked to anyone yet who knows what he's doing."

"How long till you get there?"

"I'm driving fast and running red lights. I ought to be there in five minutes."

"How long after that until we are back up and running?"

"Depends on what's wrong. I'll try restarting the web server as soon as I get there, but if someone has hacked us, or if there's some kind of attack going on, that might not do it. Did Leon tell you about the emails?"

"The 'ha, ha' emails? Yeah. Makes it sound like something deliberate."

"I'd have to agree with that."

"Can we track the emails?"

"Not soon enough. They're coming through an anonymizer that's probably in Europe or Asia. If we're lucky we'll find out sometime in the next 18 months who sent them. Then we'll discover they're originating from some DSL-connected PC in Podunk, Idaho, and that the Joe Schmo who owns it has no idea that it's been compromised by hackers."

"Any chance they're stealing credit cards?"

There was a long pause at the other end of the phone.

"There's really no way of knowing without more info."

[4] The hosting facility where the production computer equipment was housed was connected to the iPremier Company's offices via a leased "T1" line. This line would ordinarily permit people at the office to connect to production computers without traversing the public Internet.

"Can we pull the plug? Disconnect the communications lines?"

"We can. But if we start pulling cables out of the wall it may take us a while to put things back together. Right now most of our customers are asleep. Whoops." There was a pause while Ripley negotiated a traffic obstacle. "Sorry. Anyway, let me restart the web server and see what happens. Maybe we can get out of this without too much customer impact."

Turley thought about it for a moment. "Okay. But if you see something that makes you think credit cards are being stolen, I want to know that as soon as possible. We may have to take drastic actions."

"Understood. I'll call you back as soon as I know anything."

"Good. One more thing: Who else knows this is going on?"

"I haven't called anyone else. Leon might have. I'll call him and call you right back."

"Thanks."

Turley flipped his cell closed then picked up the hotel phone. After a series of transfers, he found someone who would bring coffee to his room, despite the odd hour. Never before had he so desperately wanted coffee.

Just as he replaced the hotel phone his cell rang again. He looked at the display to see who was calling.

"Damn." It was Warren Spangler, VP of business development. Turley remembered vaguely that Leon Ledbetter had come into the organization via a recommendation by Spangler. They were old high school buddies or something. Ledbetter had almost certainly called Spangler.

"Hi, Warren," said Turley, flipping the phone open.

"Hi, Bob. I hear we've got some kind of incident going on. What's the story?"

"Something's definitely going on, but we're not sure what yet. We're trying to minimize customer impact. Fortunately for us it's the middle of the night."

"Wow. So is it just a technical problem or is somebody actually doing it to us?"

Turley was eager to call the chief technology officer (CTO), so he didn't really have time to continue this discussion. But he didn't want to be abrupt. He was still getting to know his colleagues.

"We don't know. Look, I've got to—"

"Leon said something about emails—"

"Yes, there are suspicious emails coming in so it could be someone doing it."

"Oh, man. I bet the stock takes a hit tomorrow. Just when I was going to exercise some options. Shouldn't we call the police?"

"Sure, why don't you see what you can do there, that'd be a big help. Look, I've got to—"

"Seattle police? Do we know where the emails are coming from? Maybe we should call the FBI? No. Wait. If we call the police, the press might hear about this from them. Whoa. Then our stock would really take a hit."

"I've really got to go, Warren."

"Sure thing. I'll start thinking about PR. And I'll work with Leon on this end. We got you covered here, bro. Keep the faith."

"Will do, Warren. Thanks."

Turley ended that call and began searching through his cell phone's memory to find the number for Tim Mandel, the company's CTO. He and Mandel had already cemented a great working relationship. Turley wanted his opinion. Just as Turley was about to initiate the call, though, another call came in from Ripley.

Turley flipped the phone open and said: "Leon called Spanger, I know. Anything else?"

"That's it for now. Bye."

Turley dialed Mandel. At first the call switched over to voice mail, but he retried immediately. This time Mandel answered sleepily. It took five full minutes to wake Mandel and tell him what was happening.

"So what do you think, should we just pull the plug?" Turley asked.

"I wouldn't. You might lose some logging data that would help us figure out what happened. Whatever we do, we want to preserve evidence of what has happened or else we may never know exactly."

"I'm not sure that's the most important thing to me right now, knowing exactly what is happening."

"I suggest you change your mind about that. If you don't know what happened this time, it can happen again. Worse than that, if you don't know what happened you won't know what, if anything, you need to disclose publicly."

Turley thought about that for a moment. What if they halted the attack but he could not be sure of the danger, if any, to customer information? What would the company need to say publicly? It was too much to sort out on the fly. Mandel was saying something else.

"Come to think of it, Bob, preserving the logs is irrelevant because I'm pretty sure detailed logging is not enabled. Detailed logging takes up a lot of disk space on the server. To run at higher logging levels we would have to add significantly to our storage arrays and I've never been able to convince the finance guys that the expenditure was necessary. Plus detailed logging adds a performance penalty of about 20% and nobody's been game for that."

"So we aren't going to have evidence of what happened anyway."

"There'll be some, but not as much as we'll want."

Another call was coming in.

"Hold on, Tim." Turley kicked the phone over to the waiting call. It was Peter Stewart, the company's legal counsel. What was he doing awake?

"This is Turley."

"Hey, Bob, it's Pete. Pull the plug, Bob. Shut off the power, pull the comm lines out of their sockets, everything. We can't risk having credit cards stolen."

"Spangler call you?"

"Huh? No, Jack. Samuelson. He called me three minutes ago, said hackers had control of our web site. Told me in no uncertain terms to call you and 'provide a legal perspective.' That's just what he said: 'provide a legal perspective.'"

So the CEO was awake. The result, no doubt, of Spangler's "helping" from that end. Stewart continued to speak legalese at him for what seemed like an eternity. By this time, Turley was incapable of paying attention to him.

"Thanks for your thoughts, Pete. I've got to go, I've got Tim on the other line."

"Okay. For the record, though, I say pull the plug. I'll let Jack know you and I spoke."

"Thanks, Pete."

Turley switched back over to the call with Mandel.

"Spangler's got bloody everybody awake, including Jack. I recommend you get dressed and head into the office, my friend."

"Is Joanne on this?"

"Yes, she's at the colo by now." Turley's phone rang. "Got a call coming in from her now."

He switched the phone.

"What's up Joanne?"

"Well I'm at Qdata," she said in an angry voice, "and they won't let me into the NOC. There's no one here who knows anything about the network monitoring software and that's what I need to use to see the traffic coming into our site. The Qdata guy who can do it is vacationing in Aruba. I tried rebooting the web server, but we've still got a problem. My current theory is an attack directed at our firewall, but to be sure I've got to see the packets coming in, and the firewall is their equipment. You got an escalation contact to get these dudes off their butts?"

"I'm in New York, Joanne. I've got zip for Qdata contact information with me. But let me see what I can do."

"Okay. I'll keep working it from this end. The security guard doesn't look too fierce. I think I could take him."

"Do what you can."

Turley hung up. He noticed that Mandel had disconnected also. For a moment Turley just sat back in the chair, not sure what to do next. There was a knock at the door. Coffee. Good news, for a change.

5:27 AM

He had just taken his first sip of hot coffee when he got the call he'd been dreading. It was from Jack Samuelson, the CEO.

"Hi Jack."

"Bob. Exciting morning?"

"More than I like it."

"Are we working a plan?"

"Yes, sir. Not everything is going according to plan, but we are working a plan."

"Is there anything I can do?"

"Actually, Jack, there is. Call someone senior at Qdata and tell them we need their full and immediate support. They're giving Joanne the runaround about access to their NOC."

"I'll do that right now, Bob."

"Thanks, Jack."

"Bob, the stock is probably going to be impacted and we'll have to put a solid PR face on this, but that's not your concern right now. You focus on getting us back up and running. Understand?"

"I do."

The call ended. It had gone better than Turley had feared. He avoided the temptation to analyze Samuelson's every word for clues to his innermost thoughts. Instead, he dialed Joanne.

"Hi, Bob," she said, sounding mildly cheerful. "They let me in. I'm sitting in front of the console right now. It looks like a SYN flood[5] from multiple sites directed at the router[6] that runs our firewall service. It's not a proper firewall, Bob; we need to work on something better."

"Fine, but what can we do right now?"

"Well, looks like the attack is coming from about 30 sites. A classic distributed denial of service (DoS) attack. If the guys here will let me, I'm going to start shutting down traffic from those IP addresses."[7]

"Samuelson is waking up the senior guys at Qdata. If the night shift gives you any trouble, tell them it's going to be raining executives really soon."

---

[5] Each "conversation" with a web server begins with a sequence of "handshake" interactions. The initiating computer first sends a "SYNCHRONIZE" or "SYN." The contacted web server responds with a "SYNCHRONIZE-ACKNOWLEDGE" or "SYN-ACK." The initiating computer then completes the handshake with an "ACKNOWLEDGE" or "ACK." A "SYN flood" is an attack on a web server intended to make it think a very large number of "conversations" are being initiated in rapid succession. Because each interaction looks like real traffic to the web site, the web server expends resources dealing with each one. By flooding the site, an attacker can effectively paralyze the web server by trying to start too many conversations with it.

[6] As the name suggests, a "router" is a hardware platform that routes traffic across internal networks and the Internet.

[7] An "IP address" corresponds to a particular machine located somewhere on the Internet.

"Samuelson, huh? So everybody's up for our little party. Okay, I'm going to try shutting off traffic from the attacking IP addresses. I'll have to set the phone down for a minute."

There was a pause of a couple of minutes. Turley heard some muffled conversation in the background, then several exclamations. Ripley came back on the line.

"Damn it, Bob, they're spawning zombies. It's Dawn of the Dead out there."

"You're going to have to translate that one for me, Ripley."

"Every time we shut down traffic from an IP address, the zombie we've shut off automatically triggers attacks from two other sites. I'll try it a few more times, but right now it looks like that's just going to make things worse."

"If it's a denial of service attack, they haven't hacked us, right? It means it's an attack, not an intrusion. They haven't gained entry to our system. So the credit cards and other customer data are safe. Can we say that?"

"That'd be my first take on it, yeah. There's nothing that makes a DoS attack and an intrusion mutually exclusive, of course. But, yeah, the script kiddy[8] hackers who usually launch these kinds of attacks aren't sophisticated enough to get inside our firewall." She paused for a moment as if reconsidering what she had just said. "On the other hand, targeting the firewall strikes me as a fairly sophisticated attack."

It was not the straight answer he had hoped for, but it would have to do for the time being. "I'll let you get back to it. Call me with an update when there is something to tell."

Turley hung up and thought about whether to call Samuelson and what to tell him. He could say that it was a DoS attack. He could say that it therefore probably didn't put customer information at risk. But Turley wanted to think before we went on record with that position. He'd talk to Tim, see what he thought.

For a moment, everything was quiet. He put the cell phone down on the desk and poured another cup of coffee. Pacing across the room, he picked up the TV remote and hit the "ON" button. A movie appeared, an old Hitchcock film. An airplane was straifing Cary Grant. He muted the sound then walked to the window and pulled the curtain aside. There was a red glow in the sky to the east.

His cell phone rang. He went to it and picked it up. It was Ripley.

"It stopped," she said excitedly. "The attack is over."

"What did you do?"

"Nothing. It just stopped. The attack just stopped at 5:46 AM."

"So—what do we do now?"

"The website is running. A customer who visits our site now wouldn't know anything had ever been wrong. We can resume business as usual."

"Business as usual?"

---

[8] "Script kiddies" are relatively unsophisticated hackers who use automated routines—"scripts"—written by other more sophisticated hackers. These scripts are generally available to anyone willing to spend a little time searching for them on the Internet.

"Actually, I'd recommend that we give everything a proper going over after an attack like this. We really ought to do a thorough audit. I've been thinking about how they targeted the firewall, and I don't think it sounds like script kiddies."

"Sit down when you get a chance and write me an email that summarizes what you think we should do. Tell me how whatever you recommend will impact on customers, if at all. I've got to figure out what to tell Samuelson."

Exhibit 1 The iPremier Company's Technical Architecture

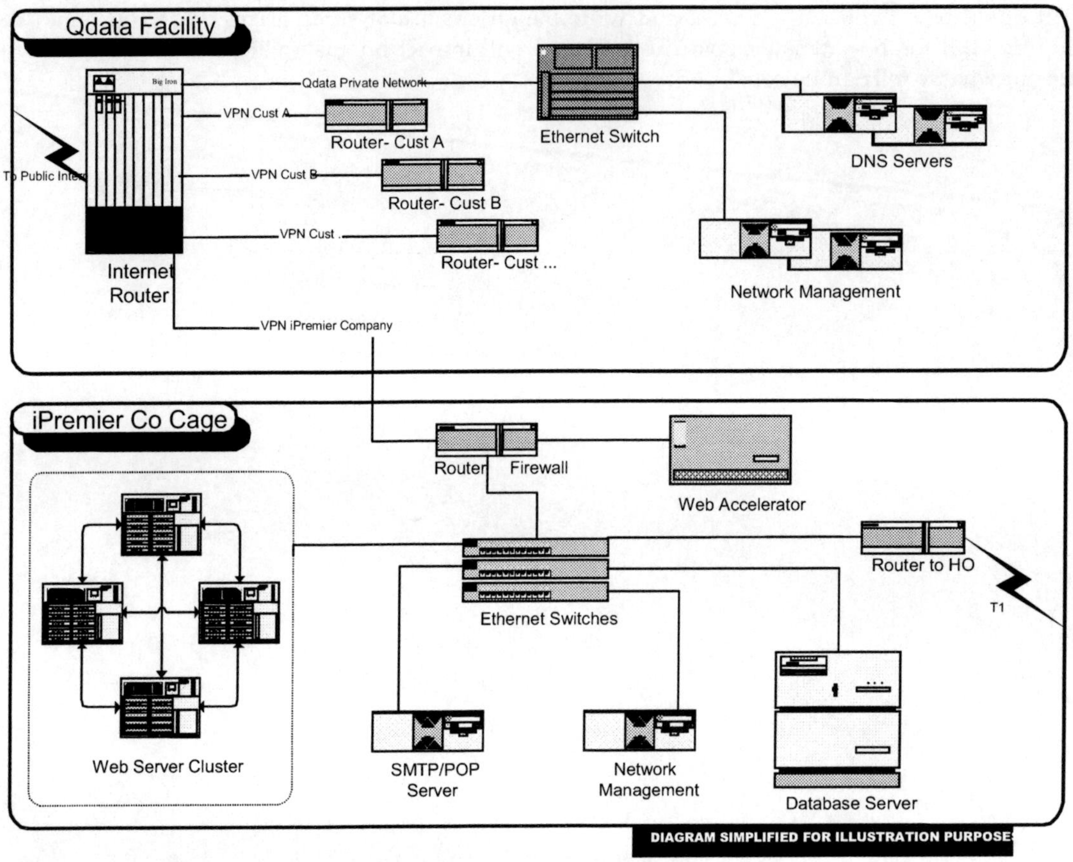

Your Next IT Strategy

by John Hagel III and John Seely Brown

Harvard Business Review

Reprint R0109G

Harvard Business Review

October 2001

HBR Case Study — R0109A
Off with His Head?
David Champion

HBR at Large — R0109B
The Leadership Lessons of Mount Everest
Michael Useem

Different Voice — R0109C
Genius at Work:
A Conversation with Mark Morris

Harnessing the Science of Persuasion — R0109D
Robert B. Cialdini

Torment Your Customers
(They'll Love It) — R0109E
Stephen Brown

Radical Change, the Quiet Way — R0109F
Debra E. Meyerson

Your Next IT Strategy — R0109G
John Hagel III and John Seely Brown

HBR Interview — R0109H
Bernard Arnault of LVMH:
The Perfect Paradox of Star Brands
Suzy Wetlaufer

Best Practice — R0109J
Speeding Up Team Learning
Amy Edmondson, Richard Bohmer, and Gary Pisano

Tool Kit — R0109K
Boost Your Marketing ROI
with Experimental Design
Eric Almquist and Gordon Wyner

The age of proprietary information systems is coming to an end, and the age of shared services is dawning. Don't panic. There's a pragmatic way to make the change pay off for your company.

Your Next IT Strategy

by John Hagel III and John Seely Brown

OVER THE PAST YEAR, AS THE HYPE OVER E-COMMERCE HAS subsided, a new chorus of promises about the potential of the Internet has been gaining volume. The singers this time are not dot-coms and their backers but rather the big providers of computer hardware, software, and services. What they're promoting, through a flurry of advertisements, white papers, and sales pitches, is a whole new approach to corporate information systems. The approach goes by many different names – Microsoft calls it ".Net," Oracle refers to "network services," IBM touts "Web services," Sun talks about an "open network environment" – but at its core is the assumption that companies will in the future buy their information technologies as services provided over the Internet rather than owning and maintaining all their own hardware and software.

No doubt, many executives are skeptical. They've heard outsized promises and indecipherable buzzwords before, and they've wasted a lot of time and money on Internet initiatives that went nowhere. This time, though, there's an important difference. The technology providers are not making empty promises: They're backing up their words with massive investments to help create the infrastructure needed to make the new IT approach work. As these efforts continue, over the next year or two, a steady stream of new, Internet-based services will come on-line, providing significant cost savings over traditional, internal systems and offering new opportunities for collaboration among companies. Slowly but surely, all your old assumptions about IT management will be overturned.

In this article, we will provide an executive's guide to the new IT strategy. We will explain what the Web services architecture is, how it differs from traditional IT architecture, and why it will create substantial benefits for companies. We will also lay out a measured, practical plan for adopting the new architecture – a step-by-step approach that will pay for itself while mitigating the potential for organizational disruption. Indeed, we believe that two of the great advantages of the Web services architecture are its openness and its modularity. Companies won't need to take high-risk, big-bang approaches to its implementation. They can focus initially on opportunities that will deliver immediate efficiency gains, incorporating new capabilities as the infrastructure becomes more robust and stable.

The New Architecture

Until now, companies have viewed their information systems as proprietary. They bought or leased their own hardware, wrote or licensed their own applications, and hired big staffs to keep everything up and running. This approach has worked, but it has not worked well. After years of piecemeal technology purchases, companies have inevitably ended up with a mishmash of disparate systems spread throughout different units. Over the last decade, in efforts to merge these "data silos," many big companies have invested large amounts of money – hundreds of millions of dollars, in some cases – in massively complex enterprise-resource-planning systems, which offer suites of interlinked applications that draw on unified databases. The ERP systems have certainly solved some problems, but they've been no panacea: Most big companies still struggle with a hodgepodge of hundreds of incompatible systems. And ERP systems have also created new problems. Because they're relatively inflexible, they tend to lock companies into rigid business processes. It becomes hard, if not impossible, to adapt quickly to changes in the marketplace, and strategic restructurings, through acquisitions, divestitures, and partnerships, become fiendishly difficult to pull off. In effect, the companies that have installed ERP systems have replaced their fragmented unit silos with more integrated but nonetheless restrictive enterprise silos.

John Hagel III *is the chief strategy officer of 12 Entrepreneuring, an operating company in San Francisco. He can be reached at jhagel@12.com.* ***John Seely Brown*** *is the chief innovation officer of 12 Entrepreneuring, where he developed the perspectives in this article, and also serves as the chief scientist of Xerox. He can be reached at jsb@12.com.*

The Web services architecture is completely different. Constructed on the Internet, it is an open rather than a proprietary architecture. Instead of building and maintaining unique internal systems, companies can rent the functionality they need – whether it's data storage, processing power, or specific applications – from outside service providers. Without getting too technical, the Web services architecture can be thought of as comprising three layers of technology, as described in the sidebar "An Overview of Web Services." At the foundation are software standards and communication protocols, such as XML and SOAP, that allow information to be exchanged easily among different applications. These tools provide the common languages for Web services, enabling applications to connect freely to other applications and to read electronic messages from them. The standards dramatically simplify and streamline information management – you no longer have to write customized code whenever communication with a new application is needed.

The service grid, the middle layer of the architecture, builds upon the protocols and standards. Analogous to an electrical power grid, the service grid provides a set of shared utilities – from security to third-party auditing to billing and payment – that makes it possible to carry out mission-critical business functions and transactions over the Internet. In addition, the service grid encompasses a set of utilities, also usually supplied and managed by third parties, that facilitates the transport of messages (such as routing and filtering), the identification of available services (such as directories and brokers), and the assurance of reliability and consistency (such as monitoring and conflict resolution). In short, the service grid plays two key roles: helping Web services users and providers find and connect with one another, and creating trusted environments essential for carrying out mission-critical business activities. The role of the service grid cannot be overemphasized: A robust service grid is vital to accelerating and broadening the potential impact of Web services. Without it, Web services will remain relatively marginal to the enterprise.

The top layer of the architecture comprises a diverse array of application services, from credit card processing to production scheduling, that automate particular business functions. It is this top layer that, day to day, will be most visible to you, your employees, your customers, and your partners. Some application services will be proprietary to a particular company or group of companies, while others will be shared among all companies. In some cases, companies may develop their own application services and then choose to sell them on a subscription basis to other enterprises, creating new and potentially lucrative sources of revenue.

An Overview of Web Services

The Web services architecture has three layers. The most fundamental layer consists of software standards (such as XML) and communication protocols (such as SOAP and its likely extensions) that make it possible for diverse applications and organizations to do business together electronically.

The middle layer is the service grid, through which specialized utilities provide key services and tools. Four types of utilities operate over the service grid.

Shared utilities provide services that support not only the application services residing in the top layer but also the other utilities within the service grid. For example, security utilities provide such services as authentication, authorization, and accounting. Performance auditing and assessment utilities assure users of Web services that they will obtain agreed-upon levels of performance and will be compensated for damages if performance falls below these levels. Billing and payment utilities aggregate charges for the use of Web services and ensure prompt and full payment.

Transport management utilities include messaging services to facilitate reliable and flexible communication among application services as well as orchestration utilities that help companies assemble sets of application services from different providers.

Resource knowledge management utilities include service directories, brokers, and common registries and repositories that describe available application services and determine correct ways of interacting with them. They also include specialized services for converting data from one format to another.

Service management utilities ensure reliable provisioning of Web services. They also manage sessions and monitor performance to ascertain conformance to service-quality specifications and service-level agreements.

The top layer encompasses a diverse array of application services that support day-to-day business activities and processes–everything from procurement and supply chain management to marketing communications and sales.

The Web Services Architecture

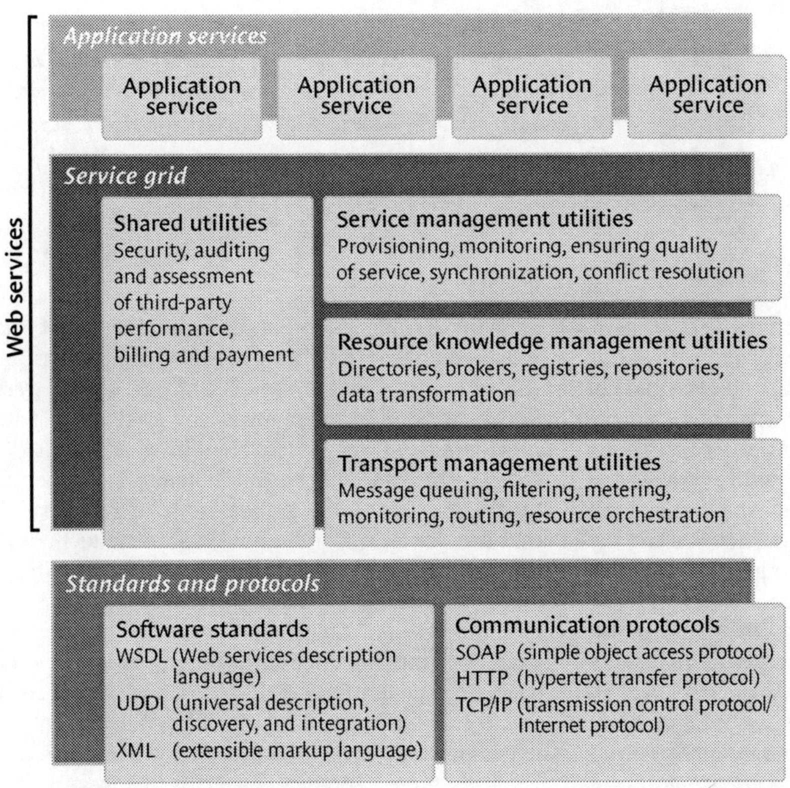

To illustrate how the architecture works, let's contrast the way a typical business activity – loan processing by a bank – would be carried out through a traditional proprietary architecture and the Web services architecture. Loan processing is a complex procedure requiring at least six steps (data gathering about an applicant, validation of data, credit scoring, risk analysis and pricing, underwriting, and closing) and involving interactions with a number of other institutions (checking an applicant's credit rating, verifying investment and loan balances, and so on). With a traditional IT architecture, the process is usually supported by one, very complicated application maintained by an individual bank; like a Swiss Army knife, the integrated application does a lot of things, but it may not do any of them particularly well. And since the costs of maintaining electronic connections with other institutions are high, requiring leased communication lines and expensive software to link different systems, the necessary interactions are often handled manually through phone calls and faxes. The process, in sum, is cumbersome, costly, and prone to errors.

With the Web services architecture, loan processing becomes much more flexible, automated, and efficient. Leased lines are replaced with the Internet, and open standards and protocols take the place of proprietary technologies. As a result, the bank can connect automatically with the most appropriate institution for each transaction, speeding up the entire process and reducing the need for manual work. And rather than maintain its own integrated loan-processing system, the bank can take a modular approach, using specialized Web services supplied by an array of providers. It can also shift easily among providers, using one service, say, for risk analysis of loans to restaurants and another for risk analysis of loans to hospitals. In other words, the bank will always be able to use the best tool for the job at hand; it will no longer have to compromise on performance to avoid the complexity of integrating proprietary applications.

Clearly, the Web services architecture offers important advantages over its predecessor. First, it represents a much more efficient way to manage information technology. By allowing companies to purchase only the functionality they need when they need it, the new architecture can substantially reduce investments in IT assets. And by shifting responsibility for maintaining systems to outside providers, it reduces the need for hiring numerous IT specialists, which itself has become a significant challenge for many companies. Using Web services also reduces the risk that companies will end up using obsolete technologies; third-party utilities and application providers will be required to offer the most up-to-date technologies in order to compete. Companies will no longer find themselves stuck with outdated or mediocre applications and hardware. The standardized, plug-and-play nature of such an architecture will also make it much easier for companies to outsource activities and processes whenever it makes economic sense. (See the sidebar "Big Changes for Your IT Department.")

Second, and perhaps more important, the Web services architecture supports more flexible collaboration, both

Big Changes for Your IT Department

The shift to the Web services architecture for corporate computing is not only a matter of adopting new technology. It will require broad organizational and managerial changes as well as the development of new kinds of capabilities. A particularly big impact will be felt in the corporate IT department. CIOs will face new challenges and assume new roles:

- IT departments will need to move in two dimensions simultaneously: outsourcing many traditional IT activities (as credible and reliable providers of services emerge) while leveraging internal capabilities to design distinctive Web services that can be sold to other companies. *CIOs will become strategists and entrepreneurs,* assessing areas of competitive advantage and focusing resources on building new IT-based businesses.
- IT departments will need to integrate new sets of skills in such areas as enterprise application architecture, enterprise application integration, application development, security, and IT operations. *CIOs will become knowledge brokers,* pulling together expertise from within and outside their companies.
- IT operations and performance will increasingly depend on the effective integration of external resources, requiring deeper skills in structuring and managing relationships. *CIOs will become relationship managers,* coordinating the efforts of an array of companies.
- IT departments will need to take the lead in shaping the standards required for industries and business communities to operate effectively. *CIOs will become negotiators,* their leadership styles shifting from command-and-control to persuade-and-influence.

among a company's own units and between a company and its business partners. When traditional information systems need to talk to each other, they do so through dedicated, point-to-point connections. For example, when a sales-force-management application needs to send information on closed sales to a payroll processing application for the computation of commissions, a programmer has to write a special piece of code–a connector–to allow the two systems to communicate. The problem with such point-to-point connections is that they are fixed and inflexible and, as they proliferate, become nightmares to manage. With the Web services architecture, tight couplings will be replaced with loose couplings. Because everyone will share the same standards for data description and connection protocols, applications will be able to talk freely with other applications, without costly reprogramming. This will make it much easier for companies to shift operations and partnerships in response to market or competitive stimuli. The loose-coupling approach of Web services also makes it an attractive option within an organization. CIOs can use the Web services architecture to more flexibly integrate the extraordinarily diverse set of applications and databases residing within most enterprises while at the same time making these resources available to business partners.

Until now, what's been called e-business has for the most part been a primitive patchwork of old technologies. Most companies that do business on the Internet have had to yoke together existing systems with new ones to create the illusion of integration. A visitor using a corporate Web site may think it's a single, streamlined system, but behind the scenes, people are often manually taking information from one application and entering it into another. Such swivel chair networks, as they have come to be known, are inefficient, slow, and mistake ridden. Merrill Lynch, like almost all large companies, has struggled to patch together hundreds of different applications to support its sites for customers. John McKinley, the company's CTO, draws an analogy to the Potemkin villages in czarist Russia, where brightly painted facades hid the unseemly reality of run-down homes. The Web services architecture promises to solve this problem. Taking the people out of the network, the architecture will enable connections between applications – both within and across enterprises–to be managed automatically.

First Steps to Success

The construction of the Web services architecture is still in its early stages, and years of investment and refinement will be required before a mature, stable architecture is in place. This does not mean, however, that companies should wait to begin the transition to a new IT strategy; even today, benefits can be gained by moving to a Web services model for certain activities and processes. But it does mean that companies should take a pragmatic, measured approach. Fortunately, the Web services architecture is ideally suited to such an approach: Because it's based on open standards and it leverages the capabilities of third parties, companies don't have to place big bets at the outset. They can carefully stage their investments, learning important lessons along the way. (See the sidebar "Five Questions You Need to Ask.")

Merrill Lynch's McKinley, for example, is currently leading a number of initiatives designed to take advantage of Web services. One initiative is the creation of an innovative portfolio-analysis system for use by brokers and selected customers. By using XML to link disparate systems

Five Questions You Need to Ask

Senior managers need to ensure that their organizations' executives are thinking ahead about the implications of the Web services architecture. Here are five questions you can use to spur your people:

Does our management team have a shared vision of the long-term (five to ten years out) business implications of the new IT architecture?

Do we have a transition plan that balances the state of the architecture's development with a clear understanding of the areas of highest business impact?

Are we moving fast enough today to build our expertise and exploit immediate opportunities for streamlining intercompany processes, outsourcing activities in which we don't have distinctive capabilities and designing Web services that we can market to other companies?

Do we have a clear understanding of the obstacles within our organization that may hinder us from exploiting the full value of the new IT architecture, and do we have initiatives under way to overcome these obstacles?

Are we exerting sufficient leadership in shaping both the functionality offered by providers of Web services (defining, for example, the performance levels required for mission-critical applications) and the standards needed to collaborate with our partners?

within Merrill Lynch as well as to integrate information from partner organizations, the new system will tie together customer information, product information, and real-time market data in a flexible, low-cost way. It will give the company's brokers up-to-the-second, integrated views of all the information they need to meet a customer's needs at any given moment. Merrill Lynch is also using a Web services approach to enable brokers and clients to access information and applications from a wide variety of devices, including computers, PDAs, cell phones, and conventional phones. Both of these projects offer immediate business benefits: They provide an important competitive advantage to the company's salespeople while delivering added value to customers.

Merrill Lynch's experience, as well as that of other early adopters such as General Motors and Dell, offers three guidelines for other companies looking to get a head start.

Build on your existing systems. The Web services architecture should initially be viewed as an adjunct to your current systems. Through a process we call node enablement, you can use Web or application servers to connect your traditional applications, one at a time, to the outside service grid, turning them, in effect, into nodes on the Internet. Node enablement is often as simple as creating an explicit record of the connection specifications of an application – documenting, in other words, its application programming interfaces, or APIs – along with the application's name, its Internet location, and procedures for connecting with it. The existing application is left intact but is "exposed" so that it can be found and accessed by other applications in the Web services architecture. The process of node enablement should be systematic, driven by near-term needs but shaped by a view of longer-term opportunities.

General Motors provides a useful example of this process. Mark Hogan, the president of eGM, a business unit created by the auto giant to oversee its consumer Internet initiatives, is a strong advocate of the Web services architecture. Like Merrill Lynch, eGM began with fairly conventional Web sites connecting the company with customers and dealers. Now, however, Hogan and his team have developed a road map for using Web services to move GM to a dramatically new build-to-order manufacturing and distribution model, which will enable the company to generate added revenue and use its assets much more efficiently. This initiative requires the ability to communicate and collaborate electronically with more than 8,000 dealers, all with information systems of widely differing specifications and sophistication. Few of the dealers have cutting-edge IT skills, and fewer still have the money to invest in major new applications. Given these constraints, says Hogan, "traditional IT architectures simply aren't up to the task. The Web services architecture provides the only way to rapidly enhance our IT platform." By applying node enablement to existing applications at GM and at the dealers, new processes can be rolled out incrementally with relatively modest investment.

For the first stage in the transition, GM is focusing on using Web services to enhance its traditional build-to-stock model, providing a broader set of options for dealers and customers. It has provided dealers, for example, with a locate-to-order functionality – a Web services–based application that quickly finds specific car models in the inventories of other dealers. GM is also planning to roll out an order-to-delivery application, which will shorten the lead time between placing a customer order and delivering the vehicle. Such interim steps will pave the way to offering the ultimate build-to-order model, which will require the reconfiguration of manufacturing operations and a more sophisticated deployment of Web services.

The payoff is expected to be enormous. GM's long-term goal is to cut in half its $25 billion investment in inventory and working capital. Analysts at Goldman Sachs estimate that supply chain initiatives using Web services could ultimately reduce GM's operating cost per vehicle by more than $1,000. Yet the staged approach to change allows GM to shift its IT architecture slowly, avoiding disruption and focusing only on systems that will deliver real economic paybacks at each stage of deployment. It also allows the company to temper the risk involved in moving to a new technology platform, since GM's efforts are tied to the evolution of the architecture.

> GM's long-term goal is to cut in half its $25 billion investment in inventory and working capital.

Start at the edge. In implementing the new architecture, early adopters are concentrating their initial efforts at the edges of their enterprises – on the applications and activities that tie their companies to customers or to other companies. Sales and customer support are obvious examples of edge activities, as are procurement and supply chain management. Less obviously, some traditionally internal functions can be pushed out to the edges as a result of outsourcing. In the electronics industry, for example, many production activities are being contracted to specialized manufacturing service providers, creating a need to share formerly proprietary applications and data.

Why is there so much focus on the edge? Because that's where the limitations of existing IT architectures are most apparent and onerous. Almost by definition, an application on the edge can benefit by being shared. As a result, it suffers most from the difficulties in connecting proprietary, heterogeneous systems. As GM found, rolling out a new set of applications to its far-flung dealer network was next to impossible before the emergence of Web services.

Dell Computer provides a great example of the benefits of starting at the edge. Dell's relationships with its suppliers of components and other direct materials are critical to the company's strategy. The total amount the company spends on direct materials equals as much as 70% of its revenue, so even modest savings in supply chain costs will have a big impact on the bottom line. A related and equally important concern to Dell is inventory management. In the personal computer industry, where product prices have recently been declining at 0.6% per week, excess inventory can become very costly.

Recognizing the huge gains possible from more effective supply-chain management, Dell focused its early Web services initiatives in this area. It began by more closely connecting its assembly operations with the network of outside logistics providers that operate the distribution centers for direct materials – the vendor-managed hubs, as Dell calls them. Traditionally, the company had to hold substantial inventory in the supply chain to ensure that products could be delivered quickly to customers. Its goal was to fill orders in five days, yet it took suppliers an average of 45 days to fill materials orders. To ensure it did not run short of key components, suppliers had to maintain ten-day inventory buffers at vendor-managed hubs, and Dell had to maintain buffers of 26 to 30 hours at its own assembly plants. In addition, every week, Dell distributed a new 52-week demand forecast to all suppliers.

Today, Dell generates a new manufacturing schedule for each of its plants every two hours, reflecting actual orders received, and publishes these schedules as a Web service via its extranet. Because the schedules are in XML format, they can be fed directly into the disparate inventory-management systems maintained by all the vendor-managed hubs. The hubs always know Dell's precise materials requirements and can deliver the materials to a specific loading dock at a specific building, from which they are fed immediately into an assembly line. With this new approach, Dell has been able to cut the inventory buffers at its plants to just three to five hours. Explains Eric Michlowitz, the company's director of supply chain e-business solutions, "We've been able to remove the stock rooms from the assembly plant, because we now pull in only materials specifically tied to customer orders. This has enabled us to add more production lines, increasing our factory utilization by one-third."

Trying to engage with too many partners too fast is one of the main reasons that so many on-line market makers have foundered: The transactions they had viewed as simple and routine actually involved many subtle distinctions in terminology and meaning.

Of course, such lean manufacturing approaches often just push inventory back from the manufacturer to the supplier. Dell's goal, however, is to eliminate excess inventory throughout the supply chain. So the company is now focusing on reducing the buffers held at the hubs. These stocks could be cut substantially if supply problems could be identified earlier. If, for example, Dell knew that one supplier was having a problem fulfilling an order for a particular part, it might be able to temporarily remove from its Web store the computer model that used the part. This would, in turn, enable a reduction in the stocks of the part held at the hubs. To establish such an early warning system for its supply chain, Dell is rolling out an "event management" Web service, again using its extranet. This service automatically sends out queries on the status of orders to suppliers, whose own systems automatically send back responses. Dell expects that this system will reduce hub inventories by as much as 40% while at the same time significantly improving gross margins by better matching demand and supply.

Create a shared terminology. The move to a shared IT architecture raises an obvious question of control: Who calls the shots? Within a single company, a CIO can impose a set of standards governing information technology (requiring, for example, that accounts always be represented in applications as "ACCTS"). But once a group of companies, each with different internal systems and standards, begins to collaborate electronically, establishing clear lines of authority becomes difficult. In some cases, one company will have the market power to impose standards on its partners, but these situations are rare and, given the increasing complexity and fluidity of corporate partnerships, usually unwise. Instead, shared meaning, and the trust it engenders, must develop much more organically among participants.

Incremental implementation of Web services can aid this process. By starting with a few long-standing business partners – as GM did with its dealers and Dell did with its logistics providers – companies gain room to experiment; they can establish through trial and error a common technical language. Then, as they learn what works and what doesn't, they can expand the orbit of their partnerships to encompass new companies. Trying to engage with too many partners too fast is one of the main reasons that so many on-line market makers have foundered: The transactions they had viewed as simple and routine actually involved many subtle distinctions in terminology and meaning. That doesn't mean that shared standards can't be established among large groups; it just can't be done easily or overnight. Traditional distributors spend years learning the shades of meaning used by different buyers and sellers. A produce distributor, for example, has to build an understanding of how each of its suppliers quantifies the ripeness of an orange as well as how each buyer evaluates ripeness. It is only then that the distributor will have the knowledge and the authority to create a standard rating system for oranges and promote its adoption throughout the community of buyers and sellers.

XML can be a powerful tool for building shared meaning in Web-based communities, but it's important to understand that XML isn't a cure-all. While XML establishes a common grammar – a framework for sharing meaning – it establishes only very limited semantics. The precise meanings of XML terms still need to be determined by the actual partners. For instance, a particular XML tag may refer to the price of a product, but that doesn't tell you if it's the net price after discounts, if it includes shipping, and so on. Subtleties of meaning have to be hashed out before business can be conducted in all its inevitable complexity. And don't expect the meanings, once established, to stay fixed. They will evolve as partners gain experience and discover shortcomings in their shared processes.

The service grid will play an important role in helping business communities build shared meaning, since a set of utilities will be established to facilitate the development of trading standards. In many cases, the dominant companies within private trading networks will provide these utilities. In other cases, industry consortia will take the lead. RosettaNet is an early example of a consortium-driven utility. It is defining and promoting the adoption of standard XML formats to describe processes in the supply chain of the electronics industry, enabling all participants to use the same terms to describe activities like issuing purchase orders. Such utilities might also be provided by independent businesses that are focused solely on developing XML or other software standards within an industry or across industries.

Shared meaning will naturally increase as the use of the Web services architecture expands. In the architecture's current, early stage of development, incentives for its adoption are limited because relatively few application services are available and the functionality of the service grid is limited. In this period, early movers like Merrill Lynch, GM, and Dell play key roles by providing their business partners with compelling reasons to use Web services. Over time, as additional resources become accessible, the benefits of adopting this architecture will become compelling to more and more companies. Newcomers will find it advantageous to adopt meanings already in use in order to tap into existing applications and utilities.

A Platform for Growth

Although many of the early uses of Web services will focus on reducing costs, efficiency-driven initiatives are only the beginning. Ultimately, the greatest beneficiaries of this new technology will be companies that harness its power for revenue growth. (See the sidebar "Unbundling and Rebundling.")

The new architecture provides, for example, a platform for companies to offer their core competencies as services to other companies. Smart businesses, in other words, won't just consume Web services; they'll also sell them. That's exactly what Citibank is doing right now. It saw that one drawback to early on-line exchanges was the inability to handle payments: Participants would use an exchange to reach agreement on the terms of a transaction but would then have to process payments either manually or through specialized banking networks. Leveraging its deep skill in electronic payments, Citibank quickly introduced CitiConnect, an XML-based payment-processing service that plugs into existing trading applications.

Here's how it works. A company purchasing supplies through an Internet exchange platform, such as one offered by Commerce One, registers information about the authorization levels for specific employees and the corporate bank accounts to be used for payment. When a purchase is made, the buyer clicks the CitiConnect icon on the Web site. An XML message containing payment instructions is automatically assembled, specifying the amount involved, the identity of the buyer, the identity of the supplier, the bank from which to withdraw funds, the bank to transfer the funds to, and the timing of payment. The message is then routed, according to predefined rules, to the appropriate specialized settlement networks.

The benefits for buyers and sellers are compelling: Sellers cut settlement times by 20% to 40%, and both buyers and sellers reduce settlement costs by 50% to 60%.

While XML establishes a common grammar – a framework for sharing meaning – it establishes only very limited semantics. The precise meanings of XML terms still need to be determined by the actual partners.

Unbundling and Rebundling

Two and a half years ago, Marc Singer and I wrote "Unbundling the Corporation" (HBR March–April 1999). In that article, we described how most companies encompass three very different types of businesses – customer relationship management, infrastructure management, and product innovation and commercialization – and how the Internet would facilitate their unbundling, leading to much more tightly focused companies.

The rise of the Web services architecture will not only speed this unbundling but will spur the growth of the new companies by letting them mobilize a greater range of resources to reach a broader set of customers. Freed from the straitjacket of existing enterprise-centric IT architectures, companies won't have to acquire new assets to grow (a slow and often treacherous process); they will be able to rent them, as Web services, from third parties. The capital-intensive model of owning resources will be supplanted by the much more efficient model of orchestrating resources. A new kind of business organization – a rebundler focusing on the assembly and coordination of business processes that stretch across entire industries and markets – will likely emerge and gain enormous power.

Of course, exploiting these new kinds of growth opportunities will require much more than just the new technology architecture. Very different organizational capabilities must be developed – not just new skills but also new performance measurement and reward systems and knowledge management approaches. Even more fundamentally, managers will need to adopt new mind-sets: They will need to focus on creating new opportunities, largely by helping to define and deploy standards, rather than simply trying to adapt to rapidly changing environments.

– John Hagel III

Citibank turned an existing operational capability into a new service line and extended its reach to a broader range of customers through its partnerships with application providers like Commerce One. And Commerce One, for its part, got happier customers while also associating itself with the respected Citibank brand.

The relationship between Citibank and Commerce One illustrates a broader pattern that will both speed the adoption of the Web services architecture and open new growth opportunities for traditional companies. All providers of inter-enterprise applications – private trading exchanges, procurement services, supply-chain management services, and so on – recognize that they need to add new functions rapidly to attract and retain customers. They have two choices: develop the added functionality themselves or source it from specialized providers. Many are choosing the latter path because it's faster and allows them to dedicate their scarce resources to acquiring customers.

In supplying these functions, traditional companies have an important advantage. When an application provider has to choose between sourcing a Web service from a well-known enterprise with a strong track record or from a small start-up with an uncertain future, it will likely go with the established company, as Commerce One did with Citibank. As traditional companies begin to make their capabilities available to other companies through Web services, the importance of the service grid will become increasingly apparent. Web services for functions like invoicing, payments, and logistics are critical to the companies that use them. Without the security, reliability, and performance auditing that service grid utilities can provide to their customers, few enterprises will be willing to offer, much less subscribe to, such mission-critical services.

As the service grid matures and companies move aggressively to exploit revenue growth opportunities created by the Web services architecture, a curious dynamic will begin to play out. The distinction between users and suppliers of Web services will fade. Companies will provide Web services to others in areas in which they have distinctive expertise while at the same time buying Web services from others in areas in which they lack special skills. Over time, the location of particular capabilities – whether inside or outside the walls of any given company – will become less important than the ability to discover and orchestrate distinctive capabilities across enterprises in order to deliver greater value to customers. In the process, many companies will find themselves turned inside out, with their formerly well-guarded core capabilities visible and accessible to all.

The authors thank Dennis Layton-Rodin, Halsey Minor, Mahmoud Falaki, and other colleagues for their contributions to this article.

Reprint R0109G
To place an order, call 1-800-988-0886.

HARVARD | BUSINESS | SCHOOL

9-301-099
REV: OCTOBER 15, 2001

RICHARD L. NOLAN

Cisco Systems Architecture: ERP and Web-enabled IT

Cisco CEO John Chamber's vision of a "New World Network"—where voice calls over the Internet will be free- is as far-reaching as Microsoft Chairman Bill Gates' decade-ago vision of "information at your finger tips, with a computer in every desk and in every home."

Pete Solvik:

> The vision is core to our perception of the marketplace. We all carry these cards in our wallets with our goal printed on them: "Internet experts: the Global Internet Company."

Founded by two Stanford computer scientists in 1984 and brought public in 1990, Cisco Systems, Inc. now dominates the exploding "Internetworking" market. In 1997—its first year on the *Fortune* 500—Cisco ranked in the top five companies in return on revenues and return on assets. (See **Exhibit 1** for Cisco's financial performance.) Only two other companies, Intel and Microsoft, have matched this feat. On July 17, 1998, just fourteen years after being founded, Cisco's market capitalization passed the significant $100 billion mark. Less than two years later, on March 27, 2000, Cisco overtook Microsoft as the most valuable business on earth with a market cap of $531 billion.

Cisco's core technology began with routers. Routers are what make the Internet work. They act as multilingual translators tying the disparate computer networks of the world together on the Internet, in much the same way that telephone networks in different countries pass calls to each other.

Cisco is at the forefront of challenging a world of three independent proprietary networks: the phone networks for voice, the local area and wide area networks for data, and the broadcast networks for video. Digitization is enabling the convergence of the three networks; the Internet, as a global network of networks, makes it possible to transmit voice, data, and video over one network in a more efficient and economical manner than transmitting signals over the three independent and proprietary networks. The Internet and its open standards are creating a new competitive battleground for the entrenched telecommunications (telecom) players, including AT&T, Verizon (GTE & Bell Atlantic), British Telecom, and Deutsche Telecom.

Professor Richard L. Nolan, William Barclay Harding Professor of Management Technology and Research Associates Kelley A. Porter and Christina Akers prepared this case with the assistance of Christina L. Darwall, Executive Director, HBs California Research Center. This case also draws on the "Cisco Systems, Inc.: Implementing ERP," HBS No. 699-022, Revised March 24, 1999, prepared by Doctoral Candidate Mark Cotteleer under the supervision of Professors Robert D. Austin and Richard L. Nolan. HBS cases are developed solely as the basis for class discussion. Cases are not intended to serve as endorsements, sources of primary data, or illustrations of effective or ineffective management.

Challengers to the incumbents have spearheaded their attacks through the Internet by offering services such as Internet access, hosting, extranets, e-mail, and search capabilities. Many—including UUNet, PSINET, GTE/BBN, and over 5,000 other ISPs (Internet Service Providers)—are competing on price for providing fax, messaging, and EDI (electronic data interchange).[1]

All of this activity signals the acceleration of the trend to IP (Internet Protocol)-based networks. This market did not exist three to five years ago. Already, in the United States it is estimated that data network traffic exceeds voice network traffic. More than 75% of all Internet traffic travels over Cisco products. In 2000, more than 275 million people are on the Internet, projected to be more than a billion by 2005.

Lucent Technologies (2001 revenues of $33 billion market cap of $60.1 billion) current leader for telecom gear has not stood still since its 1996 spin-off from AT&T. As phone companies shift their traffic from overstretched networks, which were designed to carry voice versus the 0s and 1s of computers, Lucent has been remaking itself to transition with its customers.

IP-based networks have cost advantages over traditional phone networks. In addition, the new IP-based technology providers such as Cisco are better equipped to address performance and security issues due to their constant influx of venture capital and talent. Many of the IP-based technology companies benefit from being located in Silicon Valley where there is an incredible spirit of innovation in both technology and management. Juniper Networks directly competes with Cisco by providing next generation Internet backbone routers that are specifically designed for service providers. Juniper Networks floated their IPO on June 25, 1999, and with revenues of about $100 million had a market value of $2.1 billion. In 2001, Juniper had revenues of $673.5 million and a market cap of $31,974 billion.[2]

But neither Cisco nor Lucent have the products they need to ensure a big win, nor do any of the other network companies including Northern Telecom (Nortel), Bay Networks (now a part of Nortel), or 3Com.[3] All of the network companies are racing to develop a new hybrid product with the speed and efficiency of a router and the precision of a telephone switch.

The Top Management Team at Cisco

The two founders of Cisco were long on innovation acumen. Don Valentine, Partner of Sequoia Capital and Vice Chairman of the Board of Cisco[4] was the initial venture capitalist who invested in Cisco; believing that Cisco would be a success, he took a chance when other venture capitalists were more cautious. One way in which Valentine protected his initial $2.5 million investment was by reserving the right to bring in professional management when he deemed it appropriate.

In 1988, Valentine hired John Morgridge as CEO. Morgridge, an experienced executive in the computer industry who had worked at Grid Systems, Stratus Computers, and Honeywell, immediately began to build a professional management team. This team soon clashed with the

---

[1] McKinsey 1997 Report on the Computer Industry, pp. 1-55.

[2] OneSource, February 2001.

[3] Nortel acquired Bay Networks in June 1998 for $9.1 billion in stock. At the time, Nortel had annual revenue of $15.4 billion, and a market value of $28 billion compared to Cisco's annual revenue of $6.4 billion and a market value of $85 billion.

[4] Don Valentine was previously the outside executive Chairman of the Board of Cisco. Cisco has maintained its Chairman of the Board as an outside director. Currently, John Morgridge serves as an outside director and Chairman of the Board.

founders, and after Cisco's initial public offering in 1990, both founders sold all of their stock and left the company. Some observers felt that this early exit of the founders provided a receptive environment for laying the groundwork for disciplined management, which in turn let the company capitalize on market opportunities and grow at a phenomenal rate without derailing its focus or losing control.

Morgridge believed that many Silicon Valley firms decentralized too quickly and did not appreciate the proven ability of the functional organization structure to scale without sacrificing control during high levels of growth. Accordingly, Morgridge maintained a centralized functional organization that is still in place today. While Product Marketing and R&D are now decentralized into three "Lines of Business" (Enterprise, Small/Medium Business, and Service Provider), the manufacturing, customer support, finance, human resources, Information Technology (IT) and sales organizations remain centralized. The only responsibility of sales country managers is to sell the three market segment products. They are not responsible for non-sales activities (e.g., accounting, IT, manufacturing, etc.) within a country or geography. There is a belief within Cisco that consistency of strategy, goals, organization, and management provides a huge stable benefit to a fast growing, fast moving company.

Cisco's Business Strategy

Morgridge hired John Chambers in 1991 from Wang Laboratories (Chambers had also worked for IBM for six years), and turned over the duties of CEO to Chambers in 1995. Morgridge reflects: "When Chambers took over, Cisco never lost a beat."[5] Chambers continues to execute a plan that he jointly created with Ed Kozel, chief technical officer, and Morgridge in 1993. The plan consists of four elements:[6]

1. *Assemble a broad product line so Cisco can serve as one-stop shopping for business networks.* **Exhibit 2** shows how information is routed through the Internet; Cisco's revenues and market shares for those products are also stated.

2. *Systematize acquisitions as an efficient business process.* Cisco has made more than 70 acquisitions and key strategic alliances since 1993 to fill out its product line.

3. *Set industry wide software standards for networking.* Cisco has issued IOS (Internetwork Operating System) licenses to Alcatel, Ericcson, Northern Telecom, Compaq, Hewlett-Packard (HP), Bay Networks, 3Com, Microsoft, Intel and twelve Japanese companies.

4. *Pick the right strategic partners.* Cisco is working with Microsoft to create an industry standard for security over the network, working with MCI to deliver premium Internet services, and working with HP to develop and sell Internet-based corporate computing systems built with each other's products.

If Chambers can successfully execute on this four-point plan, he believes that Cisco will be the lead architect and provider of technologies for the new Internet-based infrastructure in which voice, data and video will be delivered through one network. Further, Chambers believes that

---

5 Geoff Baum, "Cisco's CEO: John Chambers," *Forbes ASAP*, February 23, 1998, p. 52.

6 Brent Schlender, "Computing's Next Superpower," *Fortune*, May 12, 1997, p. 88.

> . . . by providing the end-to-end network plumbing, we can change the way entire companies and industries operate. Only now are businesses beginning to realize how much the network will touch their people and Customers and suppliers, and how much productivity and profitability can improve when they become truly global networked companies.[7]

In the end, Chamber's ultimate focus is on the customer, a fact that is emphasized by his directive to have the words "Dedication to Customer Success" on every Cisco worker's badge.

Building Cisco's IT Infrastructure

When Peter Solvik joined Cisco in January 1993 as their new CIO, Cisco was a $500 million company, and was running traditional financial, manufacturing, and order entry systems. Solvik, who was fresh from Apple, concluded that he had two key challenges. First, Cisco's Information Technology (IT) department was too traditional in the sense that it was viewed as a cost center that reported through the Finance department, and it was too internally oriented. As a result, the potential contribution of IT to the business was much less than it could be and Solvik believed this had to change. Solvik's second challenge was that the current systems could not scale to support Cisco's growth, nor were they flexible and robust enough to meet management requirements.

To address the first challenge, three changes were made. First, the IT-reporting relationship was changed from Accounting to the Senior Vice President of Customer Advocacy (See **Exhibit 3** for Cisco Organization Chart). Second, the IT budget pertaining to the functions were returned to the functions leaving just a small portion left in G&A (General and Administrative) expense. This created a structure where all IT application projects were client funded. Third, the central IT steering committee was disbanded, and replaced with a structure where IT investment decisions on application projects were pushed out to the line organization but still executed by central IT.

A Defining Moment

Finally, in January of 1994, Cisco's legacy environment failed so dramatically that the shortcomings of the existing systems could be ignored no longer. An unauthorized method for accessing the core application database—a workaround that was itself motivated by the inability of the system to perform—malfunctioned, corrupting Cisco's central database. As a result, the company was largely shut down for two days.

Cisco's struggle to recover from this major shutdown brought home the fact that the company's systems were on the brink of total failure. Solvik, Randy Pond, a director of manufacturing[8] and a number of other Cisco managers came to the conclusion that the autonomous approach to systems replacement they had adopted was not going to be sufficient. An alternative approach was needed. Solvik described what they did:

> We said, "we can't wait casually by while Order Entry, Finance and Manufacturing go out and make three separate decisions." It would take too long to get those applications in place. We needed to take faster action. At that point we got sponsorship from the SVP of Manufacturing, Carl Redfield. He was with Digital before Cisco, in PC manufacturing. He

[7] John Chambers as quoted in Brent Schlender, "Computing's Next Superpower," *Fortune*, May 12, 1997, p. 88.

[8] Randy Pond became Co-Director with Pete Solvik of the ERP project.

took the lead and said, "O.K., let's get on with this... let's start from the manufacturing perspective, and see if we can get the Order Entry and Financial groups in the company interested in doing a single integrated replacement of all the applications instead of taking a longer time doing separate projects." And so in February, about a month after the [company shutdown], we went about putting together a team to do an investigation to replace the application.

Redfield understood from previous large-scale implementation experiences at Digital how "monolithic" IT projects could take on lives of their own. He echoed Solvik's concerns about project size and had strong views about how Cisco should approach a large implementation project.

> I knew we wanted to do this quickly. We were not going to do a phased implementation, we would do it all at once. We were not going to allow a lot of customization either. There is a tendency in MRP systems[9] for people to want the system to mirror their method of operation instead of retraining people to do things the way the system intended them. This takes a lot longer. Also, we wanted to create a schedule that was doable and make it a priority in the company as opposed to a second tier kind of effort.

Selecting an ERP Product

Cisco's management team realized that implementing to meet *business* needs would require heavy involvement from the business community. This could not be an IT-only initiative. It was critically important to get the very best people they could find. Solvik elaborated: "It was our orientation that in pulling people out of their jobs [to work on the project] if it was easy then we were picking the wrong people. We pulled people out that the business absolutely did not want to give up."

Consistent with the need for a strong Cisco team, the company would also need strong partners. Solvik and Redfield felt it was particularly important to work with an integration partner that could assist in both the selection and implementation of whichever solution the company chose. Great technical skills and business knowledge were a prerequisite. Solvik explained the choice of KPMG as the integration partner:

> KPMG came in and saw an opportunity to really build a business around putting in these applications. They also saw this as kind of a defining opportunity, to work with us on this project. As opposed to some other firms that wanted to bring in a lot of "greenies," KPMG was building a practice of people that were very experienced in the industry. For instance, the program manager that they put on the job, Mark Lee, had been director of IT for a company in Texas that had put in various parts of an ERP system.

With KPMG on board, the team of about 20 people turned to the software market with a multi-pronged approach for identifying the best software packages. The team's strategy was to build as much knowledge as possible by leveraging the experiences of others. They asked large corporations and the "Big Six" accounting firms what they knew. They also tapped research sources such as Gartner.[10] By orienting the selection process to what people were actually using and continuing to

---

[9] MRP represents a class of systems, often thought of as predecessors of ERP, that focus on planning the material requirements for production. Forecast or actual demand is fed to MRP either manually or from other types of systems. MRP functionality is embedded in the offerings of all leading ERP vendors.

[10] The Gartner Group is a leading industry resource for information on ERP and other information systems and manufacturing related research.

emphasize decision speed, Cisco narrowed the field to five packages within two days. After a week of evaluating the packages at a high-level, the team decided on two prime candidates, Oracle and another major player in the ERP market. Pond recalled that size was an issue in the selection. "We decided that we should not put Cisco's future in the hands of a company that was significantly smaller than we were."

The team spent 10 days writing a Request For Proposals (RFP) to send to the vendors. Vendors were given two weeks to respond. While vendors prepared their responses, the Cisco team continued its "due diligence" by visiting a series of reference clients offered by each vendor. Following Cisco's analysis of the RFP responses, each vendor was invited in for a three-day software demonstration and asked to show how their package could meet Cisco's information processing requirements. Cisco provided sample data and vendors illustrated how key requirements were met (or not met) by the software.

Selection of Oracle was based on a variety of factors. Redfield described three of the major decision points:

> First, this project was being driven pretty strongly by manufacturing and Oracle had a better manufacturing capability than the other vendor. Second, they made a number of promises regarding the long term development of functionality in the package.[11] The other part of it was the flexibility offered by Oracle's being close by.[12]

Cisco also had reason to believe that Oracle was particularly motivated to make the project a success. Randy Pond provided his impression of Oracle's situation: "Oracle wanted this win badly. We ended up getting a super deal. There are, however, a lot of strings attached. We do references, allow site visits and in general talk to many companies that are involved in making this decision." The Cisco project would be the first major implementation of a new release of the Oracle ERP product. Oracle was touting the new version as having major improvements in support of manufacturing. A successful implementation at Cisco would launch the new release on a very favorable trajectory.

From inception to final selection the Cisco team had spent 75 days. The final choice was team based. Solvik described how the decision was made and presented to the vendors:

> The team internally made the choice and informed the vendors. There was no major process we had to go through with management to "approve" the selection. We just said "Oracle you won, [other vendor] you lost." Then we went on to contract negotiations with Oracle and putting a proposal together for our board of directors. The focus immediately turned to issues of how long the project would take, and how much it would cost. The team decided "yes, we will do this and we ought to go forward with the project." So now at the very end of April we were putting the whole plan together.

Going to the Board

Before going to the board for approval, the team needed to answer two very important questions: How much would it cost and how long would it take? They knew their executives were worried that a big project might spin out of control and deliver sub-standard results. Despite the risks, the team took a pragmatic approach to estimating project requirements. Solvik described the process:

---

[11] Redfield later notes that not all of these promises were met in the time frame agreed to during contract negotiations.

[12] Oracle and Cisco world headquarters are both located in the Silicon Valley approximately 20 miles from each other.

Our quarters go August to October, November to January, February to April, and May to July.[13] So right here on May 1, beginning of the fourth quarter, we are asking "how long should it take to do a project to replace all of our core systems?" This is truly how it went. We said "you know we can't implement in the fourth quarter. The auditors will have a complete cow." If it takes a year we will be implementing fourth quarter, and that won't work. We thought it really should take 15 months, July or August a year later. Tom Herbert, the program manager, said there's no way we are going to take 15 months to get this done. That's ridiculous. So we started going in the opposite direction and said well can we do it in five months? That just didn't seem right. Understand we did not have a scope yet. In the end we basically settled that we wanted to go live at the beginning of Q3, so we would be completely stable for Q4. (See **Exhibit 4** for a summary of milestone ERP implementation dates.)

That took care of setting a target date. Next came the task of estimating a project budget. Once again, Cisco was aggressive: "After we set a date, we estimated budgets. We put this whole thing together without really being that far into this program. We just looked at how much it touched" (Pete Solvik). Instead of developing a formal business case (i.e., a financial analysis) to demonstrate the impact that the project would have on the company, the team chose to focus on the issues that had sparked the analysis in the first place. In Solvik's view, Cisco had little choice but to move. He explained his approach to the situation:

> We said that we had this big outage in January. That we were the biggest customer of our current software vendor and that the vendor was being bought by another company. It was unclear who was going to support our existing systems and we needed to do something. The reliability, the scalability and the modifiability of our current applications would not support our anticipated future growth. We needed either upgrades to the new version of the current application or we needed to replace it. If we replaced it, we could either do it in parts or do it as a whole. We evaluated those three alternatives, talked about the pros and cons of each alternative, and recommended that we replace our systems, big-bang, with one ERP solution. We committed to do it in nine months for $15 million for the whole thing. (See **Exhibit 5** for a breakdown of project costs.)

Although Cisco was, to some extent, compelled to implement ERP, proceeding without a formal economic justification was also a matter of management philosophy. As Redfield put it: "You don't approach this kind of thing from a justification perspective. Cost avoidance is not an appropriate way to look at it. You really need to look at it like 'Hey, we are going to do business this way.' You are institutionalizing a business model for your organization."

At $15 million, the project would constitute the single largest capital project ever approved by the company. Members of the team prepared to take this number to senior management with some trepidation. The first meeting with CEO Morgridge did nothing to alleviate their concerns. Pond described the meeting with Morgridge this way:

> Pete Solvik, Tom Herbert, and I took the proposal to Morgridge and the reaction was pretty interesting. He made the comment "you know, careers are lost over much less money than this." Pete and I were as white as a sheet of paper. We knew that if we failed that we were going to get shot. Failure is not something the business took to well, especially with this kind of money.

But Morgridge okayed taking the project proposal to the board. Unfortunately for Pond and Solvik, the reception was not much warmer there. Pond described what happened:

---

[13] Cisco's financial year end is July 31.

Before we even get the first slide up I hear the chairman speaking from the back of the room. He says "How much?" I said I was getting to it and he responded: "I hate surprises. Just put the slide up right now." After I put it up he said "Oh my God, there better be a lot of good slides. . . ."

There were, and the board ended up approving the project[14]. In the weeks and months following the meeting, Morgridge did his part by making it clear to the rest of Cisco that the ERP project was a priority. The project emerged as one of the company's top seven goals for the year. "Everybody in the company knew this was happening and it was a priority for the business." Pond explained.

The project was completed successfully and on time and formed the centerpiece of the two-year, $100 million series of initiatives to replace all IT applications and platforms worldwide. Solvik describes the results: "In a two-year period, we literally replaced every piece of technology in the company. We have a very low-cost/high-value technology architecture. We have no mainframes, no mini computers, and no legacy technology. Everything is current."

The IT platform architecture is standardized throughout Cisco: 100% UNIX at the server level, 100% Windows NT at the LAN level, 100% Windows Toshiba and HP PCs at the client level, 100% Oracle at the database level, and 100% TCP/IP (Transmission Control Protocol/Internet Protocol) for the worldwide network. Voice-mail, e-mail, meeting schedule software, desktop and server operating systems, and office productivity suites are all standardized. Virtually all business functions utilize single applications packages worldwide. Cisco's architecture is detailed in **Exhibit 6**.

Being standardized to this degree has given the company a high level of flexibility. For example, when Cisco reorganized R&D and marketing from multiple business units to three lines of business, they completed all the changes required across all applications in less than 60 days for a cost less than $1 million. Solvik feels "that without the IP and open systems based IT architecture and standardization, we would never have been able to accomplish such a feat in the short time that we did, and at an incredibly low cost."

Although standardization means flexibility, from a scalability perspective, distributing the company's systems and yet keeping a single system image remains a daunting task. Solvik explained that

> . . . the biggest and most challenging projects we have going on are distributing our centralized core systems. We have very big UNIX servers with huge, huge databases that just don't have the inherent reliability and scalability that the same size DB2 database would have on a mainframe. A tremendous amount of our effort goes into designing our systems to be reliable and scaleable. The whole UNIX platform has a much lower cost than mainframes so we're able to spend that money to have plenty of server capability.

Completion of their IP-based open standards architecture initiative provided the centerpiece of the Cisco IT architecture. It also provided the foundation for the next phase of Solvik's strategy: incorporating the Internet.

---

[14] Pond adds that the cause for approval was aided by the fact that the legacy systems crashed on the day of the board meeting. "The day of the meeting, [the legacy system] went down. We were able to walk into the board meeting and say 'It's down again.' It was really a compelling story."

Internet and Intranet Applications and Benefits

Cisco began web development in the early 1990s when they discovered Mosaic, a public domain primitive web browser developed at the University of Illinois. Within six months of the discovery, Cisco had production and transaction web applications for itself and its customers, and a year after that they shifted from the Mosaic browser to the Netscape browser. Solvik recalls that early on "when we purchased our applications, none were web enabled. We had to web enable them all. So we did that with a standard set of tools and a smart group of people."

The initial 3 year investment cost was about $115 million ($15M for ERP and $100M for web-enablement). The following table details the key components for the Intranet and Internet applications.

Intranet	Internet
EIS (Executive Information Systems) and DSS (Decision Support Systems)	Extranet supply chain (information transparency)
Employee self-service	Customer self-service through web site
Communication and distance learning	Net commerce through the web
Collaboration and workflow management	Marketing through the web
Web-enabled legacy systems	Any place access through the web

A very high percentage of Cisco customer, partner and supplier interaction with the company is network based, and begins at Cisco's Home Page (see **Exhibit** 7). From the Cisco Connection Online (CCO), the user navigates to the information needed for the interaction work, or "publishes and subscribes"—that is, the user directly contributes information required to do business with Cisco, or enriches Cisco's intellectual asset base. This allows others (both internally and externally) to do business more efficiently and effectively with Cisco.

Cisco has built its business processes on its own global intranet, and Cisco people deployed around the world interact on this intranet to address business issues and customer needs. (See **Exhibit 8** for the "Cisco Employee Connection" home page.) Links to strategic vendors and customers allow Cisco to collaborate more efficiently with those outside the company. The intranet also provides a proving ground for new Cisco technologies and products, ensuring that they are ready for mission-critical applications before they are offered to customers.

Employee Self-Service: Internal applications

The majority of Cisco's internal applications have been web enabled. For example, almost all functions that sales people perform on the computer are done using a web browser. EIS and DSS systems, training (including distance learning), and self-service HR are all web-based.

Cisco Systems' corporate intranet Cisco Employee Connection (CEC) addressed the unique needs of its 40,000+ employees by providing centralized access to information, tools and resources needed to streamline processes, facilitate knowledge exchange and maximize employee productivity.

Cisco has leveraged the web to truly revolutionize existing process and create new, end-to end capabilities. Because the Web has integrated data and tools from a variety of sources under a unified user interface, Cisco's intranet was a key enabler of workforce optimization.

In addition to replacing its own custom designed applications, Cisco works with its vendors to help them convert the applications that Cisco has purchased for use within the company. By 2001, virtually every application in the company uses a web browser as its only user interface.

Communication and Distance Learning

The network has continued to enhance the ability to communicate with employees and added an important dimension to training. Distance learning modules available to Cisco employees can be activated at the employee's desktop. The use of these distance learning modules—as well as information about their effectiveness—can be easily tracked to determine the extent of use of the various education modules. From tracking information, the quality of the modules can be assessed to ensure high levels of effectiveness as the needs of the organization change.

An arrangement with Yahoo! (the search engine company) makes available a Cisco-tailored version of "My Yahoo!." My Yahoo! Is a type of "push" technology application whereby certain information is specified by the user, and agents search the Internet for the information and then "push" it out to the user's desktop. When the user signs onto the Internet, the information is waiting for him/her, tracking everything from breaking news reports about competitors to up-to-the-minute information about worldwide financial markets (see **Exhibit 9**).

Chambers' addresses at Cisco's Quarterly Meetings can be viewed from employee's desktops in real-time. Thousands employees tune in to view the addresses in real-time or watch them in a delayed broadcast over the Intranet—using their PC to bring up a video window. This streaming of live video provides another capability that strengthens the Cisco culture by making the company "feel" closer to each of the employees.

Customer Self-service: Electronic Connection with Customers

Cisco management never misses a chance to reinforce that the customer is the focal point of their business. The centerpiece of this strategy is Cisco.com, a comprehensive, web-based, online resource for information and networked applications. With about 590,425 active registered users from around the world, Cisco.com is accessed approximately 3.8 million times each month by registered users (as of January, 2001), making it the primary vehicle for delivering responsive, around--the-clock customer support.[15] Customers rely on Cisco.com to answer questions, diagnose network problems, and provide solutions and expert assistance worldwide. In fact, over 80% of Cisco's technical support for customers and resellers is delivered electronically, saving Cisco nearly $506 million annually and improving customer satisfaction.[16] For its international customers, portions of Cisco.com have been translated into multiple languages with nearly 68 different country pages, plus 17 languages.

Solvik reflected on the importance of the customer at Cisco:

> I have 600,000 registered Customers hooked up—those are Customers with a big "C"—compared to 42,617 Cisco employees. In contrast to most internally focused IT organizations in many other companies, my mission does not primarily focus on providing services and

---

[15] Note—As of June 2000, there were 15 million hits per month against the Cisco.com web site and this number is growing by 3.6% per month. Seventy percent of these hits are not registered users but individuals visiting the Cisco.com website for general company information. Registered users have a special login that provides them access to specific Cisco information.

[16] "Ten Minutes with John Chambers," *NASDAQ: The International Magazine*, Issue 29, January 2001, p. 18.

systems to meet the needs of the employees of the business. In fact, I refer to my employee users as clients, and not as Customers.

Customers that are using our systems directly express higher satisfaction with us and enjoy a lower cost of doing business with us than those who do not use our systems. And of course, we also lower our cost of doing business.

Seventy percent of the employees in Cisco have a very significant bonus multiplier tied to our annual customer satisfaction survey. The first thing we review at every senior staff meeting is the status of critical accounts. Every night Chambers gets a personal update on the status of every critical account. Any employee can put a Customer on the critical account list as an advocate of the Customer. So if I get a call from someone who knows me or has met me or has my business card, and they say "I'm having a problem with your company," I will find the relevant sales person and call the account team, to get the issue resolved or I can place the account on the critical account list. If you have an unhappy Customer, they stay on the critical account list until the problem is fixed.

Net Commerce—Shipping product over the Internet

Cisco was an early pioneer in using the Internet for full electronic commerce. They began with simple transactions over five years ago and have had completed configuration and order placement for the company's entire product line. Solvik recounted their experience:

> We've learned an incredible amount in the 48 months of live e-commerce. We have racked up Internet shipments of product from 0% in July of 1996, to 2% of our revenue in August of 1996, to $800 million in calendar 1997, and to $1.5 billion each quarter in 1998. As of January, 2001, Internet Commerce based revenue represents 92% of our total revenue base, a run-rate of over $25 Billion annually. Cisco operates one of the biggest electronic commerce sites in the world.

Orders can be placed via the World Wide Web from anywhere in the world. After placing an order customers can use other applications to instantly check the status of pending orders. In addition, well over 90% of Cisco's software upgrades are now delivered via the Internet at a much lower cost and in a shorter time period than in the past when traditional distribution methods were used. For example,

> At Sprint it used to take 60 days from the signing of a contract to complete a networking project. Now, thanks partly to the efficiency of ordering Cisco equipment online, it takes 35 to 45 days. Sprint has also been able to cut its order-processing staff from 21 to six, allowing the other 15 employees to work instead on installing networks.[17]

Productivity gains of 60% for Cisco and 20% for customers and resellers are being realized through online commerce.[18]

---

[17] Shawn Tully, "How Cisco Mastered the Net," *Fortune*, August 17, 1998, p. 210.

[18] Cisco 1997 Annual Report, p. 11.

Cisco's Supply Chain Management Initiative

Beginning in 1992, Cisco outsourced much of its manufacturing to contract manufacturers while still performing final assembly and test. The supply chain functions were jointly performed by Cisco and its contract manufactures, requiring them to exchange information and interact through labor-intensive processes.

As the company began implementing applications to extend to its suppliers and customers, Cisco decided that its core competencies were in design and fulfillment processes rather than physical transformation of product. As a result, Cisco chose to form partnerships with suppliers that performed physical transformation as their core competency. Central to Cisco's philosophy was to remove business barriers that would impede the flow of information within the company and its business partners, further increasing the integration with its constituents and overall power of the supply chain.

Automating Cisco's supply chain involved five initiatives:

5. *Single Enterprise*: Cisco used networked applications to integrate suppliers into its production systems, creating in effect, a "single enterprise". This enabled key suppliers to manage and operate major portions of its supply chain. The electronic links across the single enterprise allow Cisco and these suppliers to respond to customer demand in real-time. Any change in one node of the supply chain is propagated throughout the supply chain almost instantaneously. Other improvements include the elimination of purchase orders and invoice processing.

6. *New Product Introduction (NPI)*: A 1998 Cisco study revealed that as many as four to five iterations of prototype building are required, with each iteration taking, on average, one to two weeks. Two of the biggest drivers of costs and time delays in the prototype phase was the labor intensive process for gathering and disseminating information and the delays caused by manufacturability design issues. In response to this problem, Cisco automated the process for gathering product data information, thereby reducing the amount of time required from as much as one day, to less than 15 minutes. By simulating the manufacturability of the product design prior to release to the factory, Cisco caught roughly 98% of all manufacturability issues upfront, reducing the number of interactions to 2 ½. The use of networked applications in NPI has reduced time to volume by three months and reduced total cost of NPI by $49 million in 1999.

7. *Autotest*: In 1992 Cisco began to build test cells that performed tests automatically with minimal labor and standardized product tests. Testing processes were made routine and embodied in software test programs that ran the test cells. Once testing had been automated and standardized it was outsourced entirely to the suppliers, allowing quality issues to be detected at the source. However, although testing was outsourced, the intelligence behind the testing was still supplied by Cisco.

8. *Direct Fulfillment*: Originally, orders were shipped to the customer exclusively from Cisco. Therefore, products configured by partners would have to go through two shipping legs: first from the partner to Cisco, and then from Cisco to its customer. Each of these legs took approximately three days. In 1997, the first step in moving toward global direct fulfillment was launched in the United States. The manufacturing partners who have transitioned completely represent about 60% of Cisco's unit volume.

9. *Dynamic Replenishment*: Prior to supply chain automation, Cisco manufacturers and suppliers lacked real-time demand and supply information, resulting in delays and errors. To compensate, inventory levels and overhead were higher than acceptable. The dynamic replenishment model allows the market demand signal to flow through directly to the contract manufacturers without any distortion or delays. It also allows contract manufacturers to track Cisco's inventory levels in real-time.

As a result of these five initiatives, Cisco has one of the most efficient supply chain models possible. In 1997 it improved responsiveness while improving profitability by $275 million. Network-enabled applications have been key to value maximization in Cisco's supply chain. This powerful new model of managing the supply chain is referred to as "the Global Networked Business Model."

EIS (Executive Information Systems) and DSS (Decision Support Systems)

Cisco employees use the web browser as a front end for access to all executive and decision support information in the company. The company's web-based EIS system (Executive Information Systems) is used by all sales managers and executives worldwide—a total of over 2,000 users including the CEO—and provides summary and drill down Bookings, Backlog, Revenue, Not Booked, Forecast and Plan for all products, customers, channels, geographies, and markets.

Sales tracking and reporting is also via the Intranet. If a Cisco sales person would like to track certain product sales in a region on a weekly basis, that sales person merely calls up the browser template and requests the information. After several clicks of the mouse, assuming that the sales person has authority to access the information, the report will be automatically delivered to his/her desktop at the level of detail and for the period of time requested.

Integrating Acquisitions into the IP-based IT Architecture

Acquisitions have been—and will continue to be for the foreseeable future—an important part of Cisco's strategy. Approximately 2/3 of Cisco technology is from internally developed efforts, and 1/3 is from partnerships/acquisitions.[19] In addition, approximately 70% of CEO's from acquired companies remain at Cisco.

Cisco seems to have mastered the acquisition process. There are no hostile takeovers and only companies with "market congruent" visions are considered. Because Cisco wants to be assured of success, only one out of ten acquisitions that Cisco considers is actually executed.

Once an acquisition is consummated, Cisco uses a documented and repeatable process for integration. Generally, the acquired company is acquired for its R&D and developed products that contribute to providing the network customer with an end-to-end solution. The R&D and Product Organizations of each acquired company are grafted onto the product side of the organization, which includes Cisco branding, and product family integration. The manufacturing, sales, and distribution parts of the organization are integrated into Cisco's functional organization. Within Cisco's IT organization, a specific group handles acquisition integration and immediately eliminates non-standard technology, integrating the acquired company into all of Cisco's infrastructures and core applications. Because of Cisco's IP and standards based IT architecture, the company is able to

[19] Noel Lindsay, network analyst, Deutsche Morgan Grenfell.

quickly and efficiently add the capacity required to handle the administrative processes of acquired businesses. Most acquisitions can be fully integrated within 60 to 100 days.

Following cooperative initiatives in a six year relationship, in August 1999, Cisco announced that it would purchase 19.9% of a KPMG's global consulting arm for the sum of $1.05 billion,[20] which KPMG spun off in February 2000, with an intention of taking the new unit through an IPO (Initial Public Offering). KPMG will own the remaining 80% of the equity.[21]

KPMG global consulting plans to use the capital from the deal to build six technology centers that will be staffed with 4,000 of its consultants to deliver internet-based data, voice and video consulting services to Cisco's clients. If a corporate customer wants to transfer business functions like accounting or financial reporting to the web, Cisco will provide the hardware and software systems, and KPMG will provide the software required to set-up the specific application and maintain it. For Cisco, the alliance with KPMG fills a gap to help customers install and maintain its systems, which is particularly important as Cisco sells an increasing share of its systems to telecommunications providers, who are accustomed to more assistance by their equipment suppliers.[22]

Cisco has gained a competitive advantage and increased shareholder value by implementing Internet business solutions across all functional areas (including marketing, employee, manufacturing, customer support, and commerce applications). The bottom line impact in FY2000, including increased revenue, gross margin, and reduced expenses, is conservatively calculated at $1.3 billion. Solvik observed that the benefits of moving to the new architecture could be thought of as either providing the company free IT services or alternatively, as allowing the company to invest $1 billion million more in R&D than their competitors.

Beyond Cisco

It is clear that Cisco is successful in what it does, and now Chambers and Solvik believe that the principals of work using the Internet at Cisco apply in general business. Recently Solvik commented,

> The opportunity for Cisco to continue growing as a company is highly linked with the adoption of Internet-based infrastructures by other companies. We believe that we can continue to pioneer in the development and use of the Internet, and provide leadership to most traditional companies. These companies can find the same benefits that Cisco has enjoyed.

---

[20] Of the $1.05 billion, $420 million will be invested in the new unit, and the remainder will be paid to the KPMG audit and tax business.

[21] *The Wall Street Journal*, August 8, 1999, p. A3. To satisfy the SEC, KPMG has agreed to give up control of the new entity minimizing their equity holding to around 30%. Two Cisco executives will sit on the Board of Directors of the entity.

[22] *The Wall Street Journal*, August 8, 1999, p. A3.

Exhibit 1 Financials and Other Cisco Statistics

Years Ended	July 2000	July 1999	July 25, 1998	July 26, 1997	July 28, 1996	July 30, 1995
Net sales	$18,928,000,000[a]	$12,154,000,000	$8,458,780,000	$6,440,171,000	$4,096,007,000	$1,978,920,000
Income before provisions for income taxes	$ 4,343,000,000[a]	$ 3,316,000,000	$2,302,470,000	$1,888,872,000	$1,464,830,000	$ 679,046,000
Net income (Loss)	$ 2,668,000,000[a]	$ 2,096,000,000	$1,350,072,000	$1,048,680,000	$ 913,324,000	$ 421,008,000
Common Equity—Total	$26,497,000,000	$11,678,000,000	$7,106,620,000	$4,289,620,000	$2,819,620,000	$1,378,730,000
Total assets	$32,870,000,000[a]	$14,725,000,000	$8,916,710,000	$5,451,984,000	$3,630,232,000	$1,757,280,000
Price—Close Fiscal Year	$61.75[b]	$30.81	$15.958	$8.84	$5.75	$3.097
Number of employees	31,140	21,000	15,000	11,000	8,782	4,086
Net sales per employee	$607,835	$578,762	$563,918	$585,470	$466,490	$546,415
Net income per employee	$85,678	$99,809	$90,005	$95,334	$103,999	$111,720

Source: Compustat, except for

[a] www.cisco.com, August 28, 2000.

[b] www.bloomberg.com, August 28, 2000.

Exhibit 2 How Information Is Routed through the Internet

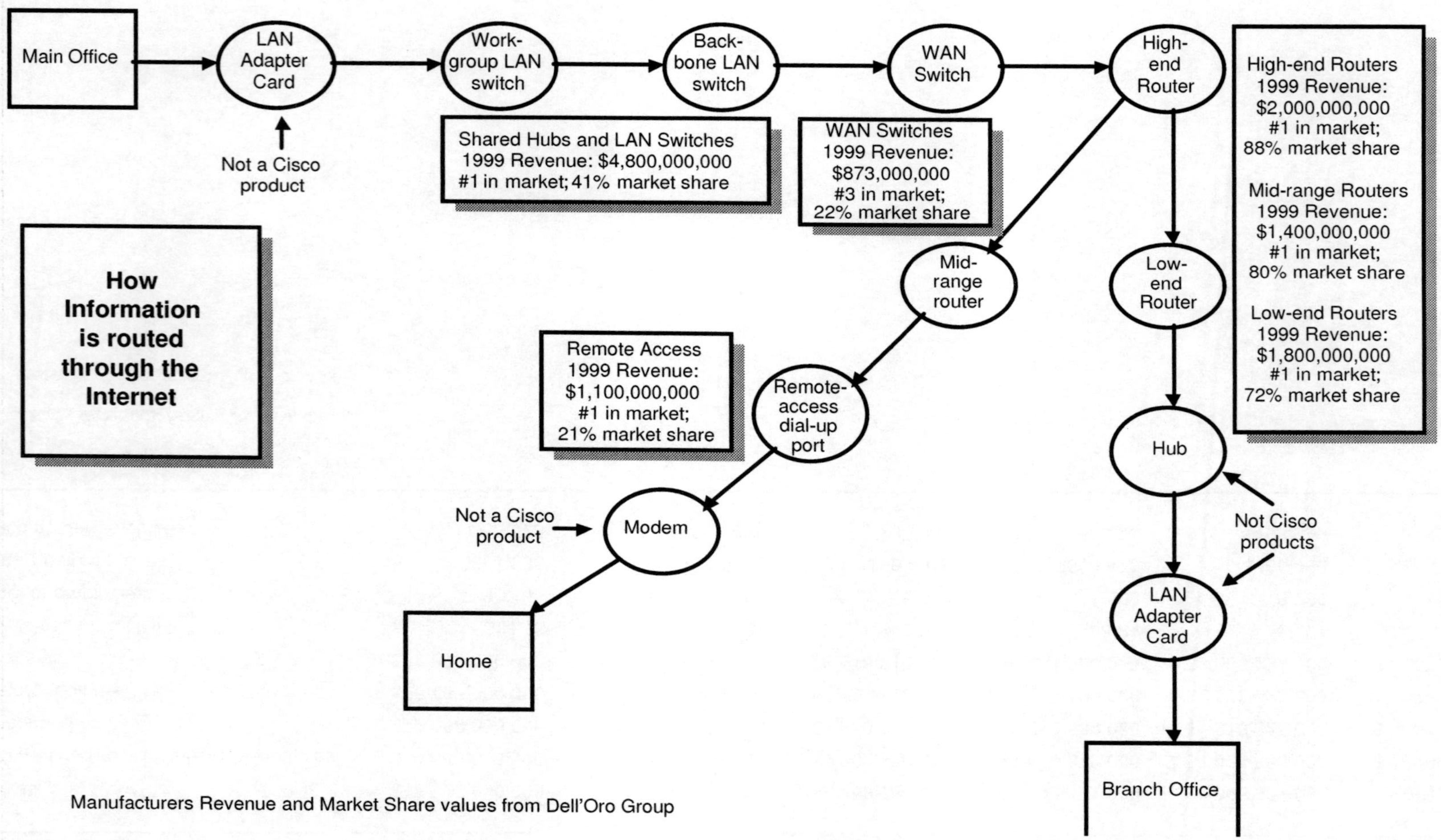

Manufacturers Revenue and Market Share values from Dell'Oro Group

Exhibit 3 Executive Level and CIO Organization Charts

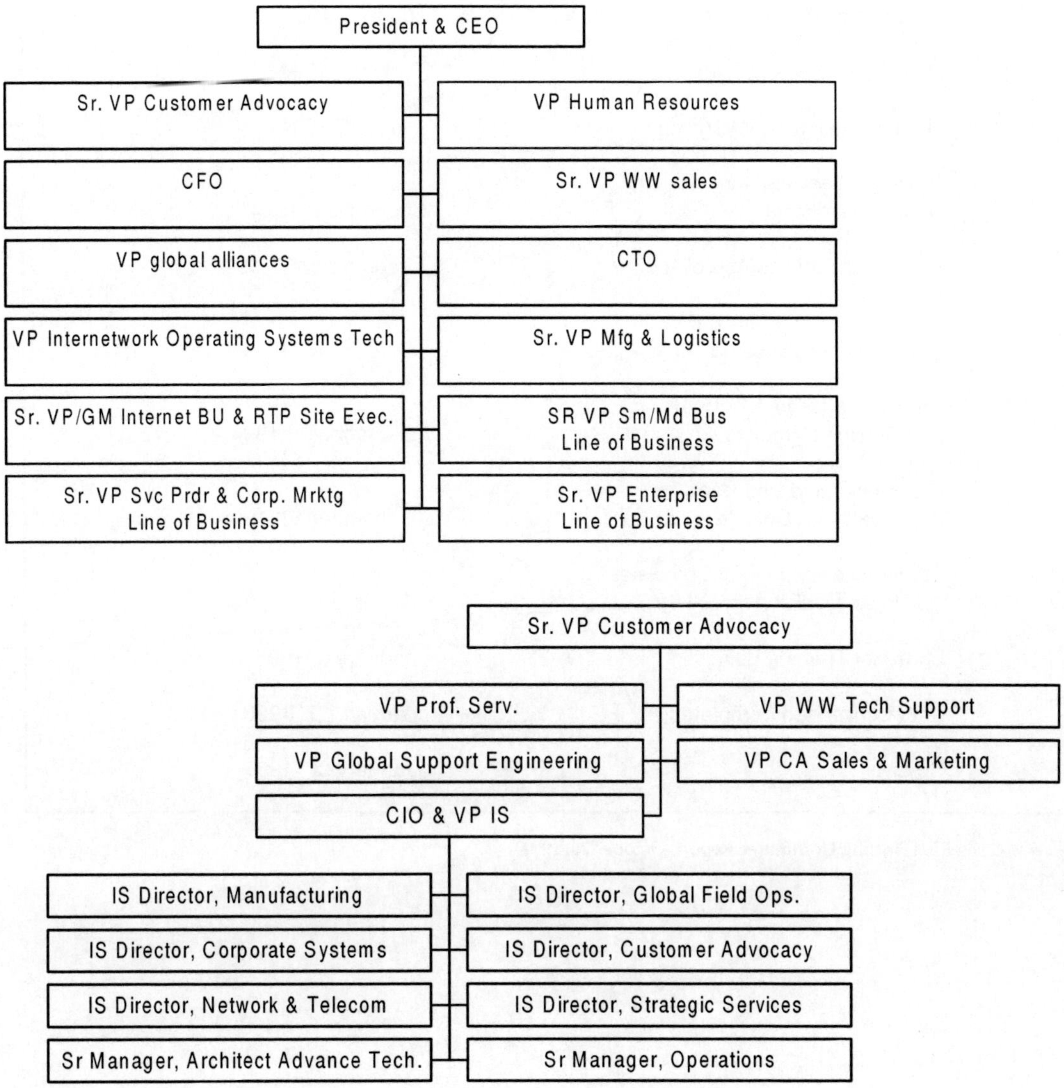

Exhibit 4 Summary of Milestone ERP Implementation Dates

Milestone	Date
Project Kickoff	June 2, 1994
Prototype Setup Complete	July 22, 1994
Implementation Team Training	July 31, 1994
Process, Key Data, Modification Designs Complete	August 31, 1994
Functional Process Approval	September 30, 1994
Hardware Benchmark and Capacity Plan Validated	October 15, 1994
Critical Interfaces, Modifications and Reports Complete	December 1, 1994
Procedures and End-User Documentation Complete	December 16, 1994
Conference Room Pilot Complete—Go/No Go Decision	December 22, 1994
End-User Training Beings	January 3, 1995
Data Conversion Complete	January 27, 1995
Go Live!	January 30, 1995

Source: Cisco ERP Steering Committee Report, October 20, 1994.

Exhibit 5 Breakdown of Implementation Costs for Cisco ERP Implementation[a]

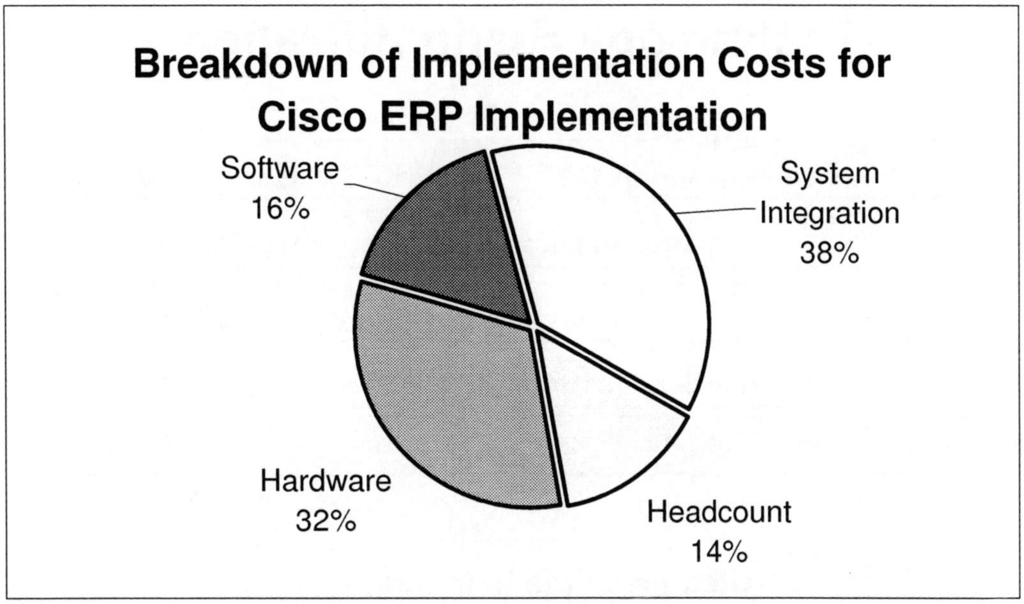

Source: Cisco ERP Steering Committee Report, October 20, 1994.

[a]The project budget estimate did not include estimates of the cost of Cisco personnel time beyond some members of the core team.

Exhibit 6 Cisco's IT Architecture

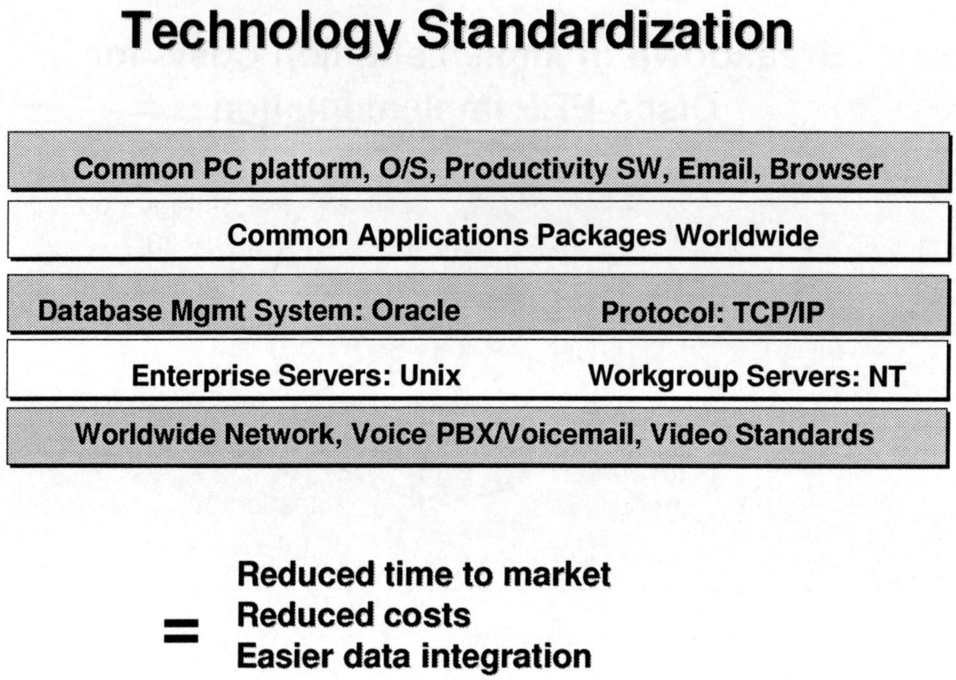

Exhibit 7 Cisco's Home Page

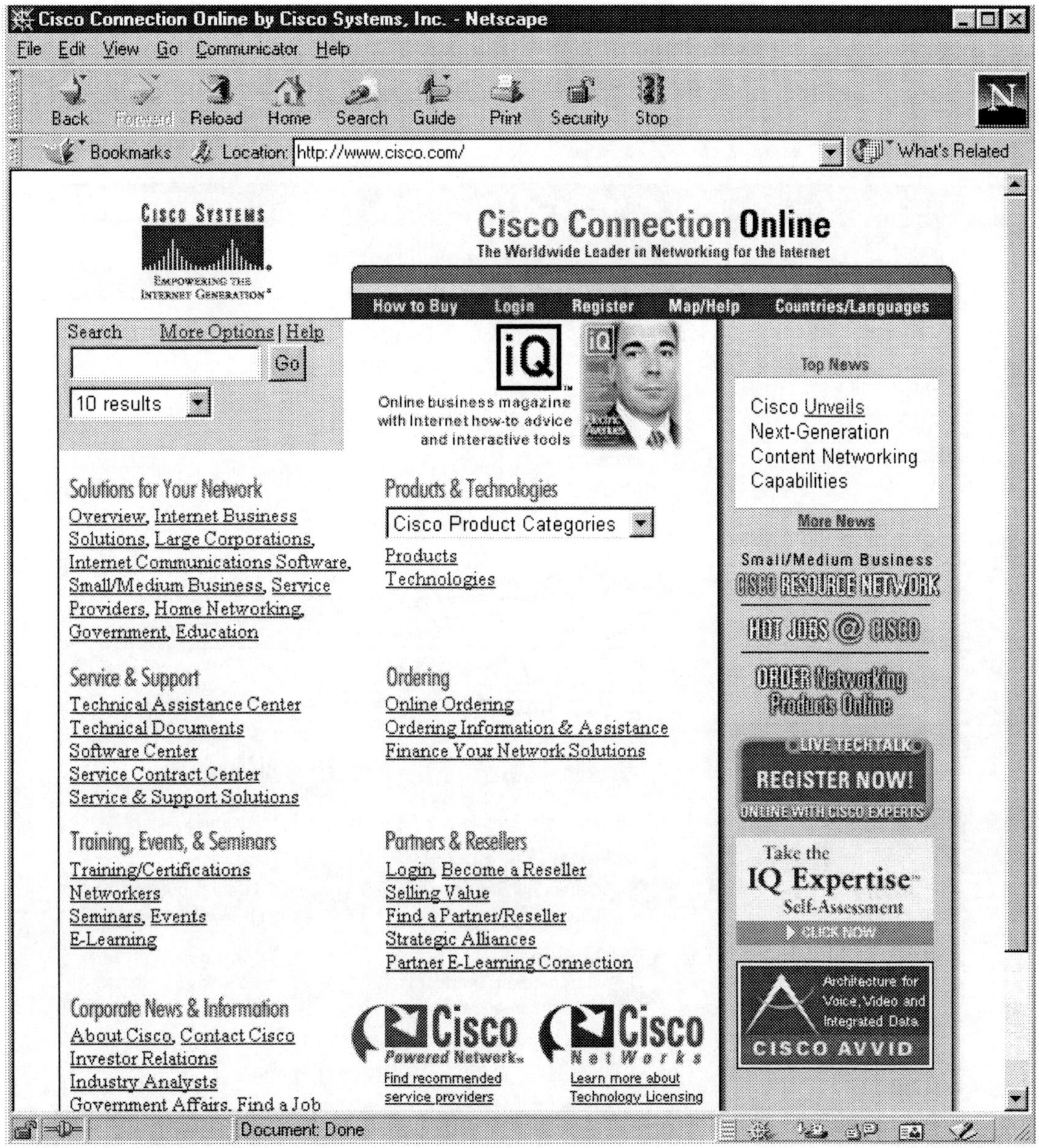

Exhibit 8 Cisco Employee Connection Home Page

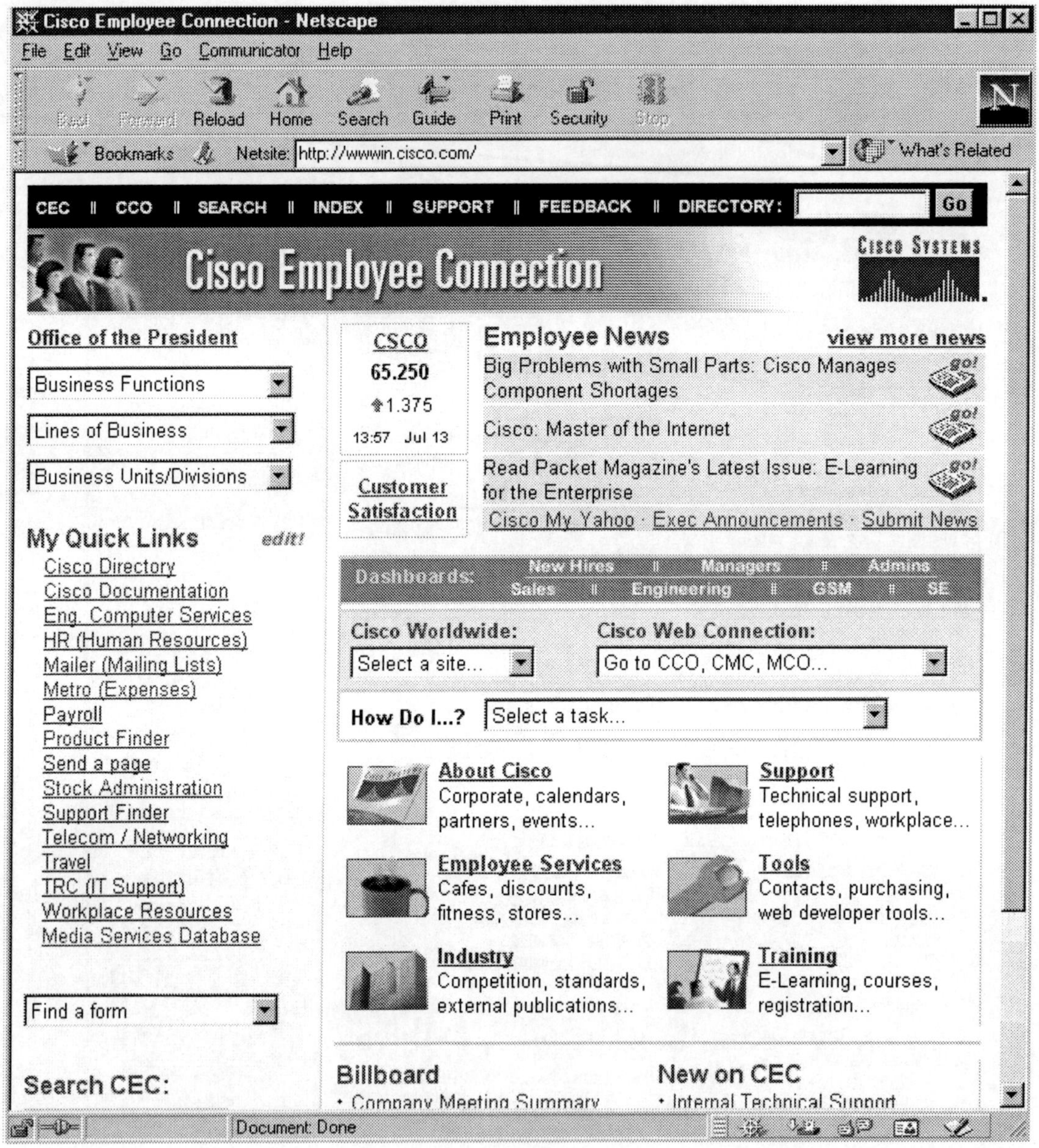

Exhibit 9 MyYahoo! at Cisco

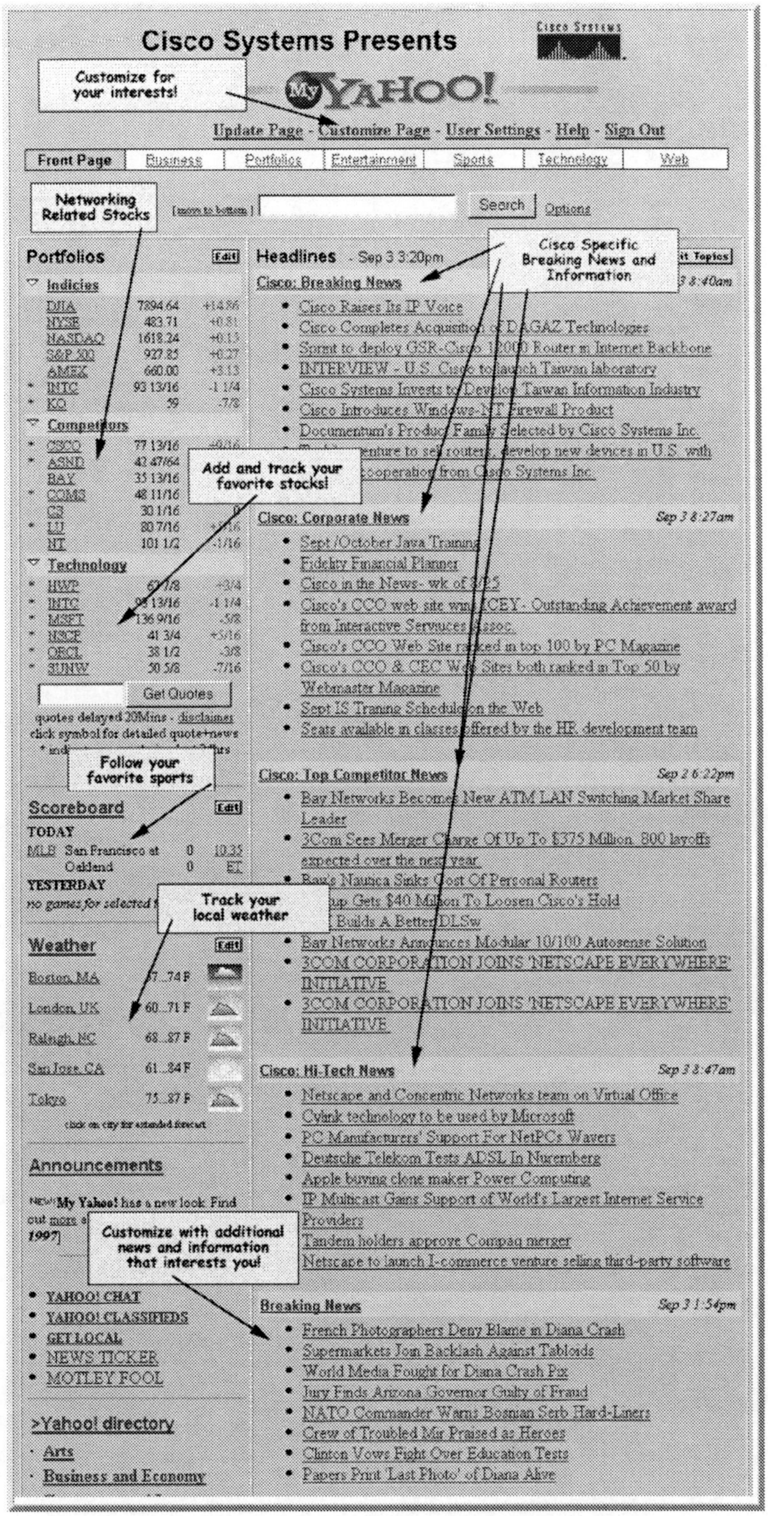

Chapter 4

Enterprise Requirements Planning

MANAGERIAL QUESTIONS

What is ERP?
How will it help my business?
What are its costs?
What are the risks?
What is ERP II and when can I expect it?

INTRODUCTION

Enterprise resource planning, usually abbreviated ERP, is a term that today covers a very large number of computer-based applications that are integrated into a single package. It is reputed to be (and actually is) a very expensive, complex, difficult to implement set of software that, at least in theory, runs the entire back office of the business. Its focus is on the firm's transactions, both with customers and internally, within the business.

ERP is the descendant of a relatively simple concept that came from the manufacturing world, material requirements planning, or MRP. MRP, which goes back to the 1970s, is based on the idea that the firms should manage the production scheduling and inventories for all their products together, not just inventory on a per product basis. The next step was to incorporate the allocation of resources and the costs associated with production. The result was MRP II. Extension to the enterprise as a whole, that is, ERP, was the next natural step.

The vision of a single integrated information system to run the back office had to overcome the way people organized computing by departmental silos. In the 1970s that was all that they could do technically. The results were "islands of automation." When new applications were added, manual interfaces needed to be created. Thus, for example, it was difficult to combine data from sales and manufacturing or to track an order from the time it arrived until payment was received. Another part of the problem was that the data were "dirty," that is, it contained duplicates and errors.

The net result was that firms wound up with a large number of separate systems whose cumulative maintenance costs exceeded the cost of the systems when new. ERP was the response. With ERP, multiple applications could share one database. Furthermore, a single transaction could flow through the ERP system without manual intervention and could automatically update financial and inventory data.

Implementation of ERP faced another barrier: large companies preferred to develop their own systems rather than buy applications packages. They had to become convinced that the packages could be bought and maintained for less than it would cost them to develop the capabilities in-house. Three other factors helped ERP:

1. The development of client-server architecture. In client-server arrangements, the main software is kept on a central computer (server) that provides data to each user. The users (clients) use PCs and are able to do both local computing and to request computing to be done on the server. The client-server arrangement also provided real-time access to data and a graphical user interface, that is, it could provide diagrams and charts in color that are much easier to understand than columns of figures.
2. The Y2K problem. As the year 2000 approached, firms became aware that they faced serious disruptions unless they either found (and then changed) all the places where they used two digits to represent a year in their programs[1] or they replaced the software they had. For many firms, much of their existing software was quite old. Faced with maintaining old, slow software or replacing it with Y2K-compliant ERP systems, many firms took the plunge and bought the new systems.
3. Most companies did not integrate their systems (see Chapter 10 on system integration) so they could work together. They wound up with custom-built systems that were stand-alone silos that could not communicate with one another. In most companies, integrating systems so they could communicate with one another was prohibitive in both cost and difficulty. ERP offered an opportunity to start over and do the job right.

The initial systems came from vendors with a particular point of view. Four of the initial large vendors were SAP, Oracle, PeopleSoft (acquired by Oracle in 2004), and Baan (now Invensys). SAP started with financial modules, PeopleSoft with personnel modules, and Baan with materials requirements planning. These companies and others that followed rapidly found that the marketplace wanted all the applications in one place, rather than needing to integrate their separate offerings. Thus, over time, each firm (and new entrants) started offering what their competitors offered.

HOW SAP WORKS

In this section we discuss SAP[2] and its main products R/2 and R/3. We choose to discuss SAP because it is the largest of the ERP firms, with 44,500 installations serving 10 million users at 17,500 organizations in 120 countries across the globe.[3] Furthermore, its competitors take similar approaches and offer similar modules. Over time, it became possible to mix and match modules, that is, to create a system that consisted of modules from several vendors. Therefore, many of the SAP installations include modules from other vendors and vice versa.

The history of SAP goes back to 1972 when a group of IBM employees in Germany developed the concept of providing integrated software to run the transactions of large firms. When IBM rejected the idea, they left and founded SAP.

---

[1] For example, if the firm wanted to determine the length of a loan, if they stored 1998 as 98 and 2008 as 08, they would compute the loan length as 08 - 99 = -91; that is, the loan lasted a negative number of years.

[2] SAP is an acronym for Systemanalyse und Programmentwicklung (German for Systems Analysis and Program Development). The full name is no longer used.

[3] Based on SAP's claims on its website http://www.sap.com/company/history.aspx. Last consulted 8-28-04.

SAP's R/2 and R/3 products differ principally in the hardware arrangements (i.e., "architecture") on which they operate. R/2 is designed for large mainframes with dumb terminals,[4] whereas R/3 is designed for client-server arrangements in which individual users are given PCs. Most systems today are R/3's. A new version, called mySAP.com, began to be marketed in recent years. This version is designed for the Internet, for e-commerce, and for collaboration with other firms.

SAP claims it supports all aspects of normal company operations with each of its three versions. SAP's core modules perform the following basic functions:

- Finance
- Sales and distribution
- Manufacturing
- Human resources

In addition, SAP offers modules for

- Enterprise portals
- Supply chain management
- Customer relationship management
- Product life cycle management
- Supplier relationship management
- Business intelligence
- Mobile business
- Hosted solutions

SAP also offers packages designed for specific industries, for small- and medium-sized businesses, and for data warehousing.

In observing the evolution of SAP's and its competitor's offerings, it is clear that each vendor tries to extend out from beyond where they started. In the case of SAP, they started in manufacturing and finance. SAP added modules to compete with Seibel, then the largest firm in sales and distribution software, and with PeopleSoft, that started out with a human resource module. Once the basic modules were in place, SAP expanded into supply chain management and into its other major offerings. Each module is designed to capture additional information systems business from firms that use several of its core modules.

Each of the modules that a firm buys connects with all of the other modules so that data do not have to be entered or stored repeatedly. The ERP system works in approximately real time, which means that the data retrieved is current.

SAP R/3 is a top-down system. That is, it assumes the firm is organized hierarchically. It is controlled by a set of thousands of tables that manage the hierarchy. These tables are set in such a way that the system reflects how the firm's processes will work. Each of the modules can access hundreds of business processes. Each of the processes is based on whatever SAP considers "best practice." The idea is that if a process changes, the tables are reset to reflect the change. Although this concept sounds ideal, in practice it is very difficult to change how SAP works once it is in place. Some claim that SAP is like concrete: flexible and easy to change when you install it but that it

[4] A dumb terminal is a display connected to a computer mainframe that can do no computing of its own. In a client-server architecture, the server stores the database being used and computing is divided between the server and the PC machines connected to it.

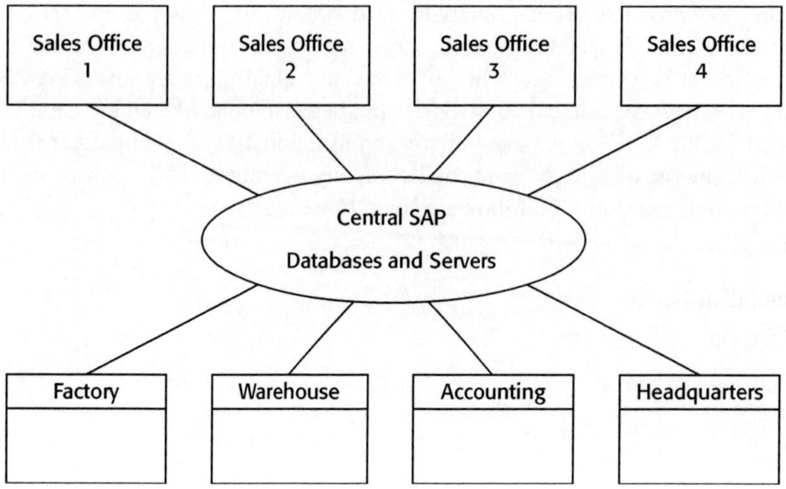

Figure 1 Handling a SAP R/3 sales order.

Based on E. Turban, E. McLean, and J. Wetherbe, *Information Technology for Management,* 2nd ed., update edition, 2001, p. 124. Used by permission, John Wiley & Sons.

hardens over time and becomes impossible to change without great expense. Thus, although the tables allow operating in a seemingly infinite number of ways, this flexibility is true only if the firm is organized in the same top-down way as SAP. Thus, for example, SAP (as do many other ERP systems) does poorly with project industries (e.g., aerospace), industries that involve product dimensions (e.g., clothing), or continuous processes (e.g., food, paper, chemicals).

Figure 1 shows how SAP works for a simple sales order. The order originates in one of the firm's sales offices and is sent to the SAP central database, which is located on SAP's servers. It then proceeds through the system:

- The factory receives the sales order and begins production.
- At the same time, the warehouse is notified and makes sure there is space to store the product as it is built. It also arranges for shipping.
- Accounting receives updated information on both sales and on each step of production. It also undertakes the billing process.
- Headquarters can obtain current data on sales, inventory, and production.

CULTURAL PROBLEMS OF IMPLEMENTATION[5]

In implementing ERP, as for many other large software systems, cultural factors must be taken into account if the system is to be used across countries or by a multiethnic workforce. Almost all ERP systems are designed in North America or Western Europe and embody the designer's cultural assumptions. However, these assumptions are not necessarily valid everywhere.

Consider best practices. ERP systems incorporate specific processes that are considered best practices in their home countries. Because of the cost to customize the ERP system to fit a company's

[5] This section is based on R. Davison, "Cultural Complications of ERP," *Communications of ACM 45*(7): pp. 109–110, July 2002.

particular way of doing business and the repeated expense of customizing each time the ERP is upgraded, these built-in processes are usually adopted. For example these processes assume that ERP will function in an online environment that is open and where standard reports are available to everyone. Yet, in Southeast Asia, information is treated as an individual rather than an organizational resource, with individuals being informed only if they have a specific need to know. The culture is highly bureaucratic, with forms for every purpose and reports that are user-specific, something which ERP does not provide. Reengineering information processes to make them open is difficult because reengineering implies (undesired) organizational change.

Another simple example is the use of numbers. ERP systems generate identification (ID) numbers for system entries. Yet in the Chinese language, the symbol for 4 is also the symbol for death and the symbol for 8 is used for wealth; one is to be avoided and the other is sought.

ERP assumes that with use of the system, employees will be empowered, able to do knowledge work rather than rote tasks. The assumption in North America is that people want responsibility for their own activities and want to make their own decisions. This assumption is not the case in high power distance cultures[6] such as Hong Kong or Singapore, where entry-level employees want to be told what to do and promotion to decision-making levels is based on seniority.

You can't simply promote or retrain. You need to shift values as well. You have two choices:

1. Try to find software that matches your culture. Recognize that the best you can do is find an ERP package that matches in some, not all, dimensions.
2. If you can't find a package that matches your culture or you choose one that is out of step with your firm, then even though ERP systems are difficult to change, it is easier to modify the system than to change the culture.

ERP VENDORS

The principal ERP vendors are shown in Table 1. They break down into vendors who offer enterprise systems for large firms and for what is called "mid-market."

Oracle competes with SAP for large installations. Oracle's PeopleSoft is in the education market aggressively because it was able to modify the personnel modules (its strength) to handle the people record keeping which is intensive in education. J.D. Edwards, acquired by PeopleSoft, concentrates on the middle-sized firm. Geac Computer, which is not well known in the United States, is a Canadian firm that moved in recent years to concentrate on business performance management (see Chapter 8). Many of the smaller companies base their ERP systems on Microsoft products.

COSTS[7]

The costs of ERP can cover a wide range. In an analysis of large-scale systems, Meta Group quoted an average cost of $15 million for large firms. That boiled down to over $53,000 per frequent user. This total included hardware, software, internal staff, and consultants plus 2 years of postimplementation support. Time to implement ranged from 6 months for small installations to several years.

---

[6] G. Hofstede, *Culture's Consequences: Comparing Values, Behaviors, Institutions, and Organizations across Nations*, 2nd ed. London: Sage, 2001.

[7] Cost data are based on reports in *CIO* magazine. Large system costs were obtained by Meta Group and quoted by *CIO* in its October 15, 1999 issue. Mid-size costs were reported November 15, 2001.

Table 1 ERP VENDORS

Firm
SAP
Oracle
PeopleSoft (acquired by Oracle)
J.D. Edwards (acquired by PeopleSoft)
Geac Computer (Canada)
Lawson Software
Microsoft (Great Plains)
QAD
SSA
Siebel
IBM
Epicor
Syspro

Notes:
J.D. Edwards was acquired by PeopleSoft who continued to service existing J.D. Edwards products. PeopleSoft (including J.D. Edwards) was then acquired by Oracle.
SSA acquired Baan software and rebranded it. Baan at one time was third/fourth in ERP sales.

Table 2 AVERAGE COST TO INSTALL ERP

Expenditure	Amount (millions)	Percentage
Hardware	1.46	13.8
Software	1.86	17.5
Internal staff	2.46	23.2
Professional services	4.82	45.5

Source: *CIO*, October 15, 1999.

In a separate estimate of cost prior to and including installation, *CIO* magazine[8] estimated an average cost of $10.8 million, with the breakdown shown in Table 2. Note the large fraction of the cost for professional services, that is, consultants.

For two mid-sized firms ($200 to $500 million revenues), costs to buy the system and install it were quoted by *CIO* magazine as $150,000 and $200,000, with implementation completed in 9 weeks. These firms used a technique called rapid ERP that is being offered by the large vendors. The cost numbers assume a bare-bones installation in which the firm purchasing the system adopts all of the "best practices" built into the system and attempts almost no customization of the ERP system to its processes. Rather, the firm must change its processes to fit the system because customization involves large additional costs. This approach is not for the trepid. The advantage is that the contract specifies both a price and a time line. Because time is money in these contracts, explicit

[8] October 15, 1999.

and accurate project planning is paramount to avoid additional charges. As it is, the firm will incur additional costs in retraining, in change management, and in integrating existing legacy systems, none of which are included in the systems price. Even in well-planned transitions, some system customization will be required. Note that these small cost numbers include only the money paid to the ERP vendor; they do not include the costs in the firm for IT, for training, and, most important, for changing processes to be compatible with the ERP system.

BENEFITS

The anticipated benefits of ERP include

- Shorter cycle time—that is the time from receipt of order to delivery
- Increased productivity
- Lower IT costs
- Better cash management
- Reduced personnel

Done right, ERP makes some processes transparent. For example, if the shipping dock does not check the packing slip, the order does not exist. The customer is not billed and accounts payable doesn't know that money is owed. With ERP that problem can be resolved.

Table 3 shows the results of a survey about achieving these benefits. The numbers indicate the percentage of respondents who expected a particular benefit and the percentage who actually achieved the benefit.

The results shown in Table 3 are mixed, in that some benefits occurred more frequently than expected, while others less frequently.

THE MARKUS AND TANIS VIEW OF THE ERP EXPERIENCE[9]

M. Lynne Markus and Cornelis Tanis described the ERP experience that firms go through. They focus on five characteristics:

- Integration
- Packages

Table 3 EXPECTED AND ACTUAL BENEFITS

Benefit	Expected (%)	Actual (%)
Shorter cycle time	19	31
Improved productivity	24	31
Lower IT costs	24	11
Better cash management	24	13
Personnel reduction	43	33

[9] Source: M L. Markus and C. Tanis, "The Enterprise System Experience—From Adoption to Success." Chapter 10 in R. W. Zmud (Ed.), *Framing the Domain of IT Management,* pp. 173-208, Cincinnati, OH: Pinnaflex Education Resources, 2000.

- Best practices
- Some assembly required
- Evolving

Integration

The promise of ERP is that all information flows through the company seamlessly by "configuring" the system to reflect the organization. Modules are chosen and software parameters are set. However, it is possible to configure the system so that the benefits are not achieved! For example, if a firm adopts only a part of ERP (such as the financial or the human resources modules) or if the firm allows SBUs to configure their system differently, most of the benefit is lost.

Packages

ERP systems, like word processors or spreadsheets, are bought as software packages rather than developed in-house. The firm is immediately faced with either accepting how the package works or customizing the package to fit the way the company worked in the past. Neither choice is ideal. If the package's rules are followed, the firm usually must change the way it performs work. This approach changes business processes, which usually results in massive employee resistance to change. It can also result in forcing the firm to standardize its business practices to that of its industry and thereby lose strategic differentiation. In addition, this choice affects the information systems group by obsolescing some in-house IS skills and changing the IS life cycle. On the other hand, if the firm chooses to customize the ERP package, it incurs large modification costs, costs that are incurred over and over for each new version as the package is upgraded. And upgrading is a routine event in the life of ERP systems.

Best Practices

The vendors want to support as many different types of firms as possible. As a result, enterprise systems contain built-in processes that are generic. The vendors, of course, claim that their processes are best practices, although it is never clear how that status was obtained. If the company follows these best practices it must, of necessity, do some business process reengineering (BPR). Unfortunately, BPR does not come for free. For example, Baan (now Invensys) required a firm to have an "integrated product team" that included contract management, project accounting, project management, and estimating. These functions were previously separate functions in aerospace. Even if a firm wanted to adopt Baan's best practice, it had first to reengineer its process. The implications of the best practice approach are

1. ERP can force substantial changes in organizational structure, job design, work sequencing, training, and more.
2. It adds considerably to the expense and the risk of implementing ERP.

Some Assembly Required

Although ERP systems claim to be integrated, this claim is overstated. For one thing, although the software is integrated, complete integration requires compatible computing platforms (e.g., hardware, operating systems, database management software, and telecommunications). For most firms, it is difficult to integrate ERP software with all of this hardware. The software also requires interfaces with the company's legacy systems and with other packages. The firm's IS group must make these connections, usually after the ERP system is installed, and incurs costs that are often not budgeted for.

REASONS FOR ADOPTING OR NOT ADOPTING ERP

The reasons for adopting or rejecting ERP depend on what the company is trying to achieve and on whether ERP capabilities are believed compatible with the company and its operations.

Adopting ERP

ERP creates a single company way of doing things. As a result, it solves both business and technical problems. The business problems solved include

- Presenting one face to the customer.
- Knowing what is "available to promise."
- Eliminating or reducing the number of applications doing the same thing (which can be used to reduce operational errors).
- Filling orders for merged businesses.

The technical problems solved include

- Handling transaction growth.
- Reducing mainframe operating costs.
- Solving maintenance problems with legacy systems.
- Providing modern transaction capabilities.

Not Adopting ERP

The prime reason for not adopting ERP is a perception that the features and functions of commercial ERP systems do not fit what the firm needs. The difficulties in some industries, such as food, paper, clothing, and aerospace were cited earlier in this chapter. Often companies will adopt only parts of an ERP system or modify it (at great expense) to increase its "feature-function" fit.

ERP's assumed top-down organizational structure is not compatible with a decentralized decision-making style. Company growth patterns and desire for strategic flexibility are other reasons for rejection. Some companies use alternative approaches for increasing systems integration such as the use of a data warehouse (Chapter 5) or middleware.[10]

Other reasons for not adopting ERP include

- ***Cost.*** As shown in the section on costs earlier in this chapter, spending over $50,000 per frequent user and multiple millions of dollars on the system as a whole can be a major deterrent. Escalating cost without closure on delivering the ERP system is often the reason why ERP projects are dropped in midcourse. Some companies, to avoid the high costs of an ERP system, undertook to integrate their transaction data in an "operational data store," a form of data warehousing discussed in the next chapter.

[10] Middleware describes software that acts as an intermediary between different components in a transactional process. The classic example of where middleware is needed is the separation that exists between the client's user and the database in a client-server system.

- ***Competitive Advantage***. Some companies believe they lose competitive advantage when they adopt ERP because their back office no longer distinguishes them. Closer investigation often shows that these companies were unwilling to change culture or to bear the pain of implementation.
- ***Resistance to Change/Lack of Management Commitment***. Like all large IS systems implementations, ERP requires change and can only occur if management is committed to the project. If change management and/or commitment are not present, an ERP system does not make sense.
- ***Company Culture***. ERP systems vendors come out of the European and American cultures. Firms that operate outside these cultures (see Cultural Problems of Implementation, page 61) or whose company cultures are not imbedded in a particular ERP package are best advised to avoid implementation.

THE ERP TEAM[11]

"After a company turns on its ERP software, the only people who understand how the business works are on the ERP implementation team." That is, the team learns both the business and the software. Team members know more about sales than the people in the sales department and more about manufacturing than the people in the manufacturing department.

A firm that adopts ERP should recognize that the team it puts in charge of creating the system is really reinventing the way the company works. Thus, when the initial project is completed, it is advantageous to keep them together rather than dispersing them back to the organizations from which they came. Furthermore, firms often experience a drop in performance for 3 to 9 months after implementation because of the need to fix glitches. As a result, firms need to keep people, resources, and money flowing for the project to meet postimplementation demands.

SUCCESS CASE STUDY: Nestlé[12]

Nestlé SA is a Swiss-based conglomerate in the food business. Founded in 1867, it is a worldwide firm with sales over $60 billion, $8 billion of which is in the United States. In June 2000, Nestlé signed a $200 million ERP contract plus $80 million for consulting. This contract was in addition to the $200 million that Nestlé USA would have spent on its ERP project. This figure includes the entire project from its inception in 1997 to its final rollout in 2003. This section explores the Nestlé USA implementation.

Nestlé USA was formed in 1991 by combining independent brands, such as Carnation and Stouffer's, which were owned by Nestlé. By 2002, Nestlé USA consisted of seven autonomous divisions, making their own decisions and reporting to Glendale, California rather than to Switzerland. The objective of the ERP installation was to create common processes, systems, and organization structures.

The need for coordination was highlighted by the 29 different prices brands paid for a common ingredient, vanilla, to the same vendor. The various computer systems didn't even have a common name for vanilla, so no one knew (except perhaps the vendor) what was going on. In the spring of 1997, a new CIO was appointed, the problems were pinpointed, and an ERP effort began. The situation was chaotic. The process involved massive reengineering, unhappy employees, and points along the way where the participants believed that the project would never end. These experiences are, of course, endemic to ERP implementations.

---

[11] Source: *CIO,* October 15, 1999.

[12] This section is based on B. Worthen, "Nestlé's ERP Odyssey" *CIO,* May 15, 2002.

The company had

- Nine different general ledgers.
- Twenty-eight points of customer entry.
- Multiple purchasing systems.
- No data on their volume of business with individual vendors since factories were autonomous.

Their key idea was that the project (named Business Excellence through System Technology, abbreviated BEST) was about change in business processes. ERP was the vehicle for that change.

A team of 50 executives and 10 senior IT professionals was formed to implement the vision. The team was to devise best practices that would be standard for every division. A separate team looked at all the data items in the divisions and standardized them. By March 1999, decisions were made to use SAP's purchasing, financial, sales and distribution, accounts payable, and accounts receivable modules as the ERP system. However, because SAP's supply chain software was new and not yet proven, Manugistics[13] software was chosen to reduce risk for the supply chain applications.

Four of the modules were to be ready by December 31, 1999, to cope with Y2K problems. Although Nestlé made the deadline, all was not smooth. Users, who had not been represented on the stakeholder teams, resisted the changes. They liked their existing processes, didn't understand the new processes, found the software complex (particularly for the supply chain), and didn't know how to use the new system. Furthermore, the team made a fundamental technical mistake. They did not integrate the modules with one another. Thus, a change in one subsystem (e.g., offering a customer a discount) did not show up in the one to which it connected (e.g., recognizing the discount in accounts payable). Thus, while replacing divisional silos, the implementation created new silos between processes.

The situation was out of hand by July 2000. A reevaluation led to changing the SAP supply chain module, which had matured in the 2 years since it was rejected.[14] The reevaluation also led to the conclusion that it had been wrong to set a date and to try to meet it rather than to set business goals, define the desired end state, and let the date be determined by how long it would take to meet the end state. Nestlé also understood that the relationships between the project team and the end user community needed to be mended so that users would know what changes were being made, why, and how. It took until the following April to define the end state and 2 more years to complete the system.

Although the cost of the system and the time spent are at the high end for ERP applications, the results more than cover the cost. Demand forecasts are more reliable, forecasts can be made down to the distribution level, inventory levels are reduced, and the supply chain is improved. Nestlé management claims it saved $325 million from its ERP.

CASE STUDIES OF FAILURE: FoxMeyer and Hershey[15]

The history of ERP, particularly early implementations, is studded with total and partial failures. They include a well-known list of firms such as appliance manufacturer Whirlpool, trash processor Allied Waste Industries, fabric maker W.L. Gore and Associates, and distributor W.W. Grainger. But perhaps the poster children for the downside of ERP failures are FoxMeyer Drugs, a pharmaceutical distributor, and Hershey Foods, best known for its chocolate kisses.

In this subsection we consider the last two cases, both of which received extensive coverage in the press.

---

[13] At the time, Manugistics was an SAP partner.

[14] The change increased the cost by 5%.

[15] This section is based in part on C. Steadman, "Failed ERP Gamble Haunts Hershey" Computerworld November 1, 1999; A. Osterland, "Blaming ERP" CFO.com, January 1, 2000; and J. E. Scott, "The FoxMeyer Drugs' Bankruptcy: Was It a Failure of ERP?" Proceedings of The Association for Information Systems Fifth Americas Conference on Information Systems, Milwaukee, WI, August 1999.

FoxMeyer Drugs

The extent of an ERP failure can be catastrophic to a company. FoxMeyer Drugs, a $5 billion company, then the fourth largest wholesale distributor of drugs and beauty aids based in Dallas, collapsed in 1996 after attempting an R/3 installation. Its bankruptcy trustees wound up suing SAP, its ERP vendor, and Andersen Consulting, its systems integrator for $500 million each.

FoxMeyer expected high growth in drug sales because of the aging population. They were operating in a market with extreme price competition, which meant eroding margins. In the early 1990s they decided their strategy should be to manage inventory efficiently, reduce operating expenses, strengthen marketing, and increase services. Their Unisys computer systems were reaching the end of their life and the vendor was discontinuing support. Given that customers sent orders electronically, that they engaged in hundreds of thousands of transactions, and needed to maintain detailed records for government compliance, ERP was deemed the appropriate solution. They selected three vendors: SAP to provide R/3, Andersen Consulting to perform integration, and Pinnacle Automation to provide a warehouse automation system. The initial total contract value was $15 million and the expected time for the system to be up was 18 months, both unrealistic goals.

The work started in 1993 with a planning effort. The plan, unfortunately, was not matched by the implementation. With two vendors (SAP for ERP software and Pinnacle for warehouse automation) FoxMeyer experienced coordination problems. They needed to change their system requirements after testing was underway. As a result, they were late and over budget. Although SAP was deemed to be implemented properly, the system did not work. The drug company was plagued by late orders, incorrect shipments, and lost shipments. In August 1996, they filed for Chapter 15 bankruptcy and were later taken over by McKesson.[16]

Analysis of the bankruptcy indicates that the problem was much more a management problem than a software problem. Although the SAP software generally worked as it was supposed to, the management choices made created many of the difficulties encountered. FoxMeyer closed three warehouses. That resulted in disgruntled workers who damaged inventory and were not able to cope with the new system. A total of $34 million worth of inventory was lost. Second, the new system initially could only process 100,000 orders per night compared to 420,000 orders with the previous system. The situation was made worse by signing a contract to supply a new customer with a high volume of transactions. FoxMeyer management assumed the ERP system could handle the increased load but it couldn't. Third, FoxMeyer did not have the necessary skills in house. They relied on their consultant to implement R/3 and to integrate it with the automated warehouse software. The consultant is alleged to have provided inexperienced people and to suffer from high turnover. FoxMeyer management did not feel it knew enough to cope with the consultants and the vendors. The project spun out of control and project costs eventually went over $100 million.

Hershey Foods

For Hershey Foods Corporation, like for most candy manufacturers, the most important part of its revenue comes in three seasonal sales periods: Halloween, Christmas, and Valentine's Day. In 1999, when a new ERP system was running late, they missed the Halloween and Christmas seasons. They issued two profit warnings in the 2 months before Christmas and their stock decreased by over 25% from their year's high at a time when the overall market was booming.

Hershey invested $112 million into ERP and related software. Not only were the ERP systems to be installed, but a CRM system (Chapter 6) and a logistics package were to be installed at the same time. The new system was supposed to replace a large number of legacy systems that the company was running. The plan was straightforward but risky. Installation, estimated to take 4 years, was scheduled for 30 months and was to be completed in July, just before Hershey's heavy shipping season. Rather than a parallel operation to begin with, a full cutover was to be made to the new system.

---

[16] As reported in The Business Journal On-Line (http://www.business-journal.com/lateJuly02/PharMorBleeding.html), the co-CEOs of FoxMeyer took over a drugstore chain, PharMor, shortly before declaring bankruptcy of FoxMeyer and also drove PharMor into its second bankruptcy from which it did not emerge. As was the case with other firms, the co-CEOs enriched themselves in the process.

Unfortunately, order processing and shipping were not ready on time. The company was still fixing problems in September. Because details of what went wrong were not available from the company, the following discussion is based on a variety of press reports and opinions.

1. Hershey tried to do too much at the same time. Going live with an ERP system is difficult enough, but trying to get three systems on line at the same time introduces daunting complexity even for the best companies.
2. Trying to cut 18 months off the normal schedule exacerbates the problem. Admittedly, Hershey was trying to beat the December 31, 1999, deadline for fixing Y2K problems. However, complex systems are best put in with a more leisurely and more flexible schedule. The schedule can most charitably be described as a bad gamble.
3. Hershey tried to go live at the peak of its shipping season. Conventional wisdom advocates selecting quiet times because, even with good implementations, it takes several weeks to find all the problems.
4. Employee training was inadequate and employee resistance to change was not dealt with fully.

Although the immediate results were dire, Hershey was able to fix its ERP troubles over time as it gained experience. In August 2002, it reported[17] that its original system was working and that they had upgraded to the SAP Internet version (mySAP.com). The firm claimed that 95% of its revenue and business transactions were being processed on the system and that 30 business processes were enhanced.

SIDEBAR 1 *Lessons Learned*

The cases indicate some of the lessons learned over the last decade of ERP implementations.

1. ERP is about changing processes and the way the business is run. Software can be made to work. Managing the resultant change is much more difficult.
2. Good general management and project management are needed. The following management practices apply not only to ERP but to most large projects that firms undertake.

- Include the people whose lives will be changed in the planning process. It will make change management easier.
- Determine the business goals and make those the objective rather than setting a time deadline for implementation. The implementation process can't be hurried.
- Avoid customizing ERP as much as possible. Customization results in recurring costs each time an upgrade occurs.
- Integrate the modules with one another and with the remaining legacy systems. The point of ERP is to have an "all-in-one" system. All the pieces must be able to understand one another and operate off the same database.
- Because additional costs are likely to be incurred, update the budget periodically to minimize surprises.
- Although it is getting easier, mixing and matching ERP modules from different vendors is still a difficult task.
- Don't stint on the training budget. ERP usually requires a mindset change on the part of employees, and that can't be done in a short training session.
- Manage your ERP consultants just as you manage your own employees. Be sure that the consultants leave enough knowledge behind when they leave so your own employees can take the job over (see Chapter 7).

3. If you can stay the course, the benefits can far exceed the costs.

[17] T. R. Weiss, "Hershey Stays the Course with mySAP.com Upgrade." *Computerworld IT Reports.* http://www/computerworld.com August 30, 2002.

THE FUTURE: ERP II

ERP was designed as an infrastructure to improve networking in the virtual communities that large organizations really are. Conventional ERP, as described in this chapter, has been available for nearly 20 years. The market for new ERP installations is shrinking and the business went through a series of shakeouts of weaker firms. It is starting to be considered "old hat" by some. As a result, ERP is slowly being transformed into ERP II. The new system, as it is envisioned by the Gartner Group,[18] expands existing ERP by adding knowledge sharing with clients and suppliers, Internet use, virtual supply chain models, customer relationship management (Chapter 6), and e-commerce models (Chapter 3). Thus, not only must additional complex technology be incorporated into ERP, but the organization must become more customer-oriented than in the past.

The present ERP systems focus on transparency of transactions, effectiveness, efficiency, and business processes. They are not designed for collaboration outside the firm in such areas as supply chain management. The objective of ERP II is a system that includes interorganizational as well as intraorganizational data. That is, ERP II systems are being touted as providing front-office as well as their present back-office[19] capabilities. In terms of products, Gartner Group expects that ERP vendors will build sector-specific capabilities that are integrated into their packages. The vision is that the systems will be able to reduce the latency that is built into them at present, that is, the ability to deliver to a customer in, say, an hour, rather than 3 days.

With ERP II, it is claimed, firms will be able to manage information to create long-term relationships both inside and outside the firm. The firm's supply chain process is integrated with their supplier's supply chain (Chapter 11). In that way, the information systems extend to the retailer's shelves and allow direct customer feedback. In addition to promoting customer loyalty by keeping the customer fully informed, ERP II uses the idea of knowledge management (Chapter 7) that knowledge sharing leads to increasing, not diminishing returns.

To make all this work requires major changes at the technology, process, and people levels. In terms of technology, the rigidity of ERP is replaced by open sourcing in which modules are components that can be connected much more easily than at present with third-party software modules such as for supply chain or customer relationship management. The hope is to introduce additional technologies that used to be considered leading edge such as voice, portals, and intelligent agents. The fundamental problem that needs to be resolved is integrating modules from multiple sources.

ERP usually results in changes in business processes. However, change is hard for organizations and is often rejected. As a result, ERP II, like ERP, will need to overcome resistance to change and lead people to think and work together.

FINAL THOUGHTS

For many firms, ERP is the single largest information technology investment they will make. The investment includes cash, resources, and reengineering processes. It will inevitably change the way the company does business. It can be a risky, "bet your company" investment that is not for the faint of heart. The good news is that most companies survive installing an ERP system and become easier to operate. Although ERP rarely, if ever, provides competitive advantage, for many firms and industries it is a competitive necessity.

---

[18] The Gartner Group of Stamford, Connecticut, is a firm that monitors the information systems business. This section is based on two reports of their findings: M. Mohamed, "Points of the Triangle," *Intelligent Enterprise*, September 3, 2002; and A. Harrington, "Gartner Touts EDRP II Vision," http//www.vunet.com/print/1115981.

[19] The term front office generally refers to customer-facing operations, such as sales, whereas back office refers to internal processes such as billing and payroll.

ANSWERS TO MANAGERIAL QUESTIONS

What is ERP?

Enterprise resource planning (ERP) is a collection of software modules that integrate with one another for running the firm's back-end transaction data processing. It focuses on both customer and internal transactions. Its promise, not fully achieved as yet, is that information flows through the organization seamlessly.

Its advantage over "islands of automation" is that multiple applications work with the same database, thereby resulting in a "single truth." The initial, basic SAP modules supported finance, sales and distribution, manufacturing, and human resources. Over time, additional modules were offered that support more specialized functions such as supply chain management and customer relationship management.

Will I need to change my business processes?

ERP incorporates processes that are judged by software vendors such as SAP to be best practices. As a result, firms must change many of their existing processes to be compatible with the ERP system or must customize the software to fit their processes. Both approaches are quite expensive.

How will it help my business?

The principal benefits claimed for ERP are

- Shorter cycle time for manufacturing
- Increased productivity
- Better data input for decision making
- Integrated financial information
- Reduced inventory
- Reduced personnel
- Lower IT costs
- Better coordination within the firm
- Integrated customer order information
- Standardized (and self-service) human resource (HR) information

With most large and many medium-sized firms now using ERP, the software itself rarely provides competitive advantage. It is a competitive necessity. What it does is allow firms to reengineer processes that can lead to competitive advantage.

What are its costs?

The expenditures for ERP can vary over a large range. Two case examples involved expenditures of over $200 million. Some smaller installations run well under $200,000. Why the disparity?

The out of pocket cost depends on such factors as

- The size of the firm and the size of the installation. The more modules that are adopted, the greater the cost.
- The extent of customization. The larger the amount of customization, the greater the cost since customization is labor intensive.
- The extent to which consultants are used.
- The skills of the internal IT shop.

The last two factors are interrelated. If ERP skills exist in-house, fewer consultants are needed and vice versa. The peak of the demand for ERP skills occurred in the late 1990s, as Y2K approached. The number and availability of people with ERP skills became better in balance as more people were trained.

Total cost of ownership for a full-time user in a large firm is estimated to be over $50,000. Hidden costs include training, the learning curve to get people up to speed on the new system after training, converting data to ERP-usable form, implementation costs beyond project completion, and the lag between installation and realizing ROI.

How long will it take?

Like cost, time from decision to operation can vary widely. For small systems and organizations using "fast-track" implementation, times as short as a few months have been observed. For large firms installing full-blown systems, 4 years is not uncommon.

What are the risks?

As with any large software project, the risks are large. Some systems were abandoned or replaced. Some companies, such as FoxMeyer (see case above), go bankrupt. Installing an ERP system is difficult. Most firms tend to underestimate the difficulty and (big mistake!) accept the vendors' promises. As a result, they overrun both budget and schedule. The good news is that many systems eventually are completed and meet their technical specifications.

The most serious risks are managerial. ERP changes business processes. Therefore, it changes the way people work. Most people, of course, don't like to learn new ways of doing things on the job. Many fear unemployment. Therefore, a deliberate effort must be made to reduce resistance to change and to integrate ERP into the firm. The resistance-to-change problem is larger for ERP than most of the other systems discussed in this book because ERP, properly implemented, affects every department in the firm.

Care must be taken in selecting the right package. If a package does not allow processes that are inherent in a business, such as continuous flow rather than discrete manufacturing, or tracking inventory you don't own outright, then adopting it is high-risk because workarounds may be unsatisfactory. Similarly, if the package assumes a top-down organizational structure and the firm is distributed, the package is not appropriate.

Most firms depend on a large contingent of outside consultants. Although the consultant firm may have many skilled people, if it assigns junior people with little experience in either ERP or your industry, serious problems can result. If knowledge is not transferred from the consultancy to in-house technical and operating people, the system may not be sustainable.

What is ERP II and when can I expect it?

ERP II is the anticipated direction in which ERP is heading. It includes knowledge sharing with clients and suppliers, Internet use, virtual supply chains, integrating CRM, and e-commerce. It moves ERP to being an interorganizational, customer-oriented system rather than being confined to the interior of the firm. ERP II was still a promise, not a reality in 2005.

PROBLEMS

1. HOW ERP WORKS

   Near the beginning of this chapter, we describe how ERP works. Pick one of the existing ERP offerings from a major vendor (e.g., SAP, Oracle, Microsoft for small and medium enterprises) and prepare a much more detailed description of the functions that ERP offers.

2. PERSONNEL FOR INSTALLING AND RUNNING ERP

   If your present or past company installed an ERP system while you were with the company, describe the team that put it together, their individual functions, how the members of the team changed over time, and the people assigned to run the system currently. Consider the improvements (if any) that could be made either by including or removing members of the team. If you don't have experience with an ERP installation, find one or more case studies that deal with the people aspects of the problem.

3. ERP FAILURES

   Two cases of ERP failure are described in this chapter. Find and summarize at least two other failures and why they occurred. Also, find a success story and compare the differences between success and failure.

4. ERP PLANNING

   The P in ERP refers to planning. Explain how ERP systems are being used in planning at the tactical and at the strategic level. Give examples.

Chapter 11

IS in Managing Business Operations: The Supply Chain

MANAGERIAL QUESTIONS

What is supply chain management?
What are the five components of supply chain management?
What is the goal of supply chain management?
How is supply chain software used?
What is the role of collaboration?
What is the relation to ERP?
What are the resistances to supply chain software?

INTRODUCTION

Businesses always dealt with their supply chain. That is, they bought raw materials, components, and supplies that they used to create their products or services and sold to a set of customers to whom they delivered their products. What is new is that the speed at which goods and services move through the supply chain increased considerably because improvements in computers and communications speeded the exchange of information.

Although a firm may see only its direct providers and its direct purchasers, as shown in Figure 1, the sets of suppliers and customers are much more complex. For example, auto manufacturers obtain almost every component of a car from someone else, although most components are built to the manufacturer's specification. The so-called manufacturer in this case is really an assembler. The suppliers (of doors, batteries, mirrors, engines, and hundreds of other pieces) in turn assemble these pieces from components bought from their own suppliers and so on back to the people who dig raw material out of the ground. If the firm is a producer of consumer products, it may sell directly to end users (e.g., acting as a retailer via e-commerce) or the goods may go through a distribution chain that can involve multiple levels of distributors and resellers. For business-to-business transactions, the sales may be direct through a sales force, through intermediaries such as jobbers, or more and more over the Internet. In other words, the supply chain extends from your supplier's supplier to your customer's customer.

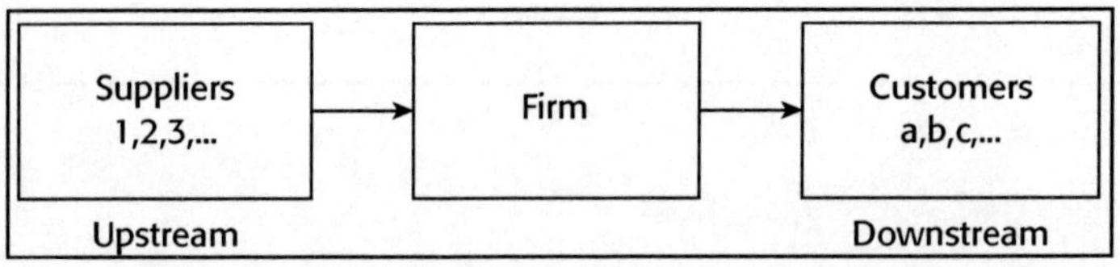

Figure 1 The supply chain as seen by the firm.

Note, too, that supply chain activities go on within the firm as goods are transferred among departments or from subsidiaries. In manufacturing, these operations are the assembly, manufacturing, and packaging that produce the finished product. Each of the subassemblies must be available to create the next level of subassembly or the finished product.

The supply chain is really a delicate mechanism that depends on everything working together at the same time. In real life, of course, everything doesn't always come together. A lot of the variables are random: the economy fluctuates; mergers and acquisitions happen upstream and downstream in the chain; suppliers and customers go in and out of business; natural and man-made disasters (e.g., hurricanes, strikes, blackouts) occur along the chain. However, decisions need to be made ahead of time, sometimes a considerable time ahead, on how many to produce and when to produce. Keeping a firm's supply chain going often seems more of an art than a science. Therefore, like an insurance policy, firms keep inventory (even with just-in-time delivery) to protect against uncertainty. They also engage in supply chain planning (SCP) to make their estimates of the future better.

THE SUPPLY CHAIN[1]

As described by the Supply Chain Council, managing the supply chain includes five components:

1. Planning
2. Sourcing
3. Making
4. Delivering
5. Returning

1. ***Planning***. Planning involves assessing what demand will be (i.e., forecasting), finding and contracting for sources of supply, and measuring how well the supply chain is running. Metrics are used to determine whether your supply chain is being run efficiently, how well cost goals are being met, and the level of quality and value being delivered to customers.

2. ***Sourcing.*** Sourcing refers to choosing suppliers that provide the needed goods and services. Pricing, delivery, and payment are considerations, as are quality and value.

3. ***Making.*** In this step, the product to be delivered to the customer is produced. The product may be a physical object (a car, a toy) or a service (insurance policy, money market account). To create a sellable product and make a profit, it is necessary to schedule its production, test it for quality, package it, and prepare it for delivery. Measures include quality level, production output, and worker productivity.

---

[1] The discussion of supply chain management is based on information at www.supply-chain.org, the website of the Supply Chain Council.

4. ***Delivering***. Delivery, also called logistics, refers to the activities that move the product to the customer. It involves coordinating shipments so they reach the customer on time, implementing warehousing strategies for storing products until they are ready to ship, selecting transportation carriers, and creating an invoicing system to get paid.

5. ***Returning***. Because customers may return part or all of a shipment, either because it is deemed defective or an excess amount was ordered, a network for receiving returns and for supporting customers must be established. In addition, for expensive, complex products, support services (e.g., a help desk) are required. (See the Section on Returns, near the end of this chapter.)

SOFTWARE'S ROLE

Many software products are on the market to help improve supply chain operations. Unfortunately, although some software vendors claim to deal with the entire process, none do. The complexity of each of the five steps described in the previous section is such that dozens of tasks need to be performed. Specific software is available that deals with individual or groups of tasks, but these software packages are not integrated with one another. Integration (see Chapter 10) is a holy grail.

In thinking about supply chain software, it is convenient to divide it into

- software that supports planning and
- software that helps execute the steps after planning.

Planning Software

Supply chain planning is intertwined with the methods of management science. Much of the planning software imbeds advanced mathematical algorithms designed to reduce inventory and improve both the efficiency and the flow through the supply chain. Being mathematical, these methods can only provide good answers if the input data from customers (e.g., present and future orders, sales by the customer to its clients, inventory on hand) and from within the organization (e.g., production, warehouse, and delivery capacity still available to commit) are current and accurate. The key parameter is demand, because if the demand estimate is right, the rest of the results will usually be right. If not, you can overproduce or underproduce, hire too many or hire too few, and make other errors. Demand forecasting turns out to be the most complex and the most likely to be wrong in quantity in the planning process.

Execution Software

Execution software automates supply chain operations. The idea is to complete steps more quickly so that the delay between the receipt of an order and its delivery to the customer is shortened. Some execution software is quite simple. For example, by sharing your estimates of demand with your suppliers, your suppliers can organize their production to meet your production needs. In theory, all that is needed is to decide which information to share, sending it regularly to suppliers, and receiving data from suppliers on their performance and their capacity. As discussed later in this chapter, coordination with suppliers is not an easy task.

WHY INSTALL SUPPLY CHAIN SOFTWARE?

Supply chain software makes it possible to gain visibility about demand. Interchanging supply chain information up and down the supply chain became easier as the Internet grew in speed and capacity, telecommunications networks expanded, and communications costs went down. In theory, supply chain software can connect the firm with its suppliers and customers in a large, optimized network. In practice, information is exchanged in only a few industries (e.g., automobiles, high technology, supermarkets, and drugstores) and even then not among all firms.
When they share demand estimates:

- suppliers don't have to guess how much material or how many subassemblies to order for meeting a particular client's needs,
- manufacturers reduce the inventory they need to keep to meet sudden or unexpected demand, and
- retailers are not out of stock of specific items in a store because the manufacturer's production falls behind the store's demand.

COOPERATION

A part of the problem is getting firms to collaborate. Most firms trust no one[2] and therefore prefer not to give anyone information about their plans. Thus, while it is technically relatively easy to share information, the culture (both in the United States and in most other countries) is not to do so, even though sharing information helps everyone. As a result, inventories all up and down the supply chain expand to guard against contingencies.

Cooperation is easier if a large firm insists on it as a condition for doing business with it. Two classic examples, Wal-Mart and Cisco Systems, are described in Sidebars 1 and 2.

SIDEBAR 1 *Wal-Mart*

Wal-Mart is, by some accounts, the gorilla of retailing. Specializing at the low cost end of the retail market, it insists on large volumes of information from suppliers who want to do business with it. They do so even with large suppliers. For example, Proctor & Gamble is connected to Wal-Mart distribution centers and, via satellite uplinks, can tell when a single unit of theirs passes through a scanner at a store. When a distribution center drops below a preset level of inventory, Wal-Mart sends an alert to Proctor & Gamble to ship more product.

The nearly real-time information (see the discussion of business activity monitoring in Chapter 8) helps Proctor & Gamble to coordinate its production and shipments with Wal-Mart's demand. In effect, Proctor & Gamble is managing Wal-Mart's inventory. The claim is that Proctor & Gamble is able to reduce its own inventory because of better knowledge of Wal-Mart's demand. Through this process, Wal-Mart, of course, shifted a large portion of its own inventory management and physical inventory costs to its suppliers.

[2] Some firms stamp everything company confidential. It is said that if you wrote force = mass times acceleration (Newton's law), some firms would consider it private information.

SIDEBAR 2 *Cisco Systems*

Cisco Systems Inc. creates network hardware for connecting to the Internet, to corporate intranets, and to extranets (see Chapter 3). By linking its own network to its suppliers, contract manufacturers, and distributors, Cisco created a just-in-time supply chain. When an order is received for a network router, for example, messages are sent to contract manufacturers (e.g., of circuit boards, final assembly) and to distributors of standard components (e.g., power supplies). That is, these firms in Cisco's supply chain receive advance warning of what demands are coming because they are logged on to Cisco's intranet and linked to Cisco's manufacturing execution system.

Once an ordered item is assembled by a subcontractor,

- Cisco receives a bar code identification,
- Cisco checks the assembly's compliance with its customer's order, and
- the unit is connected to a centralized facility for automated quality control testing.

At that point, Cisco provides the customer name and the shipping instructions to its contractor.

The foregoing process is used for items that are custom-built in response to orders. For some products, whose demand is steady, parts are built to forecasts and, if necessary, stored in warehouses.

Ideally, for custom orders, Cisco needs no inventory and hence no warehouses. Furthermore, no paper invoices (remember it is all done over the Internet) are required among members of its supply chain. If events don't happen according to plan, management by exception kicks in.

The system was set up under the assumption that demand would continue to increase. It didn't in the economic downturn of 2001 to 2003. Cisco and its supply chain partners wound up producing more units than needed and creating warehouses of unsold products. At that point, supply chain planning had to be revised to cope with the situation.

MANUFACTURING

An enormous amount of software and hardware is available to improve both engineering and manufacturing operations in a firm. These two functions are the 'make' part of the supply chain.

Overview

Factory automation, long a dream of futurists, is coming closer and closer to reality. The idea goes back to the early twentieth century. For example, the Czech play RUR (the name is a crossword puzzle favorite) opened in 1920. It told the tale of Rossum's Universal Robots. Today, lights out factories and lights out computer centers are in the early stages of implementation. Many of these operations are part-time, such as plastic factories stamping out products on third shift. Information systems are central to making this change happen.

The reality for most companies is much less than full automation. We are at the stage of computer-aided design (CAD) and computer-aided manufacturing (CAM), where many functions previously performed by hand are automated. For example, in engineering, computer-aided design is standard.

CAD

The first CAD systems in the late 1960s were typically limited to producing drawings similar to hand-drafted drawings. Since then, CAD systems grew to include

- Reuse of existing design components and automatic generation of standard components of the design.
- Validation/verification of designs against specifications and design rules.
- Simulation of designs without building a physical prototype.
- Automated design of assemblies of parts and subassemblies.
- Creation of manufacturing drawings, and bill of materials.
- Output of design drawings directly to manufacturing facilities.

Realizing these benefits requires recognizing that CAD is not a universal solution. CAD will not automate all routine design tasks. It will not generally provide a three-dimensional rendering that can be viewed from all angles, with detailed cross sections, and used to create CAM data sets or solid models. The design process is still far from paperless.

CAM

Computer-aided manufacturing uses computers to communicate work instructions directly to manufacturing machinery. The technology evolved from numerically controlled machines. Today a single computer can control banks of robotic milling machines, lathes, welding machines, and other tools, moving the product from machine to machine as each step in the manufacturing process is completed. Such systems allow easy, fast reprogramming of the machines from the computer, permitting quick implementation of design changes. As we will see below, these capabilities make customized and just-in-time manufacturing possible. The most sophisticated CAM systems, often integrated with CAD systems, can manage tasks such as parts ordering, scheduling, and tool replacement. Analysis of CAM systems indicates three critical success factors:

- a technology champion who is effective,
- systems integration (see Chapter 10), and
- cross-functional steering and implementation teams.

Just-in-Time Manufacturing[3]

Just-in-time (JIT) manufacturing, done right, is a means for increasing the return on investment by reducing the amount of inventory needed. JIT differs from traditional manufacturing in that it takes a different approach to work flow. In traditional manufacturing, production planners schedule production of a batch, that is, a fixed number of units of a given product. The key parameter is the "economic lot size," determined by trading off the cost of setup[4] and the cost of inventory. A large amount of in-process inventory (and hence cost) is created to make sure that raw materials and subassemblies are available as needed.

In just-in-time manufacturing, individual products are built from beginning to end and traditional inventory is largely eliminated. However, in just-in-time manufacturing not having materials or parts available at the time they are needed stops the entire production line. Therefore, to make

[3] Just-in-time is also discussed in the next subsection on inventory.

[4] Setup refers to making the changes needed to move from one product or model to another. If a production run is too short, more setups are required. If it is too long, too much inventory is produced and must be stored.

just-in-time work, you need to store data on where each piece of material and part is located and to make sure that parts and components arrive at the place where they are needed at the correct time.

Conversion to just-in-time means keeping accurate track of raw material and in-process inventory, including materials issued and component scrap. The goal is to keep raw material and in-process inventory as low as possible while avoiding frequent setups.

Inventory

The idea in the supply chain is to make sure that goods are available when needed. For physical goods, that results in inventory—goods kept in reserve to meet demand when it occurs. Inventory, of course, incurs cost. It ties up capital, storage space (which costs money), and requires a good data system to keep track of what is currently in stock and what is scheduled to arrive.

The movement to just-in-time inventory as part of just-in-time manufacturing, that is, the attempt to minimize inventory so that supplies are obtained only at the moment they are needed, also acts as a device to push the storage of inventory up the supply chain.[5] For example, the auto manufacturer who plans to assemble 500 units of a given model tomorrow seeks to have its suppliers bring the exact number of components needed for the 500 cars to the factory floor in the early morning or, better still, at the very moment each car is assembled.[6] In practice, the goal can be approached but not reached because some spare parts must be available in case of a defect or to rectify a mistake in assembly.

Inventory shows up in two ways: in-process and finished. In-process inventory refers to goods that are stored between stages of production or service. For example, consider the service of creating an insurance policy. The sales information (input) comes in from the insurance agents. Sales pile up (inventory) at the receiving desk. From there they are routed to individual actuaries and/or risk assessors who determine whether the policy should be written or not and, if written, should it be at the price sold by the agent or at a higher or lower price. The actuaries usually have a stack of policies to act on in their in-box (in-process inventory). As they complete individual policies, the actuaries route them to a production department whose clerks create the needed forms and send them out. Of course, there is an inventory of policies waiting to be sent out by each of the clerks.

Reducing inventory is an example of where improving the supply chain pays off. A company aims to minimize its inventory. To do so, it must produce products as close to when it is demanded as possible. Two kinds of losses can be incurred:

1. Not producing enough goods to meet demand. The penalty comes from lost sales and profits.
2. Producing more goods than are demanded. The penalty is the cost of storing (or even destroying) excess goods.

One of the fundamental formulas learned in operations management courses in business schools is the idea of an optimum lot size, that is, the number of units to produce at a time and the frequency between starting successive production batches. The idea is to balance off the two kinds of losses.

The classic example involved hiring airline stewardesses.[7] Stewardesses were trained in classes. How big should a class be (the lot size in inventory theory) and how often should a new class be

---

[5] Just-in-time manufacturing, invented at Toyota in Japan where space for keeping inventory was at a premium, was originally devised to reduce the amount of inventory on hand.

[6] Your author observed an example of the unintended consequences of just-in-time inventory in Tokyo. Arriving around 11 P.M. because of a flight delay, he found the freeways crowded with giant trucks creating traffic jams as bad as rush hour.

[7] Today, stewardesses are called flight attendants and are no longer limited to female employees

started (time between setups)? Recognize that there is a lead time (from the time a class starts to the time it graduates) before newly trained stewardesses become available. Recognize too that there are two kinds of losses: (1) salaries to stewardesses who graduated but are waiting to be assigned to flights (excess inventory) and (2) airplanes that can't fly because too few stewardesses are available[8] (loss of sales). Clearly, the latter is more expensive.

ROLE OF ERP

The role of ERP (Chapter 4) is different for supply chain planning and for supply chain execution software.

Supply Chain Planning

Enterprise requirement planning systems, which gather information from throughout the company, contain large amounts of information that are used as inputs in supply chain management planning. For a firm with an ERP system in place, it can be of great help because the system assembles needed up-to-date planning information in one place and, conversely, the planning information serves as input to the ERP system. To be useful for supply chain planning, an existing ERP system must be compatible with the supply chain software selected.

The conventional wisdom is that if a firm plans to install both ERP and supply chain planning, it should install ERP first. Part of the reason is that the ERP installation forces the firm to regularize its data. As discussed in Chapter 4, ERP is expensive and difficult to install. Therefore, if supply chain is a major problem and funds are tight, it may prove appropriate to install the supply chain software separately. However, while it is possible, it is quite difficult to create a supply chain planning system from legacy systems because information is needed quickly and reliably from many places. To do so requires great skill in integration with legacy systems (Chapter 10).

Supply Chain Execution

Execution systems don't need as much information as planning systems. Therefore, it is easier to install such systems without ERP in place. However, even in this case, it is advantageous to create compatible ERP, supply chain planning, and supply chain execution capabilities so that orders, payments, delivery, and manufacturing status are available together.

ROLE OF DATA WAREHOUSING

For firms with a large number of items in their supply chains, a data warehouse is a necessity both for planning and for execution. Wal-Mart, discussed in Sidebar 1 in this chapter, is an example. Its data warehouse in 2004 was 400 terabytes. It contains every transaction in every store, recorded within a few minutes of purchase. Data are available on new merchandise as it arrives and as it is put on the shelves. Thus, Wal-Mart is able to keep track of inventory available to sell, to plan orders, and (since they run on just-in-time deliveries) determine when goods should arrive at the stores. The data warehouse thus is the key to integrating their supply chain. Many firms also give access to selected parts of their data warehouse to their trading partners, both their suppliers and their customers.

---

[8] The problem can be ameliorated to some extent by using retired stewardesses who work part-time.

CHALLENGES TO IMPLEMENTATION

The three major challenges in implementing supply chain software are

- Gaining trust from suppliers, partners, and customers.
- Overcoming resistance to change by employees.
- Going up the learning curve.

Trust

Almost all the other large-scale software systems described in this book operate completely internal to the firm. Supply chain software, however, requires the cooperation of other firms to make it successful. Not only will your own people need to change how they work, but so will almost every one of your trading partners. That's a tall order. While large firms, simply because of their size, can force changes by threatening to replace a partner (and actually doing so, if need be), most firms do not enjoy enough market clout to enforce a behavior change. A firm embarking on improving its supply chain activities must coax, wheedle, and entice each of its trading partners to change their ways. That's a culture change, and like all culture changes, it is hard to implement. As described in Sidebar 1 for Proctor & Gamble, supply chain changes can move the management of inventory to the supplier, something suppliers did not do in the past and which they do not necessarily feel able to do.

Resistance

Not only will partners be difficult to bring on board, your own employees will resist change as well. As discussed in Chapter 12 on people issues, people don't like to deal with new ideas in their work. Precomputer supply chain operations involved long-term people-to-people contacts through phone, fax, and e-mail. People in the organization have tacit information (see Chapter 7, Knowledge Management) about likely sources in case of a crunch. Computer-based supply chain systems upset relationships and diminish individual importance. If the software doesn't perform as expected or runs into even minor problems, people return to their previous ways of solving a problem.

To overcome a lack of commitment within an enterprise and in the supply chain, it is important to provide specific, measurable goals for the effort and to make certain that the goals are clearly understood within the firm.

Learning Curve

When a commercial supply chain program is introduced, it behaves according to what the software vendor viewed as the standard way or the best practice for the purpose. Such programs do not include the company's practices and history. They follow the built-in algorithms and, as a result, seem dumb to the user. Thus, the initial forecasts often need to be modified.[9] Only after a while when a program is, in effect, trained does it develop the smarts that the vendor advertises.

---

[9] A classic tale, reported in CIO magazine, involved an auto industry supplier who received an unusually large order just after the software was installed. As a result, the program badly overestimated future demand because forecasts were based on this single order. Fortunately, a staff member who substituted his own estimate based on history caught the error.

A side effect is that initial errors reduce the trust in the program. People revert to working with their own data. Trust is only regained after the program becomes more accurate and when in-house expertise is merged into the system.

OTHER PROBLEMS ALONG THE SUPPLY CHAIN

Problems along the supply chain principally come from three sources:

- Uncertainties, particularly in demand. Decisions are made on the basis of a demand forecast, that is an estimate of what kinds of units and how many of each will be ordered and when they must be delivered.
- Difficulties in coordinating multiple activities, business partners, and internal units. That is, managing the nuts and bolts of the supply chain.
- Poor customer service, ranging from defective products to poor after-purchase support to early or late delivery.

As shown in Table 1, IT can help in reducing these sources of difficulty.

Demand Forecasting

Demand depends on competition, prices, weather (e.g., a warm or a cold winter), new technologies or fashions, the state of the economy, and much more. Modeling demand can be a tricky business. First, there is the bullwhip effect, discussed in Sidebar 3, that causes demand forecasts to escalate because of small errors made at various stages.

Table 1 IT SOLUTIONS TO SUPPLY CHAIN PROBLEMS

Supply chain problem	IT solution
Waiting times between chain segments are too long	Find reasons by using decision support software and/or groupware for collaboration
Non-value-added activities along the chain	Use supply chain management or simulation software
Slow delivery of paper documents	EDI, e-mail
Shipment errors, poor quality	Electronic verification, automation, quality alerts
Learn about delays after they occur	Shipment tracking systems, trend analysis
Excessive approvals	Work flow software, electronic approvals
Poor coordination, cooperation, and communication	Groupware, collaboration tools, e-mail
Parts obsolescence due to excessive time in warehouses	Tracking software, RFID[10]

[10] RFID is an acronym for radio frequency identification. Units are equipped with microchips in a tag or label with stored data such as unit number and date built. Transmitters send inquiries to a physical area and each unit responds with its identification information. Privacy issues for RFID are discussed in Chapter 15.

SIDEBAR 3 *The Bullwhip Effect*

The bullwhip effect is the name given to systemic problems that can arise in the supply chain where problems at one point can create problems at many others.

Originally found at Proctor & Gamble in its disposable diaper business, the bullwhip effect reflects the magnification of small errors into large ones. Specifically, Proctor & Gamble found that, while demand for its product at the retail level was relatively stable and hence predictable, the orders they received from their intermediaries, the distributors, fluctuated wildly. On investigation they found that poor demand forecasts, price fluctuations, and the batch size of orders were principal causes of the variations. The result was unnecessary inventories all along the supply chain because each firm was looking at its own interests, not the interests of the supply chain. Stockpiling against just-in-case scenarios occurred simultaneously at seven or more points, resulting in up to 100 days of inventory. The bullwhip effect can be overcome by sharing information between firms. As pointed out previously in this section (and in Chapter 7, Knowledge Management), corporate culture in the United States is ingrained against sharing. However, firms that do share, gain significant benefits.

Second, there is the issue of how the demand forecast is created. If the sales department makes it, there is a cultural tendency for salespeople to assume that only the best outcome will occur. Again, the forecast is badly overestimated. If a pessimistic manager who assumes the worst will happen makes the forecast, the forecast demand is much lower than the actual. A more neutral (and realistic) way to forecast is to run a computer model of the supply chain. Sidebar 4 describes this methodology briefly.

Note: If you are unfamiliar with simulation under uncertainty, feel free to skip Sidebar 4. It requires somewhat more mathematical understanding than the other sections of this book.

WHAT IS THE PAYOFF FROM INFORMATION SYSTEMS IN THE SUPPLY CHAIN?

The major benefits achieved from a successful supply chain software installation include

- a shorter supply chain (implying fewer suppliers to deal with),
- lower costs,
- shortened cycle times,
- ability to build to demand,
- use of more science in meeting customer demand,
- reduced overstock, and
- improved customer service.

SIDEBAR 4 *MODELING THE SUPPLY CHAIN*

Because of the uncertainties in the supply chain (e.g., in demand, in supplier performance, in manufacturing performance, in transportation, and in timing of customer payments) many firms use "stochastic risk analysis" based on simulation techniques. Stochastic is just a fancy word for saying uncertain. Simulation is the idea of creating a computer model that describes the phenomenon being studied. The idea is that you can run the computer program much, must faster than the real supply chain and that you can do so with much less expense. Thus, you can explore many more cases than by other means. Risk models fall into the class of simulation models in which randomness is represented by probability distributions.

A model allows you to create a simple generic framework that describes the supply chain. The framework is really a network with randomness in time and/or cost at many nodes and along many arcs. For example, you might consider the following uncertainties:

- Manufacturing: the time for process design, the capabilities of the resulting product design, the time to produce a component, and the quality of the product produced.
- Customer demand: the robustness of the economy, the stimulation of incentive programs.
- Customer delivery: time required to deliver the goods.
- Supplier performance: responsiveness of the supplier, cost of transportation

Figure 2 shows one distribution (a normal distribution) that an uncertainty may follow. You use your best estimate of what the distribution will look like for each uncertainty.

In a simulation, when an uncertainty is encountered, a single number is chosen from the probability distribution to represent what happens. For example, if the distribution of time for goods to reach you from a particular manufacturer is normally distributed as in Figure 2, you choose a value from that distribution.[11] By proceeding through the chain in this way, you create one possible outcome. But an individual outcome only has a small chance of occurring. Repeating this procedure many times allows you to obtain both the average and the standard deviation of the time from one end of the chain to the other. You can then do what-if analysis that allows you to see what proposed improvements in a node (e.g., time for a supplier to produce a component) or an arc (e.g., shipping time) can do to improve the average performance and the variability of your supply chain.

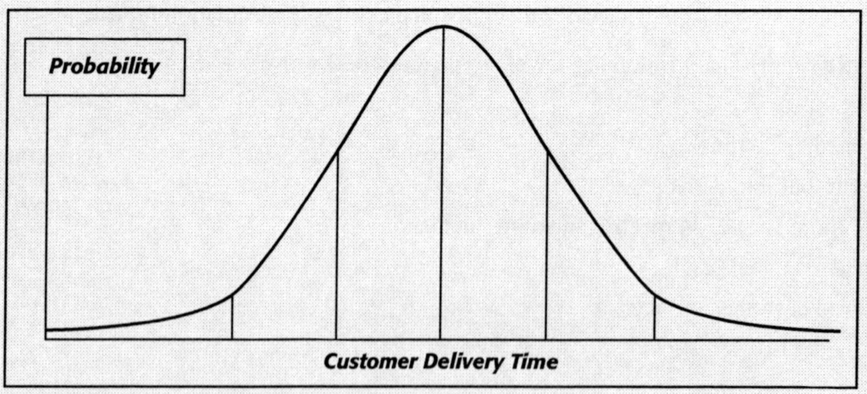

Figure 2 Normal distribution: One representation of uncertainty in a supply chain.

[11] The way the computer program is organized, it picks numbers from the probability distribution in proportion to the shape of the distribution. Thus, in a normal distribution such as shown in Figure 2, numbers from the middle are picked much more often than numbers from the end.

SIDEBAR 5 *EXAMPLES OF SUCCESS*[12]

Toy maker Mattel, who makes the Barbie doll among other products, uses supply chain optimization software in managing its seven distribution centers, seven factories, and other facilities around the world. In planning, it was able to move from monthly cycles to weekly ones and to align its production to reduce overproduction and, at the same time, meet customer demand on time. At the distribution end, it concentrated on moving product by installing a transportation management system that reduced less-than-truckload shipments and improved its shipping network.

Atari, a video game manufacturer, uses cooperative forecasting. It links its Oracle ERP system with the sales planning system to formulate weekly demand forecasts by SKU (stock keeping unit) and store. It obtains input data from customers such as Target and Best and feeds its analysis of the data to its suppliers who produce its games. Specific orders come in electronically via EDI and go through an order management system. When an order is shipped, the system sends an advance shipping notice and an invoice.

A McKinsey & Company study[13] concluded from a study of 63 high-tech companies that a firm can't and won't improve the flow of goods and information unless:

- the supply chain software is coupled with improvements in a company's most important supply chain processes,
- it improves training,
- provides clear accountability, and
- sets more realistic goals.

The difference between a successful installation and an unsuccessful one is a supply chain that is in good shape.

McKinsey & Company found that firms that didn't adopt any supply chain technologies fared better than low-performing adopters. This finding is in keeping with the idea that management must address flawed supply chain processes and practices before technology implementation can do any good. Simply throwing software at the problem won't help. It will, in fact, make things worse. It also reinforces the idea, discussed earlier, that it is wise to put ERP in place before undertaking supply change management. The ERP installation requires updating the firm's business processes so they are compatible across the firm. The McKinsey & Company study emphasizes the simple truth that implementing supply chain management technologies without a corresponding business process change makes you worse off than before. As expected, firms that adopted the supply chain technologies after improving their processes did better than the nonadopters and the low-performing adopters.

In summary, the McKinsey & Company survey found, as would be expected, that

- successful implementation occurs if broken processes are fixed first,
- rollout is incremental with repeated success rather than an all-at-once approach,
- what is promised is delivered,

[12] Examples appear in B. Bacheldor, "Steady Supply," *Information Week,* pp. 37-42, November 24, 2003.

[13] Source: McKinsey Quarterly e-mail version.

- training emphasizes improvement in decision making by using the technology, and
- a credible incentive program is instituted for adopters.

RETURNS

Returns are the last stage of the supply chain. They happen all the time. An individual receives a faulty unit (e.g., a lemon) or accepts the money back guarantee offered. A clothing store returns merchandise at the end of the season. A company upgrades its PCs to flat screens or replaces its portables with new ones that are wireless. In each case, the old merchandise must go somewhere. Usually it winds up being returned to the source. That is, returns create a supply chain in reverse.[14] Rather than pushing merchandise down the supply chain to the customer, the customer is pushing finished merchandise up the chain. The source firm's objective is to recover unsold or defective product and then resell it or send it to a liquidation outlet or a recycling center. The income derived from salvage offsets some of the losses on the returns.

In some cases, the product itself implies a reverse supply chain. A disposable camera, for example, is recycled with fresh film and resold. Manufacturers of laser printers encourage people to return their spent toner cartridge units back to the manufacturer. Recycling is being encouraged for more and more products.

Unfortunately, it is not possible simply to operate the supply chain in reverse. Forward supply chain management processes reduce transaction and transportation costs by minimizing the number of transactions in the system. For example, goods are shipped in standardized lot sizes (e.g., cases) for cost effective performance. In the reverse direction, moving unsold goods, say, from a store shelf, rarely results in standard lot sizes. That creates new problems in receiving, material handling, and stocking. Additional handling costs are incurred as individual items move to different locations in a warehouse. The computer must be able to account for small, irregular quantities.

Another technique at the retail level is to sell slow moving products at a discount either through markdowns or closeouts or outlet malls. Unfortunately, such tactics can send false signals into supply chain planning. A classic example is Volvo, whose dealers found that few people wanted their cars in green. When the dealers cut prices to move the cars, the factory took it as a signal that green Volvos were selling and started producing them in even greater quantities.

The conclusion is that reverse supply chains must be established separately from forward chains. They may take the form of third parties that act as accumulators of goods into standard lot sizes that are then shipped to the warehouse or to a plant that remanufactures the product. In either case, the goods are then treated as new product.

Computer software and infrastructure for reverse supply chains is still in its infancy. It is a business opportunity.

THE SUPPLY CHAIN MARKET

What you can do to improve the supply chain changes continually as new software comes on the market and additional supply chain functions are automated. The electronic supply chain is being credited with better customer service, more support from suppliers, and shorter production cycles.

---

[14] For a discussion of the reverse supply chain see, for example, R. Reddy, "Swimming Upstream," *Intelligent Enterprise*, p. 42, September 1, 2003.

Firms believe that they are creating ever greater levels of customer, supplier, and partner integration. To do so, however, involves challenges:

- Security
- Privacy
- Competition

Clearly, with hundreds of suppliers and customers, many of whom are small, a firm is not able to extend its supply chain end-to-end. A trade magazine, *InformationWeek*,[15] surveyed the 500 most innovative U.S. firms and found that a typical company in that cohort coordinated its supply chain in 2003 with 39% of its suppliers, 36% of its business partners, and 35% of its customers. These numbers are averages and vary by industry. At the high end is the automotive industry where the three numbers are 61%, 56%, and 54%, respectively. In some industries close connections are maintained with suppliers only.

InformationWeek found that companies provided different access to their suppliers depending on the application. The values ranged from 58% down to 35%. In rank order the applications were: order management, inventory, accounts payable, receivable status, product development specification, and production schedules.

Major Firms in the Supply Chain Market

Major vendors in the supply chain market include Manugistics and I2 which specialize in the area, and large software vendors such as SAP, Oracle, and IBM who offer supply chain software as well as ERP and other major systems. Table 2 lists the firms included in one supply chain management stock index.[16]

Table 2 COMPANIES INCLUDED IN A SUPPLY CHAIN STOCK INDEX

Company	Symbol
Amer Software A	AMSWA
Aspen Technology	AZPN
Clarus Corp	CLRS
Catalyst Intl	CLYS
Descartes Systems Group	DSGX
Exe Technologies A	EXEE
Frontstep Inc	FSTP
Industri-matematik Intl	IMIC
I2 Technologies	ITWO
Logility Inc	LGTY
Manhattan Associates	MANH
Manugistics Group	MANU
Made2manage Systems	MTMS
Qad Inc	QADI
SAP	SAP

[15] Source: *Information Week* pp. 108-110, October 27, 2003.

[16] Source: http://stocks.ittoolbox.com/ittoolbox/indices.asp?Symbol=$SCMDEX Last consulted 10-7-04. The list represents publicly traded vendors in October 2004. Some of these companies may disappear as mergers and acquisitions take place.

ANSWERS TO MANAGERIAL QUESTIONS

What is supply chain management?

Supply chain management refers to the use of the computer and analytic techniques to reduce the cost and improve the speed with which a firm obtains materials, components, and supplies for its products and services and is able to move those products to its customers.

What are the five components of supply chain management?

Supply chain management includes (1) planning to make it all happen, (2) sourcing to find the best (usually lowest cost, quickest response) vendors, (3) making the product or service, (4) delivering output, and (5) dealing with returns.

What is the goal of supply chain management?

Supply chain software allows firms to gain visibility about supplies and demand over time. As a result, they can reduce inventory, smooth out production and labor, and avoid being out of stock when a demand occurs.

How is supply chain software used?

Supply chain software is used to support planning and to help execute the supply chain steps after planning.

What is the role of collaboration?

To make the supply chain work effectively, both providers of input and consumers of output need to work together. Thus, for a given firm, vendors who sell to the firm work better if they have access to anticipated needs and clients can plan better if they can obtain accurate forecasts of what outputs will be available.

What is the relation to ERP?

Although ERP is not required, it usually makes it easier to manage the supply chain because an ERP system provides much of the data needed for managing the supply chain.

What are the resistances to installing supply chain software?

The resistance to supply chain software is similar to that for other innovations. People don't like to learn new things, and fear their job will be displaced.

PROBLEMS

1. SUPPLY CHAIN PAYOFF

   Discuss the supply chain in your current firm or a firm that you worked for previously. Describe what parts of the supply chain and inventory records were automated and which were not. Suggest ways in which the supply chain could be improved.

2. MATHEMATICAL AND COMPUTER MODELS (ONLY FOR STUDENTS WITH ANALYTIC BACKGROUNDS)

   A large amount of effort in creating mathematical optimization models and simulation models is underway by firms specializing in operations research and industrial engineering. Discuss the models and the firms building and selling them.

3. VENDORS

   For four of the vendors listed in Table 2, determine the extent of their offerings of products for supply chain management. Include the products produced, the market they seek to serve, what they claim their market distinction is, and (if available) the dollar volume of their shipments.

4. REVERSE SUPPLY CHAIN

   Discuss how your company deals with returns. Frame your explanation in terms of the reverse supply chain discussed in the section on returns.

9-601-099
REV: MARCH 31, 2003

ANDREW MCAFEE

Quantum Corporation: eSupplyChain Group

In May 2000, Mike Wais, the director of Quantum Corporation's recently formed eSupplyChain Group, read a press release announcing that his company was forming an alliance with eleven other computer makers and suppliers. The alliance—including Quantum, Advanced Micro Devices Inc., Compaq Computer, Gateway, Hitachi America, Infineon Technologies AG, NEC, Samsung, SEI, and Western Digital Corporation—had banded together to form a group that would build new B2B exchange for supply chain management.[1] This was news to Wais, as well as to most of his colleagues within the company. As the release stated, the new venture had been formed very quickly, and initial discussions had involved only the most senior executives at involved companies.

According to the release, the exchange would "build a new business-to-business (B2B) exchange for supply chain management. Its ultimate goal will be to capitalize on greater efficiencies, thus driving prices lower for PC and electronics buyers and sellers, all via the Internet. . . Representatives from the founding companies said they believe that the exchange could help them save between 5 percent and 7 percent of their costs of procuring parts. . . The new venture will start off by developing a method by which member companies will share basic parts catalogs. This would give the companies faster, more direct access to the components they need to turn out products. . ."[2]

The only additional information Wais knew was that the exchange had been named eHITEX. He knew, however, that he and his team would have to quickly figure out how to incorporate eHITEX into their work. The eSupplyChain group was tasked with designing a new vision and new approaches for supply chain collaboration and fulfillment of customer orders. Clearly, eHITEX could, and probably should, be part of that process—but how?

Company History and Structure

Products and Markets

Founded in 1980 in Milpitas, California, Quantum Corporation captured 25% of the hard disk drive market share within two years. The company accomplished this in part by concentrating on two dimensions of operational performance—quality and time to volume, or the time required to

[1] "ZDNet News from ZDWire," ZD, Inc., May 1, 2000.

[2] Ibid.

Professor Andrew McAfee prepared this case with the assistance of Research Associate Greg Bounds. HBS cases are developed solely as the basis for class discussion. Cases are not intended to serve as endorsements, sources of primary data, or illustrations of effective or ineffective management.

"ramp up" production to meet customers' requirements. By 2000, the company employed 6,300 people and had developed solutions for every digital storage need, from consumer electronics to home and office PCs to corporate workgroups and data centers (see **Exhibit 1**). Quantum was the only supplier selling to the world's top 10 PC manufacturers and offered the industry's broadest range of desktop products. Quantum operated globally, selling its wide range of storage products through both OEM and distribution channels. In addition to computer manufacturers, OEM customers included makers of novel consumer products such as the personal video recorders made by ReplayTV and TiVo. Most of the world's major electronic components distributors were also customers.

Quantum shipped 30 million desktop drives in fiscal year 2000 and remained the market share leader for the seventh consecutive year, accounting for 24% of total sales. However, excellent products and a dominant position in the market were not enough to ensure excellent financial performance for the company. [See **Exhibit 2** for company financial information.]

HDDG and HDDO

On August 4, 1999, Quantum became the first Silicon Valley company to issue tracking stock when it replaced its existing common stock with the ticker symbols DSS, which tracked the performance of Quantum's DLTtape & Storage Systems Group (DSSG), and HDD, which tracked the performance of Quantum's Hard Disk Drive Group (HDDG). Both tracking stocks were traded on the New York Stock Exchange. At that time, Quantum made organizational structure changes that mirrored the tracking stock entities. HDDG was comprised of the three business units providing desktop storage, consumer electronics storage and high-end storage: DSSG was comprised of the four business units providing DLTtape drives and media, solid state storage systems (such as ATL tape automation products and the Snap! Server), network-attached storage solutions, and enterprise storage solutions. As an explanation for the stock split and reorganization, Quantum stated that it wanted "to offer investors a choice between their two distinct businesses, which serve different markets and are subject to very different trends and opportunities."[3] The split also allowed investors to track the separate performance of HDDG and DSSG. Sales for the fiscal year 2000 were $1.4 billion for DSSG and $3.3 billion HDDG. [See **Exhibit 3** for a history of Quantum stocks.]

Within HDDG, each of the three business units had its own marketing, engineering, and finance functions, along with dedicated product development teams. However, Hard Disk Drive Operations (HDDO) served all the businesses units (see **Exhibit 4** for the Group's organization chart). HDDO was established as a shared service because the supply chain, or set of activities involved in procuring disk drives and delivering them to customers to meet their needs, was largely the same across product lines. All HDDG products, for example, were manufactured by a single supplier, which had Quantum as its only customer for hard disk drives.

MKE Relationship

Quantum had a unique partnership with its supplier, Matsushita-Kotobuki Electronics Industries Ltd. (MKE). Based in Japan, MKE was founded in 1969 as an independent subsidiary of the Matsushita Electrical Industrial Co., Ltd. MKE focused on manufacturing as an OEM product supplier and grew to employ about 5,300 employees worldwide. In 1984, Quantum began using MKE

[3] Source: Quantum.com, HDDG Letter.

as an exclusive supplier for desktop products, and MKE agreed to sell disk drive products only to Quantum. In 1997, when Quantum closed down its high-end manufacturing line, Quantum and MKE signed agreements making the relationship exclusive on both sides. Because of this unique relationship with MKE, Quantum did not have the component procurement process of a typical manufacturing company. Instead, Quantum and MKE selected suppliers jointly for key components such as heads, media, motors, and integrated circuits (ICs). For other components, MKE made the selections. MKE managed the purchasing process for all components.

This arrangement combined Quantum's strengths in product design, marketing, customer service, and demand management with MKE's strengths in high-quality, high-volume, electromechanical manufacturing. Over the years, Quantum became convinced that this partnership enabled it to become the volume leader in the desktop hard disk drive market and to boast of the fastest manufacturing ramps and the highest product quality and reliability in the industry.

MKE operated in an almost pure build-to-schedule environment where production plans were fixed far enough in advance to ensure materials supply and preparation of the plant's extensive automation. MKE then executed these plans, typically with extremely high reliability. Quantum took ownership of the drives as soon as they were completed. This approach to manufacturing was very efficient and allowed Quantum to offer its customers a desirable combination of high quality and large volume production. In the late 1990s, however, changes and pressures in Quantum's markets exposed weaknesses in this approach and throughout the companies' supply chains.

Supply Chain Initiatives

Pressures

In the late 1990s, Quantum, like other disk drive manufacturers, experienced a sharp deterioration in the prices it was able to charge for its products. An analyst with International Data Corp. explained at the time that "companies are all very aggressively looking for the right formula to make the business model work. Everyone realizes that prices are never going to go up again."[4] Many observers attributed this decline to a number of factors:

- A widespread disk drive glut hurt prices, which remained suppressed even though excess inventory came down steadily.
- Disk drive manufacturers placed a higher priority on market share than on profits, leading to price competition.
- PC prices plummeted as companies tried to competitively serve the emerging sub-$1,000 PC market, which put additional downward pressure on prices for components such as drives.
- Manufacturers moved toward somewhat lower performing, high capacity hardware, with fewer, lower cost components and higher reliability.

Figure A, below, shows that while shipment volumes increased during this period, revenue decreased. Quantum's margins suffered during this period partially because component prices were

[4] Source: "Seagate Reports 4% Profit Rise, Hurt by Disk Drive Price Cuts," by Lee Gomes, *The Wall Street Journal Europe*, (UK5A), July 16, 1999.

not declining as rapidly as prices for completed drives, and the company as a whole reported losses in several quarters during this time. In May of 2000, Quantum's average selling price for a disk drive was approximately $128; component costs averaged 75% of this price.

Figure A Recent Quarterly Revenues, Net Income, and Units Shipped

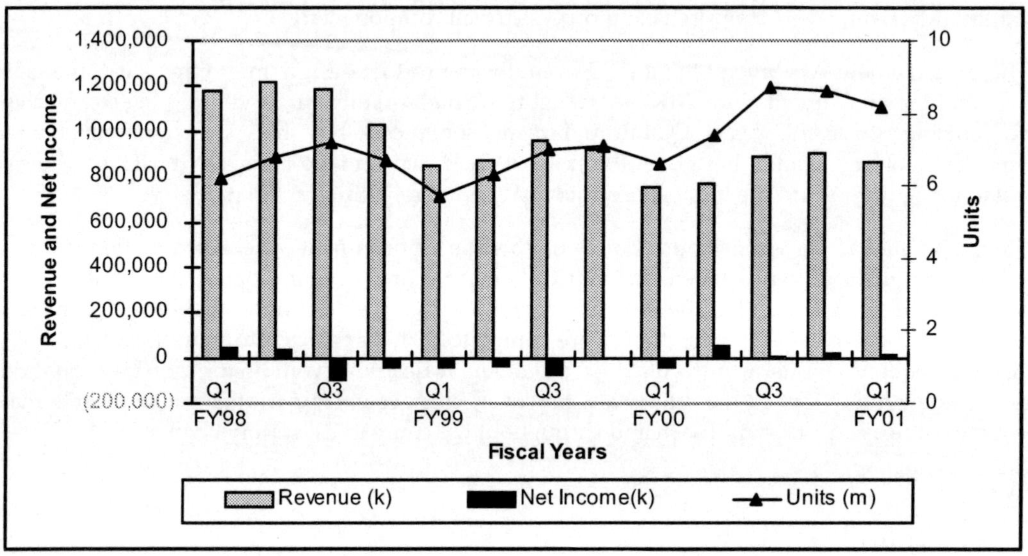

Source: Company documents.

At the same time that they were demanding cheaper products, Quantum's customers were also creating challenges in other ways. They became, for example, less willing to make amends when changes in their orders or forecasts had a negative impact on Quantum. Wais recalled that:

> Going back three or four years, we have seen a real degradation in the effort of our customers to commit to forecast. I have been at Quantum for nine years and I can remember a meeting six or seven years ago where we had a customer's forecast change dramatically. I actually met with them, mapped out the lead times for the material that was therefore excess, did all the math, added it up, etc. and said, "Here's how much money you just cost us. Now what are we going to do about that?" And they felt obligated that their forecast changed and generated scrap for us. That's the obligation that they had. That kind of discussion is science fiction today.

Also during this time, Quantum's large customers began demanding that stockpiles of finished disk drives be maintained near their factories to ensure a steady supply of this critical PC component, pulled into their factories on a just-in-time basis. These "local inventories" were still owned by Quantum, who therefore bore all risks (obsolescence, damage, etc.) associated with them. Local inventories typically comprised two to four weeks of supply.

Phase 1 Initiatives

In response to these pressures, in the summer of 1998 HDDO began a series of efforts aimed at reducing supply chain costs while improving fulfillment efficiency. Initial work, dubbed "Phase 1," concentrated on improving Quantum's ability to get finished drives from the MKE factories to customers quickly and cheaply. The two primary projects within Phase 1 were direct shipment and generic drives. These were intended to help HDDO move away from using what Wais termed a "classic postponement model" where, as he described it:

> We built product in our factories according to a forecast, sent it to regional logistic sites, customized it at the very last moment as necessary to meet customer orders (hence the term "postponement"), and sent it to the customer. Customization means putting a label on it, or unique packaging, or special firmware[5] for a customer, or its own label that has identifying markers that match their system. It may also be special testing that the customer is interested in.

Quantum's Steve Herrick, a supply chain re-engineering consultant, explained the basic problems with a postponement model in Quantum's markets:

> We were building to forecast, but we were sending this inventory to regional inventory centers when we weren't quite sure who was going to get the product. We could have piles of inventory in Europe when the real orders were coming in from the United States and not even know it. So we would have to send it all over the world a second time. Our basic inventory metric is what we call Time Of Ownership or TOO. That is the number of days from when we take ownership of the drive until the customer takes ownership of the drive. A year and a half ago, we were running up to several weeks of TOO. When you are talking about more than 100,000 disk drives a day; that's a lot of cash tied up in inventory around the world. We did an analysis when we started the Phase I activities that showed that TOO was costing Quantum hundreds of millions of dollars a year.

TOO was costly because prices for both finished drives and their components declined over time. Quantum estimated that the selling price for a completed disk drive declined 8% per quarter.[6] The longer a drive sat in inventory, in other words, the less valuable it became. At the same time, Quantum missed out on the opportunity to pay *less* for the drive's components, which declined in price 6.5% per quarter. In May of 2000, Quantum's TOO averaged 30 working days.

Generic drives HDDO managers felt that the Group was producing too many different drive models, or SKUs.[7] This worsened the problem outlined by Herrick: it was often the case that the specific SKU desired by a customer in Texas, for example, was sitting in Quantum's Singapore logistics center. To get around this problem, the Group engaged in a major effort to reduce the number of different drives manufactured by replacing several similar SKUs with a single generic one. To entice customers to give up the drives that had been tailored for them and accept generic ones instead, Quantum convinced customers both on the increased flexibility they would get from their supply base and also a cost reduction of up to a few dollars per drive depending on the complexity of

---

[5] Firmware is programming instructions that are stored in a read-only memory unit rather than being implemented through software.

[6] Quantum based its calculations on 80 working days per quarter.

[7] A stock-keeping unit (SKU) was, in Quantum's case, a discrete finished drive that could be sold to a customer.

their configuration. Moving to generic drives also improved quality, since configuration, or any post-production handling of disk drives, added opportunity for damage. As a result the number of SKUs was reduced to less than half of what it had been. As of May 2000, about 70% of MKE's output was a generic product.

Direct shipment Quantum's other Phase 1 effort involved changing how the company worked with MKE. Direct shipment meant that MKE, rather than shipping all product to Quantum directly, had to create a more complex shipping and invoicing process to handle shipments to all of Quantum's many customers. Direct shipment would not have been possible without the generic drive program, which allowed drives to go to customers right off the production line. Quantum was able to convince MKE to take on the added logistics complexity because, as Quantum manager Gillian Verga explained, "MKE knew this was the company strategy and they would have to do it sooner or later. They understood that the cost pressures in our industry required us to streamline the supply chain, and they were also investigating similar efforts further upstream in their suppliers' supply chains." Like the generic drive program, the direct-ship program was highlighted to customers for its improvement of quality through reduced handling, as well as for lower costs. After one year, Quantum went from 35% to 70% generic drives, and from 0% direct ship to 35% direct ship. Quantum also found a significant reduction in operating expense and improvement in cash flow each quarter after these changes were implemented.

Information Technology Initiatives

At the same time that Quantum was pursuing these phase one initiatives, the company was also implementing a comprehensive information system intended to improve fulfillment-related decisions. This advanced planning and scheduling (APS) software was made by i2, a Dallas-based company, and sold under the name RHYTHM. RHYTHM added value by applying sophisticated algorithms to HDDO data to make improved (and in some cases mathematically "optimal") decisions around such questions as how to develop more accurate forecasts for Quantum's markets, how to plan production across MKE factories given customer demands and constraints on capacity and material availability, and how to allocate short-supply products across the many customers that wanted them. Using the software, Quantum hoped that it would be able to make more effective use of its operations resources (materials, production capacity, warehouse space, shipping and trucking routes, etc.), lowering costs while simultaneously increasing its ability to satisfy customers.

The i2 software leveraged investments Quantum had previously made in a company-wide enterprise information system. This system, built around software produced by Oracle, Inc., provided a common information technology platform for transactions and data. With Oracle in place, common transactions (such as receiving product into inventory, taking a customer order, paying a supplier, and closing the books each month) were performed the same way throughout the company, and therefore yielded consistent data. These transactions were recorded in the single database that supported the system, so information was always up-to-date and widely available. These data could also be used to create reports that summarized and tracked performance, providing important visibility to managers throughout the corporation. Quantum went live on the Oracle system in May 1996. The cutover from the previous system to Oracle happened over a week's time, although the whole project, including the time spent writing the RFQ and selecting a vendor, took more than two years. During that time Quantum acquired the disk drive unit of Digital Equipment Corporation, which significantly delayed the project.

The Oracle and i2 projects were time-consuming and required a great deal of commitment, resources, and follow-up work to resolve issues for several months after system implementation. However, the projects were perceived as important building blocks for future supply chain efforts within the company. **Figure B** combines the Phase 1 initiatives with this IT-based work, and shows resulting benefits to customers. By the spring of 2000, HDDO managers were able to take advantage of standardized data and transactions and improved decision-making capabilities within their organization. They also saw new opportunities in their operating environment that could potentially be seized with the aid of these capabilities.

Figure B Supply Chain Integration: Processes, Benefits, and Initiatives

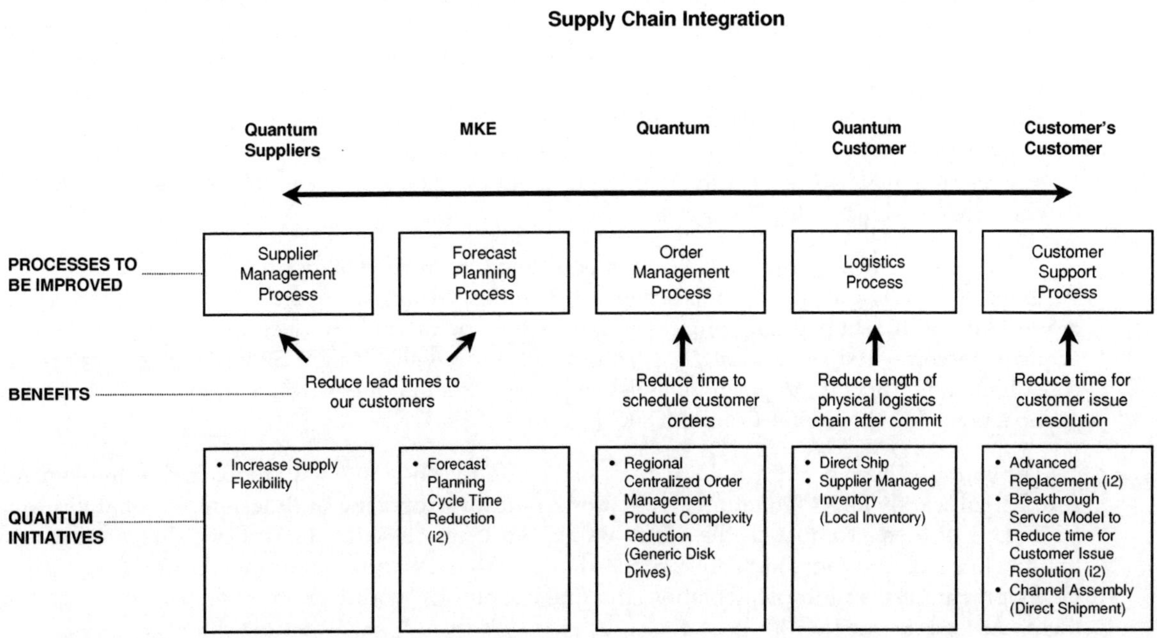

Source: Company documents.

The eSupplyChain Group

Formation

At the same time that the i2 implementation and the generic drive and direct-ship efforts were maturing in the second half of 1999, Mike Wais and his colleagues in HDDO began to hear more about new models for Internet-based supply chain collaboration within their industry. Many of Quantum's customers and other partners were expressing strong interest in these models, and were announcing and launching efforts to explore them. These developments clearly brought substantial opportunities and challenges to Quantum's operations, but it was not clear how to respond to them, or even how to start formulating a response. HDDO managers were being kept extremely busy with their existing initiatives, and with managing the fulfillment process on a daily basis. As Wais explained the situation:

> At the beginning of this year, we were still implementing final stages of i2 systems and we were still finishing the restructuring of the Supply Chain. So those efforts weren't finished yet, but it was time to think ahead to Phase II. Starting with the idea of exchanging information for assets and combining some of the trends in other industries, we thought, "There is a real intersection with some of the work we have done so far." And the capabilities for collaboration that initially we would have thought would have been through privately hosted tools like i2 were really going to be accelerated through some of the Web-based exchanges. Our senior staff spent several days together over a couple of off-sites trying to get a handle on these trends and what our vision should be, because we all felt that they would revolutionize the way we do business. It's another step function, it's as dramatic a change as the one that we had been through in the past year or so and we don't really understand all potential applications of it yet. So at the end of the second off-site, we came to the conclusion as a group that "This is big, and we can't just have everybody doing a little bit of it while at the same time trying to do their regular job—fighting to fulfill orders for customers every day and trying to finish this re-engineering that we've already launched." And we started to think, "We need dedicated resources working on this."

The eSupplyChain group at Quantum was formed in April 2000, with Mike Wais as its director. Wais was formerly director of the Fulfillment Planning Group, an operational group managing the day-to-day fulfillment planning process as well as the operational interface with MKE. The rest of the group was composed of Gillian Verga, manager of strategic design, Steve Herrick, supply chain consultant, and Raj Oza, organizational development consultant. [**Exhibit 4** shows the eSupplyChain group's position within HDDO and HDDG.]

The eSupplyChain group would be responsible for investigating new trends and technologies that could significantly affect Quantum's operations, and for proposing and designing initiatives to take advantage of them. To do this, the group would work closely with the rest of HDDO to make sure that the line functions agreed on the proposed approaches. As initiatives moved from design through development, test, and implementation, the line operations would progressively take ownership of them. As Oza described:

> It's all about alignment. A start-up environment has built-in alignment, and thus the resistance to change is low. The eSupplyChain team's challenge was to be entrepreneurial in an established company. This entailed creating alignment within Operations, between Operations and other parts of Quantum, and between Quantum and its customers and key partners. To be sure, cascading commitment was a part of the change management strategy. More importantly, the team approached pilot implementations with an eye on low organizational resistance and high organizational learning. Involvement with OEMs in dynamic trading exchanges ensured that the voice of the customer was present. Ultimately, operationalizing the change in the business model would require that the new policies and processes would be co-developed with stakeholders from Sales, Marketing, and Manufacturing.

Vision

The eSupplyChain group worked throughout the first quarter of 2000 to develop a vision for Internet-enabled fulfillment within HDDO. They began by summarizing the factors that were compelling this effort; these are drawn below in **Figure C**. The group felt that a combination of newly available technologies, industry trends, and external customer and internal Quantum needs were combining to drive the need for a new vision within operations.

Figure C HDDO Vision for the eSupplyChain

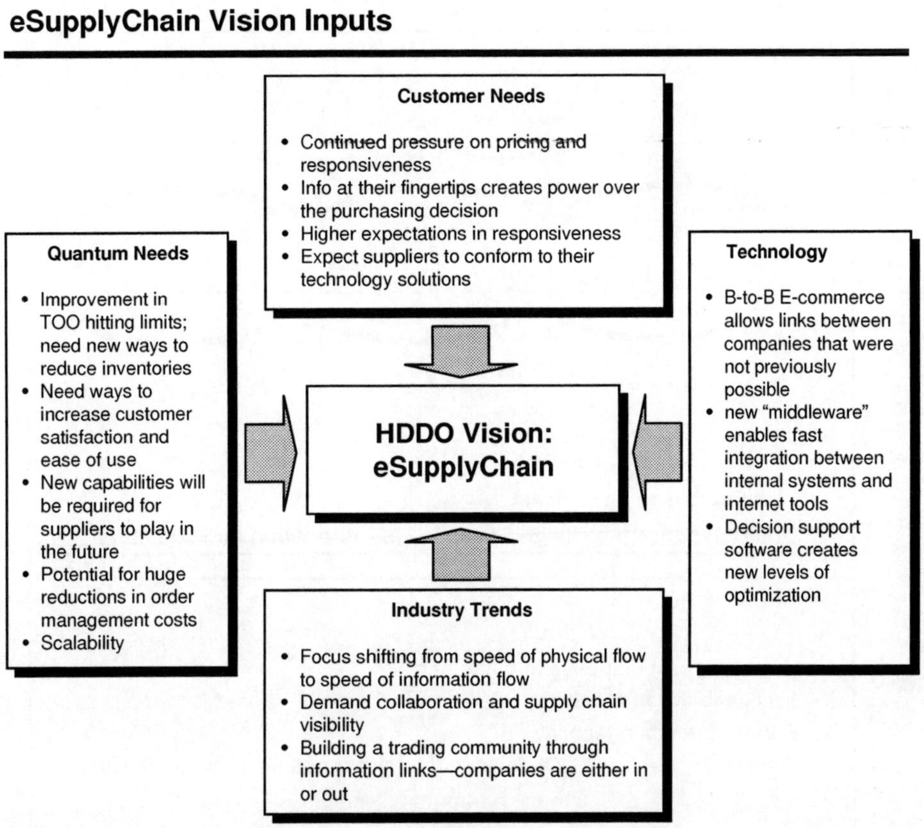

Source: Company documents.

The difference between this vision and Quantum's existing practice is shown below in **Figure D.** Traditional supply chains consisted of sequential flows of information in one direction through the chain, followed by sequential flows of product in the other direction, culminating in finished goods delivery to the customer in response to an order placed earlier. The eSupplyChain group felt that this model was slow, inefficient, and unnecessarily inflexible, and wanted to replace it with one that looked more like a loop than a chain. While product would still flow sequentially from suppliers to MKE to customers in this model, information would flow much more quickly and freely among all involved parties.

The group also felt that Quantum's markets were forcing them to adopt new practices. It seemed clear that the Internet, and business-to-business (B2B) communication channels built on top of it, were quickly becoming mainstream for Quantum's customers, partners, and competitors. It also seemed that the speeds required for effective communication and decision-making were constantly increasing, and that it was imperative to have technologies and practices in place that would enable

HDDO to move at these speeds. The eSupplyChain group's charter was to define these technologies and practices.

Figure D The Difference Between the eSupply Chain Vision and Current Practice

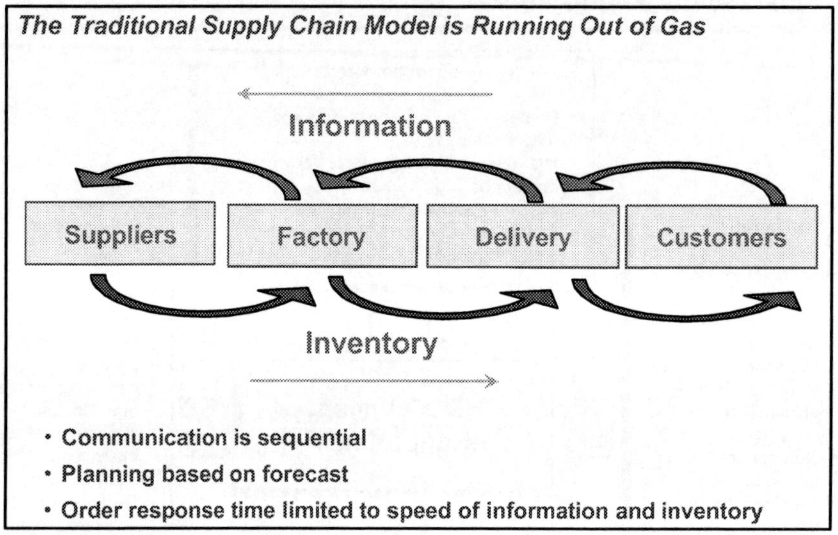

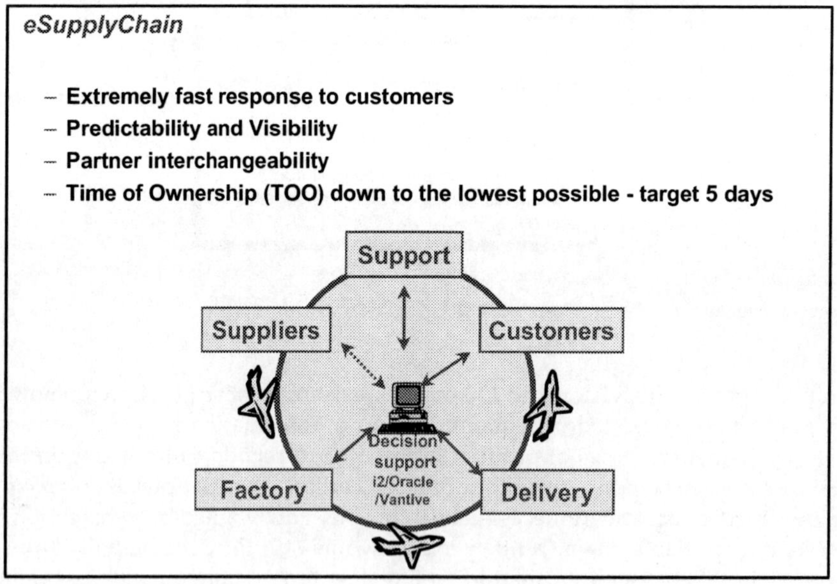

Source: Company documents.

Benefits

The group felt that if eSupplyChain efforts were successful, Quantum, its customers, and its other business partners would all benefit. Customers would get more rapid and accurate responses about available inventory, delivery dates, and other parameters of interest as well as more rapid fulfillmentof orders placed. These orders, as well as Quantum's forecasts, would quickly flow throughout the company's supply chain, so that component suppliers would have accurate and timely information about market needs, allowing them to shift mix and volume more quickly and accurately.

The immediate benefit to Quantum from the eSupplyChain efforts would be a reduction in TOO. In fact, in the final vision all drives would be shipped in their final configurations directly from an MKE factory to the customer, resulting in a TOO of approximately five days. This would yield better financial performance, higher customer satisfaction, a much simpler and less expensive logistics network, and a perception that Quantum's operations were the most responsive and progressive of any disk drive manufacturer. [**Exhibit 5** lists other advantages and possibilities from these efforts, as perceived by the eSupplyChain group.]

Efforts

The eSupplyChain group categorized HDDO's current and future efforts into three areas: getting and sharing information more quickly, making more rapid decisions in response to customer demands, and delivering completed product to customers more quickly. While maintaining and improving accuracy was also important, the primary driver for each was increased speed. The group felt that success in these areas would allow Quantum to move far away from its current postponement model toward one of continuous replenishment of requested products.

Information speed The vision shown in **Figure C** above was largely one of ideal information flows among Quantum and all of its partners. Demand signals in the form of orders and, to a lesser extent, forecasts would arrive continuously from customers, and be immediately shared throughout the loop. The results of Quantum's internal decisions—for example, long-term production plans—would also be quickly shared using this loop, as would information from other partners (for example, notification from a supplier that a component was in short supply.

In the summer of 1998, Quantum had begun an initial project toward this goal with one of its largest customers. This project, called Quantum Supply Online, established a direct, dedicated link between the customer and Quantum; orders, acknowledgement, and other fulfillment communications were automatically sent between the two companies over this link. The Quantum Supply Online project was the most advanced effort within Quantum to increase information speed; most other customer communications were less automated, relying on a mixture of electronic transmissions, phone calls, faxes, and documents sent through the mail.

Decision speed The main goal of the ongoing i2 implementation within Quantum was improved fulfillment-related decisions, and improvement was often a matter of speed. Under previous practices, for example, Quantum could typically not provide a firm delivery date commitment at the time an order was placed, and instead had to re-contact the customer with this information. If the order exceeded that customer's allocation, or amount of current inventory and future production capacity "set aside" for the customer, the delay could be quite long.

Decisions about over-allocation orders went through a complicated process, which started with the Quantum order taker checking for extra allocation from other "instances" of the same customer. Quantum's existing order management system (which was to be replaced by i2) allowed a single customer to have many instances, or separate order-placing entities. An instance could correspond, for example, to a customer's factory, division, or geographic region. If an instance exceeded its allocation, Quantum order takers would use their familiarity with the system and the customer's configuration on it to check if there were other instances with spare allocation. If so, the spare allocation was transferred from one instance to the other.

If not, the order takers broadened their search, starting with other customers in the same region. If one of these had allocation to spare, the order taker contacted the customer (or, in some cases, the sales rep responsible for that customer) to see if they would be willing to surrender part of their allocation.

For products that were greatly in demand, this process of searching for allocation would be progressively widened, including more geographies and more customers. It would also involve more groups within Quantum, including order management, the production liaisons with MKE, marketing, and the sales reps responsible for different customer accounts. In many cases, these groups would come together in meetings where final allocation decisions were made. Weeks could elapse between the time an over-allocation request was made, and the time a final decision was made, because of the many steps in the process and the many players involved in making the decision.

In contrast, the i2 system offered a much more streamlined process for over-allocation decisions. The i2 software could, in real-time, check both unused MKE production capacity and the allocation status of all customers. It could also take into account customer priorities, as determined by historical sales volumes, prospective sales volumes, subjective rankings of importance, or other factors. With this information, the system could immediately decide if the customer's request would be granted, partially granted, or rejected.

Fulfillment speed MKE's production schedule had historically changed once a month based on the planning cycle, with only exception-driven changes in between. MKE's planning process was done manually, and was generally targeted at minimizing production changeovers and optimizing factory output. To provide more rapid customer response without stockpiling inventory, the eSupplyChain group envisioned a different production process, which divided the work at the factory into forecast-driven and order-driven segments. Component purchasing and production planning would still be based on forecast. However, as customers pulled drives from warehouses for their factory consumption, that demand information would be captured real time and fed to MKE so that they could adjust their factory output to more closely match final demand. Any testing and configuration required would be moved to the end of the line at MKE, and combined with the generic drive and direct-ship programs, this would allow MKE's production to be shipped directly to customers each day. In this vision, Quantum's TOO would be approximately five days.

From Postponement to Replenishment

Together, the efforts to improve information, decision-making, and fulfillment speed would, the eSupplyChain group felt, allow HDDO to shift from a postponement production model to one of continuous replenishment of actual customer demand. Both of them relied on forecasting demand and planning production capacity in advance, but the postponement model relied heavily on a weekly cycle of updates to these plans and decisions around customer requests, while the replenishment model rested on real-time decisions about customer orders.

eHITEX

Wais reviewed his group's vision and the efforts underway and proposed within HDDO as he read about eHITEX. [See **Exhibit 6** for another press release and the Frequently Asked Questions in **Exhibit 7** for more information about the exchange.] He knew that many people, including senior executives, were excited about Quantum's participation and expected it to yield substantial benefits to the company. He also knew that many colleagues with HDDO were expecting the eSupplyChain group to articulate how eHITEX would fit within the current vision, and what specific projects would best begin the work of integrating eHITEX into Quantum's operations. Wais knew he and his team would have to very quickly begin answering these questions.

Exhibit 1 Products

	Desktop hard disk drives
3.5-inch drives	5.1GB to 40GB drives for entry-level, mid-range and high-end PCs.
	High end hard disk drives
3.5-inch drives	9.1GB to 73.4GB high-performance drives for mainstream and performance workstations, servers and storage subsystems, and storage intensive applications such as networked databases, graphics, imaging, digital video, transaction processing, and CAD/CAM.
	Consumer electronics disk drives
Quantum QuickView Technologies	Quantum QuickView technologies enable consumer products to record, store and play audio and video content with instant access, live broadcast pause, and instant replay options.
	Tape drives and tape automation
.5-inch cartridge DLTtape™ drives	20, 35 and 40GB (native) cartridge streaming tape drives.
	Solid state disks
3.5-inch SSD drives	134MB to 3.2GB Ultra SCSI
Quantum eSystem Accelerator	536MB to 3.2GB solid-state technology with tools, service, and consulting for time-critical applications including Web page access and e-commerce transactions.
	Network-Attached Storage (NAS) servers
Snap Server™	15GB to 120GB servers for workgroups of all sizes. Uses include data storage, backup, general purpose and cross-platform file sharing, remote storage, and software distribution.

Source: Company documents.

Exhibit 2 Selected Financial Information

Pro forma net income (loss) per share for DSSG and HDDG assumes the recapitalization occurred at the beginning of the earliest period presented.

	At or For the Year Ended March 31,				
	1996	1997	1998	1999	2000
	(in thousands, except per-share amounts)				
Statement of Operations Data					
Revenue	$4,422,726	$5,319,457	$5,805,235	$4,902,056	$4,727,204
Gross profit	542,417	768,741	875,521	871,338	878,960
Research and development expenses	239,116	291,332	321,741	353,223	365,204
Sales and marketing, general and administrative expenses	207,558	235,878	258,395	284,876	357,768
Restructuring/special charges included in operating expenses	209,122	--	--	--	42,421
Purchased in-process research and development expense	--	--	--	89,000	37,000
Income (loss) from operations	(113,379)	241,531	295,385	14,239	76,567
Loss from investee	--	--	(66,060)	(142,050)	--
Net income (loss)	$(90,456)	$148,515	$170,801	$(29,535)	$40,844
Net income (loss) per share:					
Basic	$(0.87)	$1.27	$1.25	$(0.18)	$NM
Diluted	$(0.87)	$1.04	$1.07	$(0.18)	$NM
DLT & Storage Systems Group					
Pro forma net income per share:					
Basic	$0.34	$0.92	$1.64	$0.77	$0.89
Diluted	$0.31	$0.75	$1.37	$0.73	$0.86
Hard Disk Drive Group					
Pro forma net income (loss) per share:					
Basic	$(2.43)	$0.70	$(0.78)	$(0.90)	$(1.26)
Diluted	$(2.43)	$0.58	$(0.78)	$(0.90)	$(1.26)
Balance Sheet Data:					
Property, plant and equipment, net	$364,111	$407,206	$285,159	$271,928	$236,685
Total assets	1,975,355	2,158,263	2,438,411	2,483,596	2,533,952
Total long-term debt, convertible debt, and redeemable preferred stock	598,158	422,906	327,485	344,461	325,338

NM = Not meaningful

Net income (loss) per share for Quantum common stock for fiscal year 2000 is not meaningful because the amount is for the period April 11, 1999 through August 3, 1999, and therefore would not be comparable with the preceding fiscal years. Net loss for Quantum common stock for this period, basic and diluted, is $(0.10).

Exhibit 2 (continued)

Pro forma net income (loss) per share for HDDG assumes the recapitalization occurred at the beginning of the earliest period presented.

	At or For the Year Ended March 31,				
	1996	1997	1998	1999	2000
	(in thousands, except per-share amounts)				
Statement of Operations Data					
Business unit:					
Desktop:					
Revenue	$3,349,735	$4,004,828	$3,981,614	$3,079,437	$2,784,808
Gross profit	511,390	565,681	453,278	232,036	129,429
Unit operating profit (loss)	290,767	300,287	184,331	(49,132)	(154,963)
High-end:					
Revenue	$737,426	$586,616	$633,821	$519,883	$526,771
Gross profit (loss)	(73,974)	(10,721)	(80,790)	59,383	100,641
Unit operating profit	(416,620)	(154,184)	(250,136)	(93,323)	(35,961)
Recording heads:					
Unit operating loss	(69,967)	(109,632)	(8,592)	--	--
Loss from investee	--	--	(66,060)	(142,050)	--
Combined group:					
Revenue	$4,087,161	$4,591,444	$4,615,435	$3,599,320	$3,311,579
Gross profit	415,807	498,402	373,307	291,419	230,070
Research and development expenses	214,148	261,293	258,916	253,893	242,383
Sales and marketing, general and administrative expenses	188,357	200,638	188,788	169,981	176,273
Restructuring/special charge	209,122	--	--	--	2,338
Income (loss) from operations	(195,820)	36,471	(73,397)	(132,455)	(190,924)
Net income (loss)	$(125,429)	$41,055	$(52,858)	$(152,526)	$(104,770)
Pro forma net income (loss) per share:					
Basic	$(2.43)	$0.70	$(0.78)	$(1.90)	$(1.26)
Diluted	$(2.43)	$0.58	$(0.78)	$(1.90)	$(1.26)
Balance Sheet Data:					
Property, plant and equipment, net	$333,976	$368,092	$227,760	$198,806	$158,548
Total assets	1,740,949	1,721,402	1,646,340	1,469,953	1,478,048
Total long-term debt, convertible debt, and redeemable preferred stock	288,008	140,969	109,161	114,820	108,446

Source: Quantum.com Annual Report: Confidential Financials.

Exhibit 3 Stock Values Before and After the Stock Split

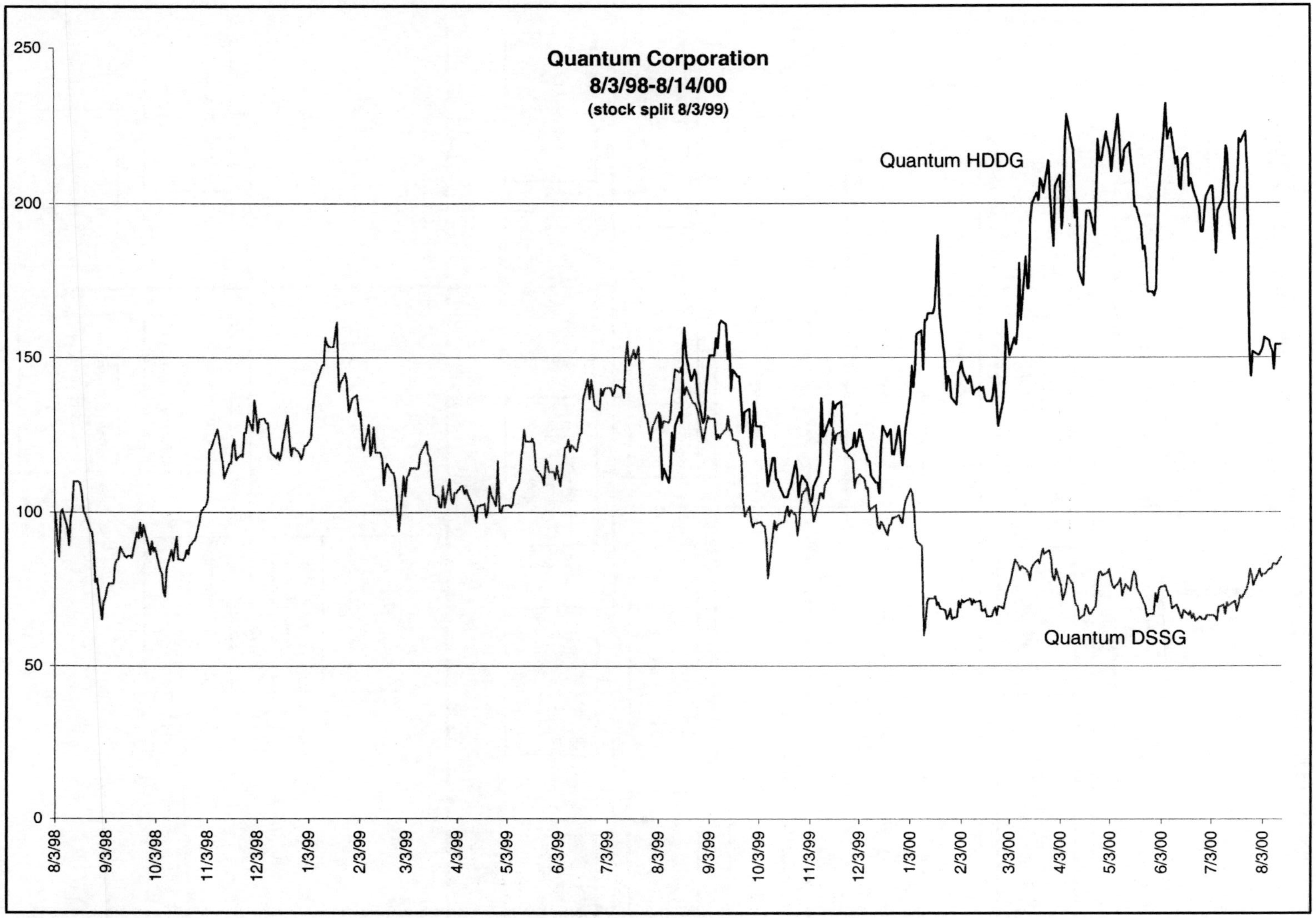

Source: Datastream.

Exhibit 4 HDD Leadership

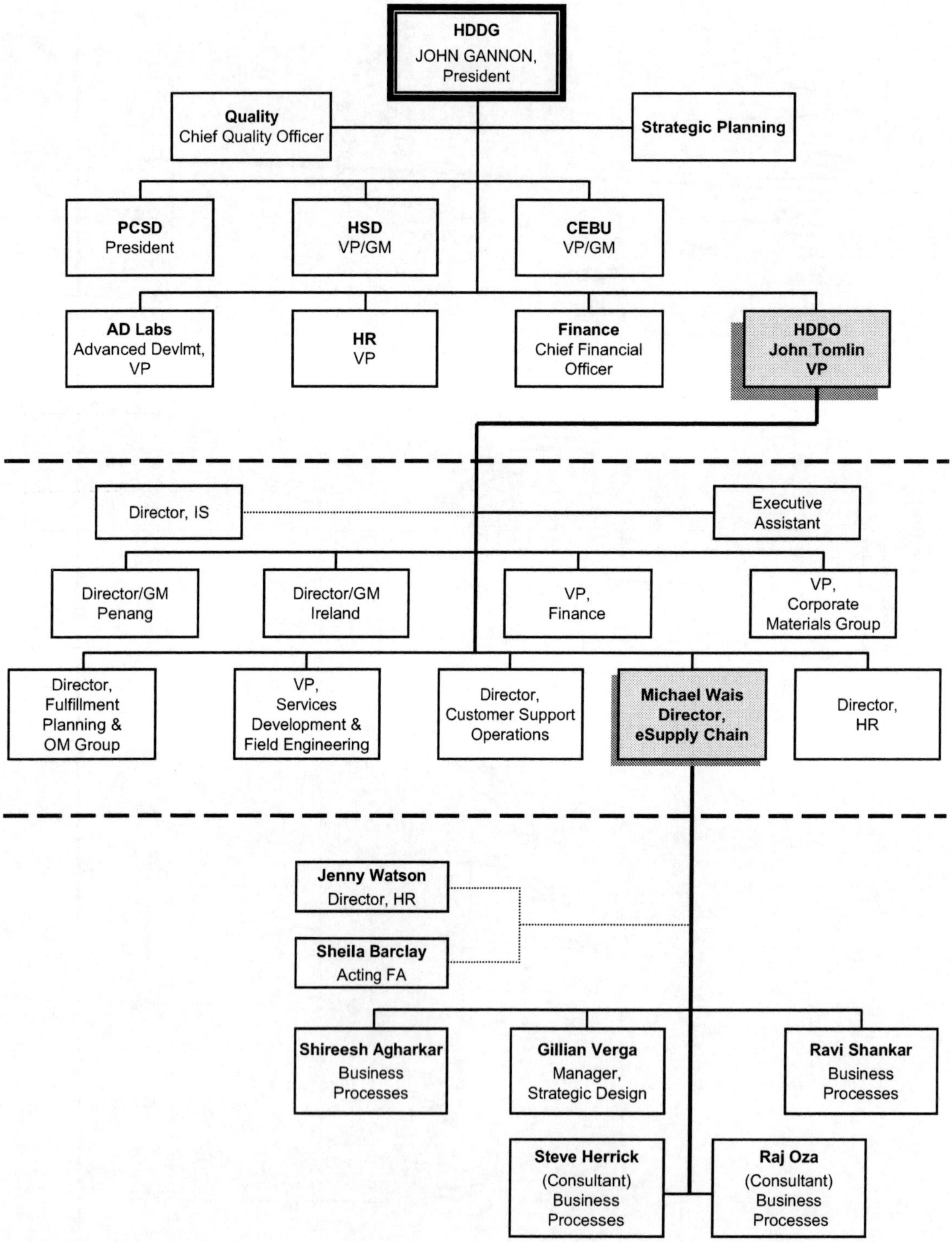

Source: Company documents.

Exhibit 5 Possible Changes in the Supply Chain

Future Possibilities

FROM	TO
Forecast-Driven	Order-Driven
OEM & Disti	Multiple Channels
Physical Inventory	Information
Closed Systems	Collaborative Systems
Predictability	Responsiveness and Flexibility
Manual Reporting	Collaborative Information Sharing
Allocation	Quick Response to Market Trends
Fixed Priority list	Profit/Priority Optimization
Weekly Planning	Event-driven Planning
Plan Changed By Local Managers	Plan Executed Consistently
Regional Allocation Buckets	Global Availability
Difficult to Establish New Accounts	Plug-n-Play Links with Partners
Call Center	Multi-Technology Support
Onsite Tech Support	Remote Tech Support

Source: Company documents.

Exhibit 6 Press Release

HIGH-TECH INDUSTRY LEADERS ANNOUNCE OPEN INTERNET EXCHANGE FOR COMPUTER AND ELECTRONICS MARKETPLACE

AMD, Compaq, Gateway, Hitachi, HP, Infineon, NEC, Quantum, Samsung, SCI Systems, Solectron, Western Digital to form independent company for high-tech supply chain, increasing business efficiency and customer value

NEW YORK, May 1, 2000—Twelve high-tech industry leaders today announced their intent to launch an independent company that will operate an open Internet exchange to serve the needs of the high-tech supply-chain community.

The new venture will provide services to buyers and sellers involved in computing and electronics-related industries. The exchange is expected to enable these businesses to manage their supply chains more efficiently and effectively, improve delivery of products and services to the marketplace, and increase customer satisfaction.

An estimated $600 billion* in online business-to-business sales of high-tech components and parts will occur over the next few years, making this the world's largest e-marketplace opportunity. The founding companies are some of the world's largest buyers and suppliers of computer and electronics components and products and have developed considerable expertise in efficient procurement and sales.

The exchange's end-to-end services will be open and available to all parties in the supply-chain process—consumer and business electronics makers, contract manufacturers, suppliers, and distributors. All participants in this electronic marketplace will be able to manage a wide array of their e-procurement purchases and sales through this new exchange.

"The creation of such an exchange can improve supply-chain efficiency tremendously through cost reduction, timely transactions, inventory savings, and higher-value services," said Dr. Hau Lee, professor of Operations, Information and Technology, Stanford Business School. "But most importantly, it will enable supply-chain partners to fundamentally redesign their business processes and create new business opportunities from end to end. This is a major step toward a virtual economy for the high-tech industry."

In addition to delivering the traditional benefits of the Web, such as continuous global reach and open industry-standard interfaces, the new high-tech exchange is expected to: lower manufacturing and purchasing transaction costs through process efficiencies; reduce levels of inventory throughout the entire supply chain by better matching supply and demand via the online marketplace; increase customer satisfaction by improving the ability to deliver products more quickly and predictably; provide expertise on supply chain "best practices" to help participants achieve better results from product design to customer delivery.

The new company will use best-in-class technology to deliver a variety of services to participants, including open sourcing, e-catalogs, auctions and dynamic pricing, supply planning and logistics. It will acquire some of this capability from its founders, who have already developed services for efficient buying and selling over the Internet. The exchange will use this expertise to start delivering immediate value to all members.

The exchange is expected to begin operations within 90 days. The founders plan to contribute resources and an initial total of $100 million to the new company and will have equal ownership in it. They intend to use the exchange for their own supply-chain activities, driving significant transaction volumes through it.

A full-time interim management team, comprised of representatives from the founders, has been chartered to finalize the formation of the new company and launch the business. More details on the exchange are available at www.converge.com.

* Data point from "eMarketplaces Boost B2B Trade," Forrester Research, Inc. Feb. 2000.

This press release contains statements that are forward-looking. These statements are based on current expectations as of the date of release.

Exhibit 7 Converge Frequently Asked Questions

Q: Who are the founders of the High-Tech Exchange?

A: Founders represent every stage of the high-technology supply chain: global OEMs, CEMs, Suppliers and Distributors. The companies are AMD, Agilent, Canon, Compaq, Gateway, Hiatchi, HP, NEC, Quantum, Samsung, SCI Systems, Solectron, Synnex, Tatung, and Western Digital.

Q: Do the founders include technology partners and venture capitalists?

A: The High-Tech Exchange is committed to operate independently, free from influences outside the high-tech supply chain—"by the industry, for the industry." The exchange will be built on best-in-class solutions from a variety of vendors, not locked in to one or two partners. and while an IPO is always a possibility, it is not a focus of the company, so venture capital participation seems inappropriate at this time.

Q: Will the founders jointly operate the exchange?

A: Founders will be equal shareholders in an open, independent exchange. The exchange will select an independent Board of Directors from outside the founders group. The exchange is now recruiting a management team to handle day-to-day operations, replacing an Interim Launch Team of over 50 executives and specialists on loan from the founding companies.

Q: What services will the exchange offer at its launch?

A: At launch, the exchange will offer services focused on procurement: auctions, catalog management, information services and administration (workflow, audience selection). Additional services to enable supply chain collaboration, advanced logistics and collaborative product design will be added on an aggressive schedule.

Q: How will the new company generate revenue?

A: Revenues will come from transaction fees as well as value-added services such as consulting and information services. Exchange fees will be competitively priced—given the value of these services, the exchange expects strong participation.

Q: Will the High-Tech Exchange be primarily a buyer's or seller's marketplace?

A: Both. In the same way as leading financial exchanges, the exchange will provide a confidential and secure way of transacting business for both buyers and sellers, together with information and other services to support those transactions.

Q: Will the exchange adopt open standards, or develop its own?

A: The High-Tech Exchange is committed to integrate its systems seamlessly with its participants' procurement, manufacturing and logistics systems. The exchange has standardized on XML, and is working actively with RosettaNet to standardize its supply-chain interface.

Q: How will the exchange assure confidentiality and security of participants' transactions?

A: The exchange must be a trusted place for high-tech companies to transact business. Consistent with its "best-in-class" approach to technology, the High-Tech Exchange is working with top security, authentication and industry experts to develop an infrastructure that exceeds its participants' requirements. The exchange will also offer options including anonymous transactions and bidder selection to assure transaction confidentiality where requested.

Q: Who is the contact for companies who want to join the High-Tech Exchange?

A: Companies may join the exchange by registering at the website.

Source: www.converge.com

HARVARD | BUSINESS | SCHOOL

9-802-024
REV: JANUARY 7, 2002

ROGER HALLOWELL
CATE REAVIS

Monster.com: Success Beyond the Bubble

In Fall 2001, Jeff Taylor, founder and CEO of Monster.com (Monster), the leading online career search service provider, noted that growth, while still remarkable, was slowing. After achieving growth rates of 25% per quarter in 1999 and 2000 (see **Exhibit 1**), he predicted Monster's revenue would grow 50% in all of 2001 with 75% of that growth coming from new clients. Despite the slowdown, Taylor believed great opportunities lay ahead for Monster:

> With the baby boomers nearing retirement, we are facing severe labor shortages. Companies could very well go out of business because of the mass exodus of employees. Employees are going to be the main driver in the hiring shift we will be witnessing. We need to put employees at the center. Our aim is to empower the job seeker.

Maynard, Massachusetts-based Monster was the leading online job site with 485,000 job postings. In June 2001, Media Metrix[1] rated Monster the number one destination for career seekers and the forty-ninth most visited U.S. Internet site. Monster had a reach of 7.3% (percent of U.S. population that visited the site), an average of 31.1 pages viewed per user, and a power ranking of 227 (reach multiplied by average page views), more than six times the power ranking of its closest career site competitor. The site drew 6.5 million unique visitors in June 2001, up from 4.4 million in June 2000.[2] Through its four-year, $100 million deal with AOL (signed at the end of 1999), Monster was the exclusive provider of career search services to AOL's 27 million subscribers in the United States and Canada. Monster accounted for 50% of the online recruitment advertising market.[3]

In 2000, Monster's total gross billings were $364 million; 99% of Monster's revenue came from employers via job postings and subscriptions to the resume database. Based on feedback received from a May 2001 survey sent by a third party to 8,500 Monster customers that included questions such as, "Would you recommend our site?" Monster managers boasted that they had achieved 93% customer loyalty.

---

[1] Media Metrix analyzed and measured the impact of the Internet and new technologies on commerce and marketing.

[2] "Monster.com strengthens lead in career category," *Business Wire*, July 12, 2001.

[3] Market share refers to percentage of eyeball minutes compared with other career sites.

Senior Researcher Cate Reavis, Global Research Group, prepared this case under the supervision of Professor Roger Hallowell. HBS cases are developed solely as the basis for class discussion. Cases are not intended to serve as endorsements, sources of primary data, or illustrations of effective or ineffective management.

Taylor and his team were faced with how best to grow going forward, keeping in mind the objectives of both clientele groups Monster served: job seekers who aimed to "earn, learn, and yearn"(earn a salary, learn new career enhancing skills, and yearn for a higher position and salary) and employers who aimed to "obtain, train, and retain" (find employees, provide them opportunities to improve their skills, and, as a result, reduce employee turnover).

Genesis of Monster

In May 1989, Taylor and six investors founded ADION, a niche-advertising agency that designed and placed recruitment advertisements in traditional media for Boston-area high-tech companies. By mid-1993, ADION employed 30 people and the company was billing $6 million annually. The demand for high-tech staffing and the fast growth of ADION were catalysts for building something bigger and more efficient. Taylor recalled:

> For weeks we'd been trying to come up with something big and different to offer our clients, who were really pushing us for new ideas. But all we came up with was print-based solutions. One day, I woke up with this "monster" idea. So with a little bit of knowledge about the Internet and a dream-induced brainstorm, I began to sketch out this completely new platform for matching job seekers with employers, and The Monster Board was born. The monster theme was important because we were talking about something really big, with attitude, that would stand out, like a monster.[4]

The Monster Board, along with its official monster mascot, Trump, was officially launched in 1994. Taylor recalled the public's initial reaction: "We were the first company to advertise on the radio with a URL. After that we received email from some MIT students saying 'Welcome!' and one email from an engineering student saying, 'No! Stop this commercialization of the Web!', as a response to our radio advertising."[5] Launching The Monster Board, Taylor explained, proved challenging since its existence depended on attracting content from both job seekers and employers, and eyeball minutes from job seekers:

> We convinced 30 of our best (ADION) clients to let us "use" their jobs for free, and then we spent $50,000 on radio advertising to jumpstart the applicant flow. And we got no response. As a result, we gave free job postings to about 50 companies.
>
> By Fall of 1994, we had about 400 jobs on the board and 100 visitors a day. We hit a tense moment when employers wanted to take their jobs down, and the newspapers wouldn't run advertising for our site. But we made sure we had good jobs. We kept doing radio and emphasizing our brand. Eventually we turned the corner.[6]

In 1995, TMP Worldwide, a nearly 20-year-old global recruitment advertising company with offices worldwide, approached Taylor about a possible acquisition. At the time, Monster was struggling with creating a solid national operation and was contemplating hiring local salespeople to develop a client base in major cities. TMP's global presence and large client base—especially through its portfolio of recruitment agencies—provided Monster immediate access to a wide array of human

[4] "Monster.com," HBS No. 801-145, written by Dickson L. Louie under the supervision of Professor Jeffrey F. Rayport.

[5] Ibid.

[6] Ibid.

capital and potential clients.[7] Two months after TMP's proposal, Taylor agreed to the deal. Marketing of The Monster Board to TMP clients began prior to the acquisition, which was finalized in November 1995.

TMP

TMP, which originally stood for Telephone Marketing Program, was founded in 1967. By 2001, TMP had over 17,000 clients, including 90 *Fortune* 100 companies and 450 of all *Fortune* 500 companies.[8] Its 9,000 employees served the yellow pages advertising market, and the intern-to-CEO job-recruitment markets through its Directional Marketing, Advertising and Communications, eResourcing, Interactive, and Executive Search businesses (see **Exhibit 2**).

Yellow Pages Directional Marketing, TMP's original business, created classified advertisements for roughly 7,000 yellow page directories. With $98 million in revenue in 2000 and a 90% retention rate, TMP was the leading yellow page agency in the world, accounting for 30% of the U.S. market.

Recruitment Advertising In 1993, TMP launched its Recruitment Advertising business (later renamed Advertising and Communications), that offered clients comprehensive recruitment advertising services, including creation and placement of classified advertising, development of employer and corporate image campaigns and recruitment materials, and implementation of alternative recruitment programs, such as job fairs and campus recruiting.[9]

Temporary and Mid-Market Recruiting TMP's eResourcing business was a temporary contracting (one day up to 12 months) and mid-market recruitment service (annual salary range $50,000 to $150,000) that relied on classified ads and database searches as well as direct telephone solicitation to attract candidates.

TMP's Interactive division included Monster.com and Monstermoving.com (an online relocation and moving service). Total Interactive commissions and fees were $435 million in 2000.[10]

Executive Search Finally, TMP's Executive Search business ranked number six in the world with $178 million in revenue in 2000. This division provided senior-level search services for professionals earning over $250,000.

In 2000, Monster accounted for 83% of Interactive's revenue and 28% of TMP's total revenue; Monster's revenue was predicted to reach 50% of TMP's total revenue in 2001. (See **Exhibits 3** and **4** for selected TMP and Monster financials and stock performance.)

---

[7] T. Brett Manderfield, Brian Gesuale, and Gina M. Parizek, "TMP Worldwide," *U.S. Bancorp Piper Jaffray*, August 2001.

[8] "Monster.com," HBS No. 801-145, written by Dickson L. Louie under the supervision of Professor Jeffrey F. Rayport.

[9] Ibid.

[10] Represents all fees earned by TMP's businesses via the Internet.

The Recruitment Industry[11]

Approximately 15% of the U.S. full-time workforce turned over every year (see **Table A**). In addition, Monster's managers believed that globalization, technology, and the retirement of baby boomers were providing firms and organizations involved in the recruitment industry new growth opportunities (see **Exhibit 5**).

Table A U.S. Employee Churn

	Overall Workforce
U.S. total full-time workforce	131,000,000
Average turnover/Year	15%
Annual turnover	19,650,000
Average salary/Year	$31,063
Average cost to replace/Employee	$10,871
Cost to replace employees	$213.6 billion

Source: U.S. Bancorp Piper Jaffray via *Monster.com* (accessed October 4, 2001).

The recruitment industry was comprised of firms such as Manpower that found temporary help to fill short-term office/clerical positions and received a portion of their hourly charge, permanent placement firms that placed individuals in permanent clerical, administrative, and entry-level management positions and were paid on a contingency basis (only after successfully placing a candidate), and retainer firms such as Korn Ferry International that filled upper management and senior executive positions. Retainer firms received part of their fee at the beginning of a search and billed on an installment basis. Fees generally ended up being equivalent to one-third of the individual's starting salary. Two of the largest publicly-traded firms, Korn Ferry International and Heidrick & Struggles, had lost 66% and 75% of their value, respectively, since early 2000.[12]

Companies seeking to recruit new employees often placed "help wanted" ads in the classified sections of newspapers (TMP's recruitment advertising division facilitated this process). The average price for a two-inch by five-inch help wanted ad in a major metropolitan paper was $5,000 a day. For many local newspapers, recruitment classified advertising made the difference between profit and loss. Help wanted advertising accounted for 17.9% ($8.7 billion) of newspaper ad revenues in 2000.[13]

By 2001, online recruiting was gaining in popularity and cutting into the profit margins that newspapers historically relied on (see **Exhibit 6**). Many newspapers were scaling down their operations as a result. In June 2001, 185 employees at *The Boston Globe* took advantage of a voluntary buyout/early retirement plan; 70 were reporters, editors, or photographers. *The Boston Globe* acknowledged that a severe drop in ad revenues from classifieds was the main cause for the forced

[11] Portions of this section were adapted from "Monster.com", HBS No. 801-145, written by Dickson L. Louie under the supervision of Professor Jeffrey F. Rayport.

[12] Reed Abelson, "Executive search fall with dot-coms," *The New York Times*, August 12, 2001.

[13] Lanny Baker, William G. Bird, and Eileen Furukawa, "TMP Worldwide: Monster quietly devours help wanted marketshare," *Salomon Smith Barney*, July 16, 2001.

cuts. In addition to the buyout plan, the paper had scaled down the number of printed articles and cut back on certain special interest sections. A number of other newspapers were also cutting back.[14] Salomon Smith Barney estimated that by 2003, online advertising would erode newspaper recruitment revenues by $3 billion and would account for 11.6% of total recruitment industry revenue (newspaper and online recruitment advertising) in 2001, up from 6.1% in 2000.[15] In 2000, Monster generated more than 50% of the equivalent recruitment revenue earned by *The New York Times*, the largest help wanted franchise in the United States.[16]

Between January 1998 and 1999, the use of online recruitment by *Fortune 500* companies grew from 17% to 45% spanning high-tech and low-tech industries. Salomon Smith Barney predicted that by 2003, 100% of large, 60% of medium-sized, and 20% of small companies would run online recruitment advertising.[17]

Online corporate boards were also becoming popular. Job openings at Microsoft were posted on its *Microsoft.com/jobs* site. In a 2001 survey, 40% of job seekers queried responded that seeking employment listings on corporate websites was the most useful online search method, up from 30% in 2000. [18]

There were also a number of niche online recruiters: dice.com was an online job site for the high-tech industry; guru.com and SkillsVillage were online recruiters for independent contractors (free agents); and Korn Ferry International's FutureStep focused on online senior executive searches.

One study by an executive recruiting research firm found that Internet recruiting cut the recruiting cycle from 90 to 28 days, 30 to 7 days for candidate identification, 30 to 14 days for interview and assessment, and 30 to 7 days for closing. Average cost per hire using online recruitment was $1,000, compared to permanent placement/executive search ($12,000), newspapers ($5,000), job fairs ($3,000), and campus recruiting ($2,000) (see **Exhibit 7**).

Industry Consolidation

In 2001, there was consolidation among the leading online job boards. CareerBuilder, a joint venture between the Tribune Company and Knight Ridder, agreed to buy HeadHunter.net for $200 million. The new company would be able to cross sell ads between the site and Knight Ridder's 32 daily papers and the Tribune's 11. The papers planned to rename their Sunday employment section, CareerBuilder. The combined company was expected to have revenue of $100 million in 2002. CareerBuilder's CEO said the HeadHunter deal would create a Coke vs. Pepsi rivalry between CareerBuilder and Monster.[19] See **Exhibit 8** for marketshare of the leading U.S. online job boards.

---

14 Monica Brady, "Boston Globe cuts staff, cuts size," WBUR: *Morning Edition*, July 16, 2001.

15 Lanny Baker, William G. Bird, and Eileen Furukawa, "TMP Worldwide: Monster quietly devours help wanted marketshare," *Salomon Smith Barney*, July 16, 2001.

16 Ibid.

17 Ibid.

18 Jennifer Gill, "Now Hiring," *Business Week*, July 18, 2001.

19 Patricia Callahan, "CareerBuilder venture to buy online recruiter headhunter," *The Wall Street Journal*, August 27, 2001.

Monster in 2001

Organization

In Spring 2001, Monster underwent an organizational restructuring. The number of executives reporting directly to Taylor fell from 17 to three. The three were new positions including Group President Global Sales, Marketing, Customer Service and Partnerships; Group President Finance, HR and Administration; and, Group President Strategy, Product and Technology. All three group presidents had been promoted from the Monster management team and had worked for other TMP divisions or had extensive experience in the recruitment industry. Many of Monster's other senior executives came from TMP.

Products/Services and Pricing

For Job Seekers The Monster site offered a number of services for job seekers, at no cost to them. The most popular service was MonsterSearch, which granted seekers access to the Monster.com database of job postings. Seekers could search for jobs by location, career level, discipline (administrative, finance, healthcare, human resources, Internet, legal, retail, sales, technology), and special interests (self-employment, work abroad). A keyword search option enabled users to enter specific keywords to match skills, job titles, and other requirements. All matches would immediately be displayed. Through the site's MyMonster feature, seekers could create automatic job search agents that would send email notification when a job listing matched their criteria and store up to five online resumes and cover letters to use to apply online to jobs.

Also popular was Resume City, a portion of Monster's website where job seekers could post their resumes. A seeker could post his resume in three ways: (1) Public, a seeker's complete resume could be reviewed by member companies (employers). (2) Confidential, a seeker's skills and employment history could be reviewed by employers, but his name and current employer were withheld. Note that if an employer indicated an interest in a seeker's skills, an e-mail could be sent to the seeker asking for permission to divulge his identify to that particular employer. (3) Private, no employer could review any data through searches. However, the seeker could send his resume to selected companies. Monster's database contained over 13.5 million resumes with more than 20,000 received daily.

ChiefMonster was a career resource for senior executives. A five-minute validation process screened applicants for senior-level positions and granted approved executives access to the premium-content portion of the website. Approved executives could explore senior-level opportunities posted by a wide range of employers and search firms, create a personal profile, and access content on the latest industry trends and salary levels for senior-level positions. As of Fall 2001, 150,000 members had posted resumes on ChiefMonster. ChiefMonster accounted for $1.2 million in revenue in 2000.

Through Monster's TalentMarket site, contractors, independent professionals, consultants, and freelancers seeking nonpermanent employment positions could auction their skills and talents to the highest bidder. Seekers used the site to build a personal profile, receive and accept bids from employers, and negotiate contract terms. On average, there were 40,000 auctions per day, although many did not result in a placement; Monster received $1,000 for each match made.

The Monster site also provided job seekers with resume advice, tips on interviewing, and overall career guidance.

For Employers Monster.com served employers (called "members") in a number of ways. Employers could post jobs on the site. While prices varied depending on the number of positions posted, single job postings were priced at $295 a month. Approximately 52% of Monster's revenue in 2000 came from job postings, down from 73% in 1998. Employers could also buy access to Monster's database of resumes that job seekers had posted on the site. Roughly 36% of Monster's revenue came from database subscriptions, up from 8% in 1998. For an additional fee per job search of $2,250, companies could subscribe to WebDragon, Monster's electronic search service. In WebDragon, an employee of both TMP and Monster matched job postings with resumes in the Monster database; Monster would then email employers "hand" selected resumes that fit the qualifications indicated on the job posting.

Monster provided a number of "memberships" that varied in length and products/services offered. For $5,500, employers could purchase Monster's three-month introductory membership that included 15 job postings and three-months access to the resume database. Salespeople could customize memberships to meet a client's particular needs (see **Exhibit 9**).

Monster also sold private label applications of its interactive products. This software enabled companies to adopt the Monster.com technology when posting jobs on their corporate intranet sites.

Serving Job Posters (Employers)

Monster's sales force made up 35% of its 2,700 employees. The U.S. sales force was divided into field and telesales representatives. Roughly 36% of Monster's sales came from the field sales channel. Monster's 36 field representatives typically worked with companies with 500 or more employees. Average order size in the field was over $70,000. Monster's 140 U.S. telesales representatives worked mainly with start-ups and small and mid-sized companies. Telesales accounted for 55% of Monster's revenue. Average order size in telesales was approximately $3,000. Remaining sales came from Monster's e-commerce channel, a self-service sales link on the Monster site accessible by any employer. The e-commerce channel was typically used by first-time Monster job posters who then became leads for the telesales force.

Top field sales representatives could make over $500,000 per year, but on average, field sales representatives earned cash compensation of $200,000 per year. Top telesales representatives could make over $125,000 per year; on average telesales representatives made $100,000. Total sales costs were approximately 10% of revenues. Additional costs associated with sales (telephone, travel, occupancy, etc.) were often 50% of personnel costs in sales intensive organizations.

Sales representatives' performance was measured on a number of metrics presented in **Table B.** As one executive noted, sales representatives were trained to offer customized solutions based on a potential client's needs: "Our sales people don't go in and boast about the Monster site. Instead they tell clients 'This is what we can do for you.' We are focused on the relationship." Monster's and TMP's sales representatives were encouraged to cross sell each other's services. By Fall 2001, 8% of Monster's clients came from existing relationships with TMP.

Table B Monster's Sales Force Performance Measurements

Telesales	Field
Number new accounts	Number new accounts
Average order size	Average contract size
Renewal percentage	Account growth
Number of outbound calls	Renewal percentage
Minutes of outbound talk time	New product sales
Number of zero days (zero sales)	Customer touch points
New product sales	Global sales (non-U.S. company accounts)

Source: Monster.com.

Monster also operated two call centers with a staff of over 100 client-relations representatives in the United States who provided service to existing employer customers: one in Maynard, Massachusetts and a second in Indianapolis, Indiana. (The company also had call centers in Glasgow, Scotland and Sydney, Australia.) Client relations representatives made under $50,000 annually and could earn an additional $1,000 per quarter in bonus if they exceeded certain performance goals, including quick response time to incoming calls. Outside observers estimated total customer service costs (salaries and related variable overhead) were approximately 6% of revenues. Total client-relations-representative turnover at Monster was less than 10%; managers noted that average turnover at U.S. call centers was approximately 40%.

Marketing

Monster managers believed that marketing costs would decrease as a percentage of total revenues as the company continued to grow and the industry experienced further consolidation. In 2001, marketing costs were expected to reach $220 million up from $161 million in 2000. [20] Taylor was committed to delivering a 25% operating profit in 2001 on estimated revenues of $543 million, with marketing consuming 41% of total revenue for the year.

Growth Opportunities

Early Growth

During the late 1990s, Taylor and his team focused on getting out the Monster message. In 1999, Monster launched its *When I Grow Up* campaign, a series of ads quoting fresh-faced, elementary-aged school children with low career expectations: "When I grow up, I want to claw my way up to middle management," stated one. This statement was followed by, "When I grow up, I want to be forced into early retirement." "When I grow up, I want to have a brown nose," stated another. The ads were first shown during a 30-second commercial during the 1999 Super Bowl. Monster spent 15% of

[20] T. Brett Manderfield, Brian Gesuale, and Gina M. Parizek, "TMP Worldwide," *U.S. Bancorp Piper Jaffray*, August 2001.

its $32 million 1999 advertising budget on the Super Bowl spot. Within a 24-hour period after the spot's airing, searches on Monster's site increased 450%. Between 1995 and 1999, Monster's revenue grew from $6.9 million to $133.5 million (CAGR of 80.85%).

In Fall 2001, Taylor and his team were investing in new markets and products to further leverage the Monster brand.

New Products/Services

Monster began offering employers additional services to help them create more efficient recruiting operations. Employers communicated their desire for additional services through a survey Monster sent out in the Fall of 2000. "One thing we learned," explained a manager, "was that employers need help screening and tracking applicants. Sourcing applicants is no longer the challenge that it was when the employment market was incredibly tight."

MonsterMomentum Through MonsterMomentum, Monster's Web-based hiring management system, employers could access screening, tracking and reporting services. Screening enabled companies to create a customized questionnaire for a particular position that was automatically linked to its job posting. Upon applying for a position, applicants would have to complete the questionnaire. As a Monster manager noted, screening allowed companies to quickly identify the most qualified candidates without having to review every resume while it enabled Monster to better understand employers who used the site: "By analyzing the relationship between (1) candidates companies ultimately hire, and (2) questionnaire results of those recruited, we will eventually have a clearer picture of what a company using our services is looking for. We will then be in a better position to help that company create a more efficient recruiting system."

The tracking feature enabled employers to see where candidates were in the interview/hiring process (i.e., how many interviews they had completed and with whom, whether an offer had been made, etc.). Reporting allowed employers to track every dimension of the recruiting process. Progress reports presented employers with up-to-the-minute status on recruiting efforts. Employers could request a summary report that monitored and measured the effectiveness (both in time and overall cost) of a particular recruiting effort. While these services were components of MonsterMomentum, one executive explained that they would eventually be broken up and offered in a number of different "bundles" in the future. Prices for the new services had not been determined. MonsterMomentum was launched in November 2000 and had Q1 2001 revenue of $657,000.

Site Seminars Monster also provided seminars to employers on using the Monster site (and the Internet overall) to create a more efficient recruitment system. Monster offered both free sessions that lasted a couple of hours and a one-day *Power Recruiting on the Internet* seminar (for $995 per person) which focused on more advanced techniques.

Job-Posting Services Resulting from TMP's May 2001 acquisition of Hiring Tools, a Web-based, HR software application provider, Monster's Job Posting Services offered employers a tool to help them create effective job descriptions and interview guidelines for both internal use and external job postings. The tool could be purchased for a 15% premium on the standard membership packages Monster offered. It would eventually be offered as a private label product so that companies could use it at will in-house.

While there was consensus among Monster's senior executives on the value of offering more services, executives believed that Monster needed to be clearer in communicating its array of services and products to its clients, particularly employers: "Many clients are unaware of the scope of services and products available," one noted.

Broadening Clientele

Monster was exploring a number of new recruitment segments. One was the hourly job market (66% of the U.S. workforce, according to Taylor) in which employers sought to fill paid-by-the-hour positions in, for example, grocery stores, video stores, or other local retail. "We want to create a system that allows all candidates to search by geographic location and pay," explained one manager. He continued, "For those without Internet access, we want to create an Interactive Voice Response system through which they can answer basic questions, create a personal profile, and have it posted on the Web. The job agent will then pass on the information to appropriate employers who then call the candidate if interested."

Monster was also exploring the government and military sectors as other potential clientele. In June 2001, Monster formed a partnership with the U.S. Department of Labor, to develop a global standard to classify jobs and the skills they required. Another partnership was formed with Janes.com, an online resource for information on the defense, aerospace, transport, and security industries. The goal of the partnership was to create a co-branded site that would provide job information for those particular sectors. Approximately 23.5 million people worked in the aerospace, defense, transport and security industries in Europe and the United States alone.[21]

Geographic Expansion

Monster.com operated sites in the United States and 20 other countries.[22] According to one Monster executive, the company entered markets where TMP already had an infrastructure.

In Fall 2001, Monster's global expansion strategy was focused on European profitability. Noted one executive, "We want our European operations to be as profitable as our U.S. operations. That will help fuel further expansion. This will take size." In July 2001, TMP completed its $115 million cash acquisition of Sweden-based JobLine, one of Europe's leading online professional search companies with operations in 11 European countries. The acquisition gave Monster a presence in 14 European countries.

Each Monster site was tailored to the local language and culture. For example, not every country site had the same category/industry selections. Although Monster retained one advertising agency to serve all of its European sites, the company relied on local country managers to create sites based on local industry trends. The way in which Monster sold its services was also based largely on local customs. As a manager explained, "In France, sales are generally made through recruitment advertising agencies. We learned from one company we recently acquired that their French site had failed because they were targeting companies directly as opposed to reaching them through recruitment advertising agencies. Now we focus our marketing dollars on agencies." Monster had over one million job seeker accounts (500,000 resumes) and was the leading career site (based on power ranking) in the United Kingdom, the Netherlands, and Italy. (See **Exhibits 10** and **11** for information on Monster's international growth and data on European online job recruiters.)

---

[21] "Monster.com, Janes tie-up to launch job channel," *Business Standard*, June 13, 2001.

[22] Australia, Belgium, Canada, Denmark, Finland, France, Germany, Hong Kong, India, Ireland, Italy, Luxembourg, the Netherlands, New Zealand, Norway, Singapore, Spain, Sweden, Switzerland, and the United Kingdom.

Lifelong Relationships

Creating life-long relationships, particularly with job seekers, was considered a key strategy. "As part of our intern-to-CEO strategy, we would like to form relationships early and retain them through various product/service offerings," explained one manager. As a result, TMP acquired CollegeLink and FastWeb, providing Monster the opportunity to capture a new segment of pre-career clientele. Both of the acquired sites provided information on colleges and scholarships and were merged into Monster's campus offerings (the "Monstertrak" site). Through these two services, as one manager stated, Monster could "start building relationships with potential job seekers before the beginning of their careers, and help schools and career counselors direct students toward the appropriate schools and jobs."

TMP also acquired Jobtrak, a site that served students at more than 1,000 colleges, as well as alumni associations and MBA programs, providing job listings and a resume database. More than 500,000 employers used Jobtrak (renamed Monstertrak) to target college students for internships as well as part-time and full-time positions. As of Fall 2001, 600,000 resumes and 300,000 jobs were posted on the site.[23]

Monster's partnership with the U.S. Olympic Committee, according to one Monster executive, was another example of attempts at building lifelong relationships. TeamUSAnet, a partnership formed in July 2001 between Monster and the U.S. Olympic Committee, was the first career management website created specifically for Olympic athletes. The sight would include a number of career management tools such as resume builders, job search access, and an Olympic mentoring network to help athletes find careers after the conclusion of their Olympic experience. Monster planned to host an iFair (online career fair) to connect Olympic athletes with potential employers.[24]

Complementary Businesses

In 2000, Monster launched two new businesses to compliment Monster's core career management site: MonsterMoving.com and MonsterLearning.com.

MonsterMoving MonsterMoving, a portal for relocation information and services, was launched in October 2000. As one executive explained, "MonsterMoving is a natural extension of Monster.com since many job seekers are willing to move for a new job. In addition, TMP's yellow page division receives 35% of its revenues from the placement of yellow page advertisements for moving services." According to Tom Zorn, the head of MonsterMoving, 17 million families spent up to $100 billion moving each year. He added that moving companies spent 4% to 5% of their revenue on advertising.

MonsterMoving featured information on moving companies. It also facilitated home and apartment searches (the site profiled 1.4 million new and existing houses and 45,000 rental properties), and mortgage and insurance quotes (1,400 participating lenders covering more than 124 loan programs). Also provided was information on schools and community resources including relocation information on 1,500 cities in the United States.

Roughly 25% of MonsterMoving's revenue came from banner advertisements. Another 25% came from listings in which clients (such as mortgage companies) paid MonsterMoving $199 a year to be

[23] T. Brett Manderfield, Brian Gesuale, and Gina M. Parizek, "TMP Worldwide," *U.S. Bancorp Piper Jaffray*, August 2001.

[24] "Monster.com debuts first career management website for U.S. Olympic athletes and hopefuls," *Business Wire*, July 11, 2001.

listed in its directory. Another 20% of revenue came from private label fees paid by companies that included MonsterMoving's relocation information on their intranet sites; a year's subscription was priced at $25,000.

A small percentage of revenue came from referral fees. MonsterMoving received referral fees for services ordered through the site including truck rental, storage space reservations, and credit reports. Referral fees varied depending on the service. For example, MonsterMoving received $35 from one major truck rental company for each truck rental reservation made by a visitor that originated from the site. The company was paid an $8 referral fee when a visitor clicked on the PersonalCredit center through to one of MonsterMoving's financial partners who provided credit reports to MonsterMoving's users for a fee. Zorn, who reported to Taylor, believed the company's growth would come largely from transaction fees, "We would like to be involved in all transactions in the moving process: from helping families find a mortgage, to scheduling a moving company, arranging storage, and assisting with child care arrangements in their new community."

MonsterMoving maintained its own sales force (55 of 120 MonsterMoving employees were sales representatives), marketing group, and financial planning/analysis team. MonsterMoving shared legal, HR, and finance operations with TMP. MonsterMoving had a link on its site to Monster.com, and shared back-office technology with Monster.

As of Fall 2001, 250 companies used MonsterMoving's relocation tools including General Motors, Ford, Goldman Sachs, AOL/Time Warner, Microsoft, and Disney. The site received approximately 1 million new visitors a month. Zorn believed that by 2004, the company would have a pretax profit margin of 25%, and that 70% of incremental revenue would fall to the bottom line. He predicted that as a percentage of incremental revenue, cost of sales (sales force and sales administration) would be 15%; marketing, 10%; and technology, 5%.

MonsterLearning Launched in Fall 2001 as a business unit within Monster.com, MonsterLearning was an online learning resource serving individual and corporate learning seekers (corporate trainers and hiring managers). Linda Natansohn, the head of MonsterLearning, explained the rationale for its creation:

> Monster's value proposition has always been to help people manage their career from intern to CEO. To date, we've fulfilled that commitment primarily by helping people change jobs. But as earning and learning go hand in hand, we can become even more valuable to our users by providing them with tools and information that allow them to manage their skills and knowledge as it relates to career advancement. Our research showed that consumers think this is a very logical extension for Monster.

MonsterLearning's search function allowed individual and corporate learning seekers to search the site by selecting what they wanted to learn, how they wanted to learn (classroom, online), and the types of learning they preferred (conferences, seminars, degree programs). Once an appealing learning opportunity was found, the seeker simply clicked on a link that would take them to the provider's website for more information or to enroll. In this way, managers believed that MonsterLearning enabled learning providers to extend their reach and broaden their audience. If the provider did not have a website, the link would automatically generate an email window so seekers could contact the provider for more information.

Learning providers could purchase memberships (ranging anywhere from $1,000 to $10,000+) that were tiered depending on the number of learning opportunities the provider had to offer. MonsterLearning also had an *a la carte* selection of ad offerings that providers could purchase, such as placing ads in MonsterLearning's newsletters. While MonsterLearning had its own dedicated telesales force, TMP's Educational Marketing Group, part of TMP's Advertising and Communications division that focused on helping learning institutions brand and recruit more successfully, was cross-trained to sell offerings on MonsterLearning. With a link to Monster.com on its site, managers noted that MonsterLearning supported Monster's core business of helping people manage their careers. The primary source of MonsterLearning's website traffic was Monster.com.

Although MonsterLearning initially served both the individual and corporate learning seeker, it planned to launch a B2B product of online course offerings that would enable corporate trainers and hiring managers "to manage their company's human capital needs in an efficient, accessible, cost effective, Web-based system."[25] Corporate online training was predicted to grow from $1.1 billion in 1999 to $11.4 billion in 2003.[26] Manager's believed Monster would be able to cross-sell its e-learning services to the more than 35,000 corporate (job-posting) customers Monster served as of Fall 2001 in its core business.

According to Natansohn, one of MonsterLearning's biggest challenges, especially with its pending Monster Learning System, was Monster's lack of credibility in the learning market:

> I've worked at Monster for five years and while we have always referred to ourselves as a "career management" destination, the market has—and in many ways still does—perceive us as a "job board" specializing in employment listings. As we build out an entirely new client base comprised of learning providers—from traditional institutions to for-profit education organizations—we will have to prove everyday that we understand their diverse recruiting needs and that it is more cost-effective to spend their dollars with Monster than with traditional media or other online competitors. Our tremendous brand awareness helps get attention, but it does not close sales for us.

An Inconsistent, Insecure Job Market

In Fall 2001, the U.S. job market was experiencing rising unemployment (between July and August unemployment rose from 4.5% to 4.9%) coupled with a shortage in skilled labor that was expected to increase until 2008 with the retirement of baby-boomers. It remained unseen how companies' short-term and long-term recruiting practices would handle these two conflicting pressures.[27]

While Taylor was concerned about Monster's short-term growth, he remained optimistic on the long-term outlook:

> Employers are not complaining about prices or going to our competitors. They are simply in a holding pattern. On hold is a hard place for them—and for us—to be. But mark my words, we will not only be a survivor, we will have a lot more to say in the future. As the Monster brand has grown, we've come to believe we can expand the platform to a broader definition of career management. We're not going to start an on-line car wash, but we can deliver more value to our job seekers and employer members, and capture value for ourselves in the process.

---

[25] MonsterLearning internal document, September 2001.

[26] "The Knowledge Web," *Merrill Lynch*, May 2000.

[27] William Bird, "Who's been eating my newspaper?" *Salomon Smith Barney*, July 1, 2001.

Exhibit 1 Monster Revenue and Profitability ($ millions)

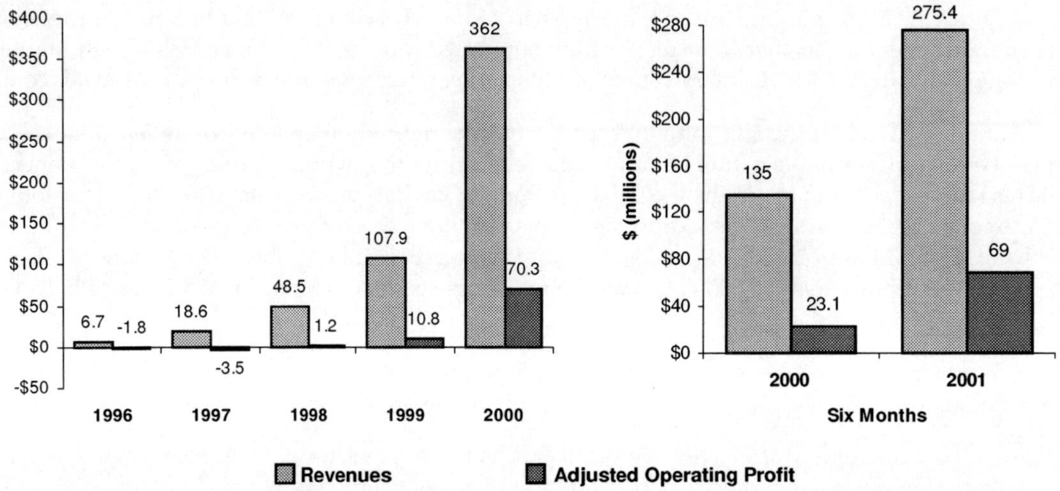

Note: As originally reported without adjustements for subsequent poolings

Source: Monster.com

Exhibit 2 TMP Human Resource Market Segments (excludes Yellow Pages advertising)

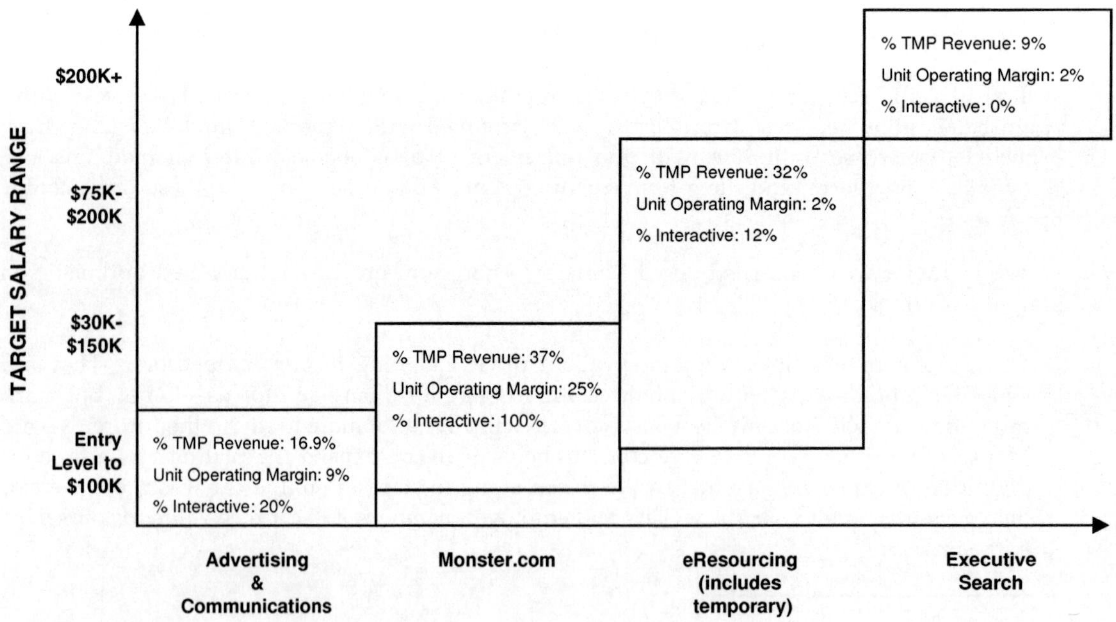

Source: Adapted from U.S. Bancorp Piper Jaffray.

Exhibit 3a TMP Financials (in thousands)

Information by Business Segment	Year Ended December 31, 1998		Year Ended December 31, 1999		Year Ended December 31, 2000	
	Monster.com	TMP[a]	Monster.com	TMP[a]	Monster.com	TMP[a]
Commissions and Fees:						
Traditional sources	--	$706,980	--	$ 750,740	--	$ 856,554
Interactive	$59,410	64,858	$126,121	158,215	$361,950	435,183
Total Commissions and Fees	59,410	771,838	126,121	908,955	361,950	1,291,731
Operating Expenses:						
Traditional[b]	--	603,473	--	647,478	--	752,933
Interactive[b]	57,916	62,673	112,674	157,682	291,195	363,260
Merger and acquisition costs	--	22,412	--	63,054	4,668	64,604
Restructuring charges	--	3,543	--	2,789	445	16,536
Amortization of intangibles	234	11,281	236	12,894	296,308	1,197,333
Total Operating Expenses	58,150	703,382	112,910	883,897		883,897
Operating Income (loss):						
Traditional sources	--	66,515	--	24,778	--	33,829
Interactive	1,260	1,941	13,211	280	65,642	60,575
Total Operating Income (loss)	$ 1,260	68,456	$ 13,211	25,058	$ 65,642	94,404
Total Assets	$ 38,775	$933,873	$ 99,920	$1,098,765	$200,544	$1,991,843

Source: TMP

[a] Including Monster.com.

[b] Is comprised of salaries & related; office & general; marketing & promotion; CEO special bonus; and allocated overhead.

Exhibit 3b Selected TMP Divisional Financials (in thousands)

Year Ended December 31, 2000	Monster.com	Advertising & Communications	Executive Search
Total commissions and fees	$361,950	$225,727	$178,429
Total operating income	$ 65,642	$ 19,792	$ 2,779
Total operating income as a % of commissions and fees	18.1%	8.7%	1.6%
Total operating income as a % of assets allocated to the segment	33%	2%	1.2%

Source: TMP

Exhibit 4a TMP Worldwide Relative Stock Price Performance, December 1996-September 2001

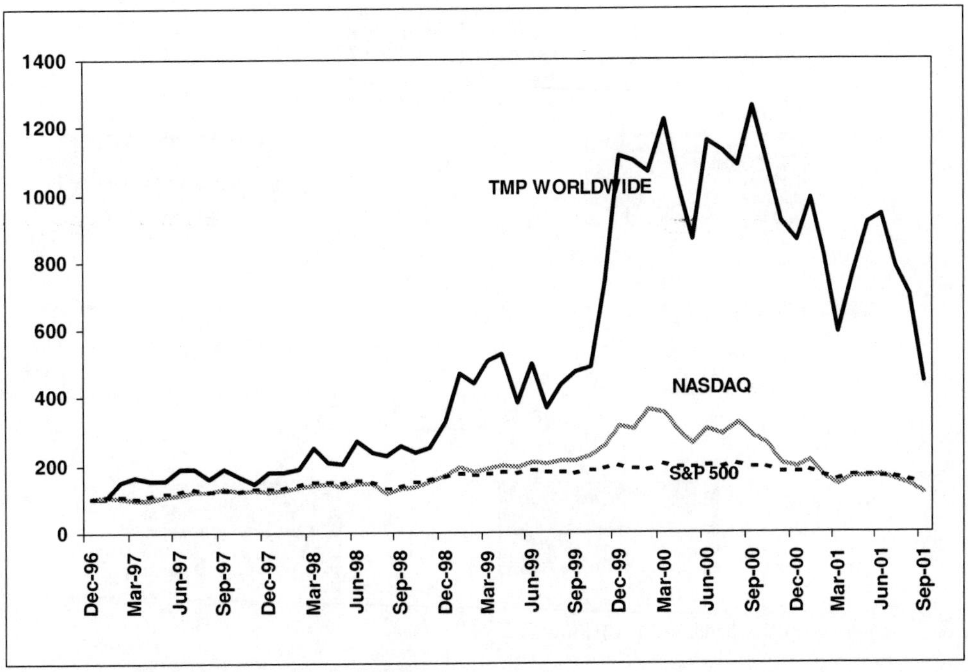

Exhibit 4b TMP Worldwide Price Earnings Ratio

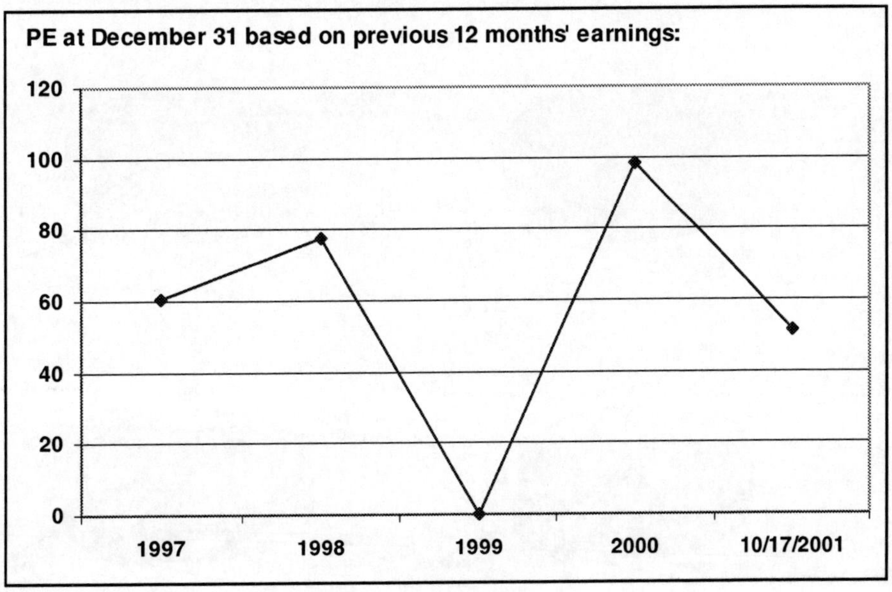

Source: *Datastream*

Note: TMP went public in December 1996. 1999 PE is not applicable due to a loss incurred that year.

Exhibit 5 Growth Drivers for Human Capital Firms

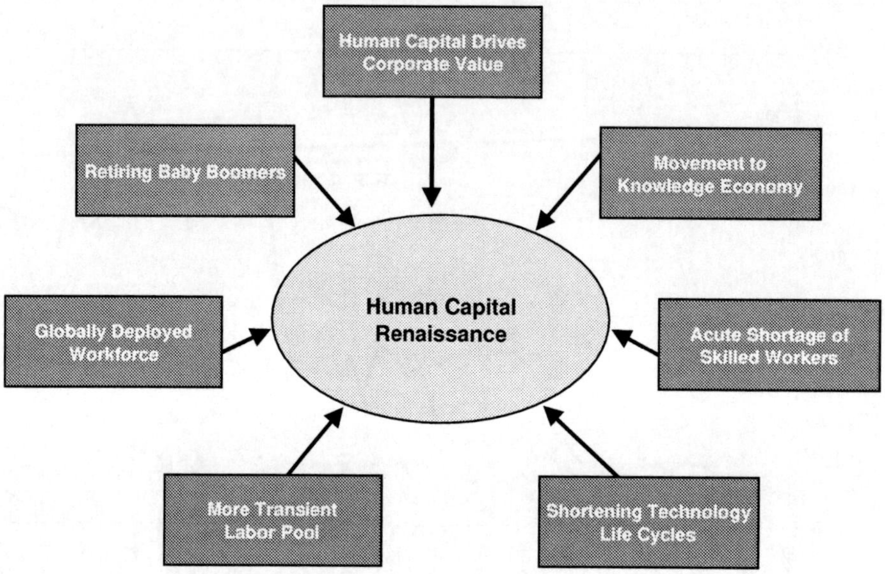

Source: Adapted from U.S. Bancorp Piper Jaffray.

Exhibit 6 U.S. Job Recruiting Spending Share

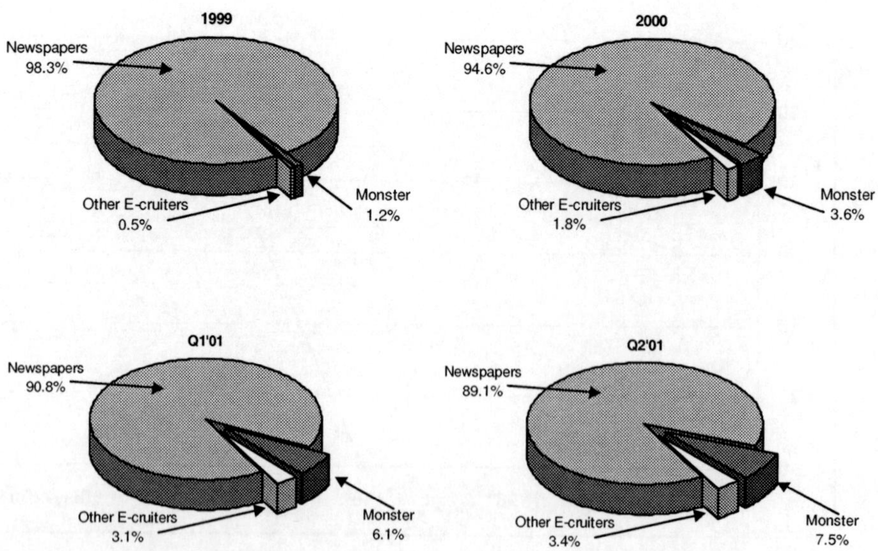

Source: Adapted from First Union Securities, Company Reports, NAA.

Exhibit 7 Average Cost/Time per Hire

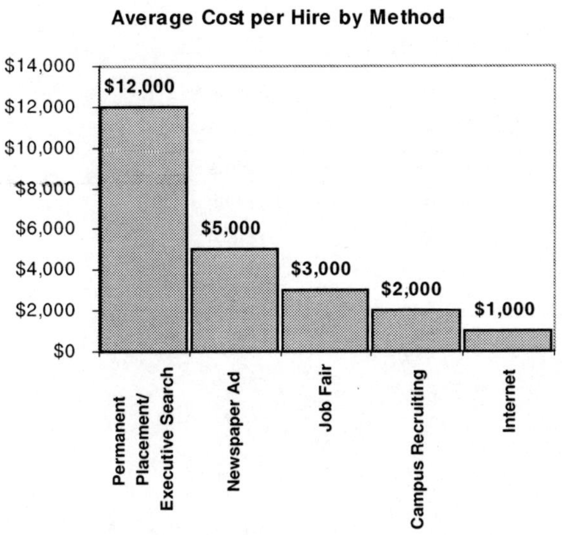

Source: Adapted from recruitsoft.com/iLogos 1998 Survey via Monster.com site.

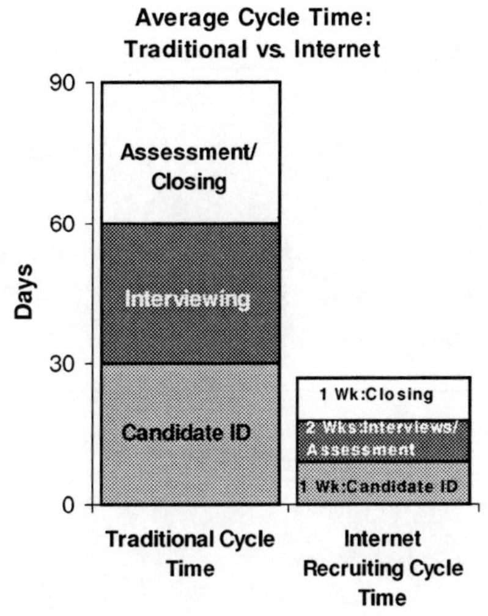

Source: Adapted from Kennedy Information via Monster.com site.

Exhibit 8 Online Recruitment Advertisement Market Share

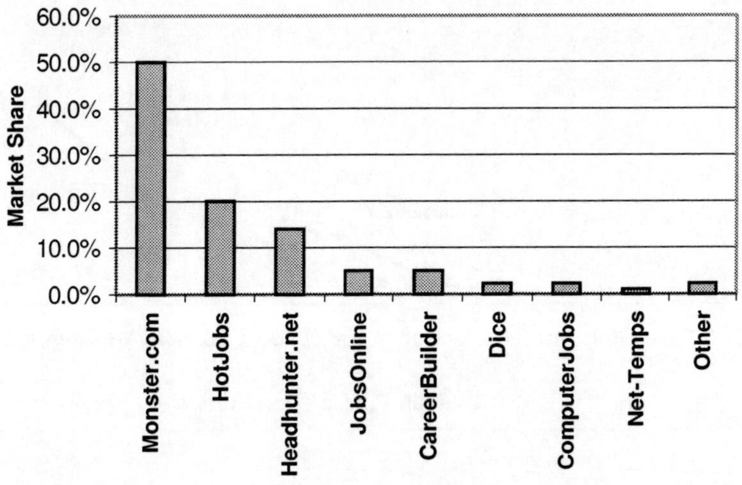

Source: Adapted from U.S. Bancorp Piper Jaffray and Media Metrix.

Exhibit 9 Sample of Monster's Membership Pricing

Membership	Price	Jobs Listed	Resume Database Access
1 month	$2,500	5	1 month
1 month	$1,500	3	1 month
3 months	$5,500	15	3 months
6 months	$7,500	30	6 months
3-month resume access only	$4,800	NA	NA
Additional user for 3 months	$2,750		

Source: Monster.com

Exhibit 10 Monster Resume Database in Europe and Asia: September 1999 to August 2001 (thousands of resumes)

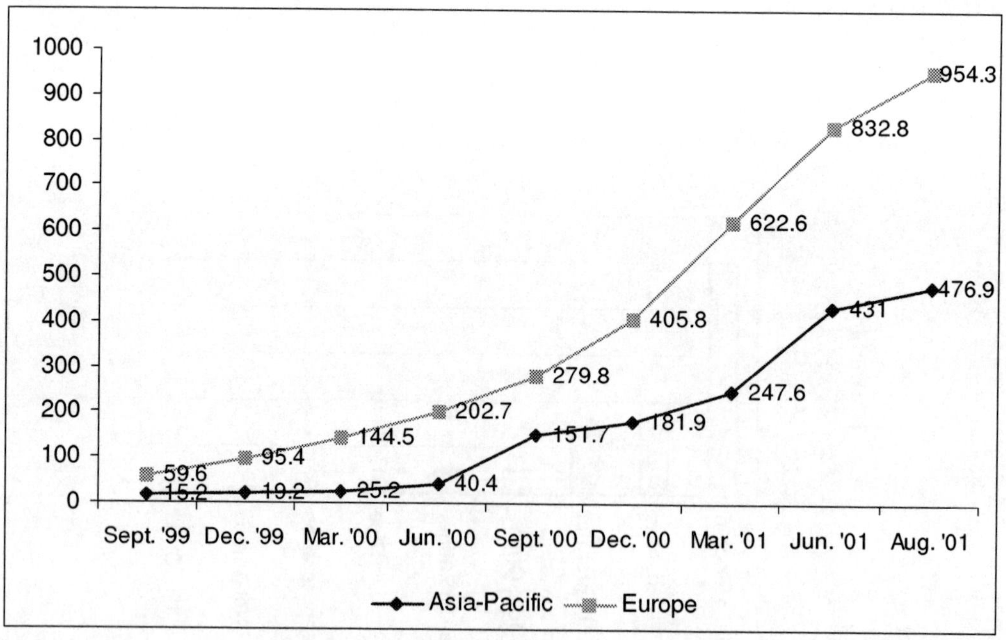

Source: Monster.com

Exhibit 11 Selected European Markets Power Ranking (August 2001)

Belgium		Spain		Netherlands		Italy		United Kingdom		France		Germany	
Vdab	353.3	Infojobs	203.9	Monster	57.5	Monster	34.7	Monster	28.3	ANPE	274.0	Arbeitsamt	226.2
Stepstone	165.0	Monster	14.4	Werk	57.0	Stepstone	31.7	Workthing	17.0	Monster	48.7	Jobpilot	41.4
Monster	60.8	Jobpilot	10.5	Stepstone	16.7	BancaLavora	14.5	TotalJobs	14.4	Jobpilot	25.3	Stepstone	33.6
Jobs-career	56.5	Infoempleo/CdP	10.2	Clickwork	14.8	Jobpilot	9.5	Stepstone	12.0	Cadremploi	21.6	Monster	22.9
Vacature	35.8	Laboris.net	1.5	Jobpilot	7.4	Cliccalavoro	3.6	Reed	11.9	Emailjob	18.7	Jobscout24	12.7
Jobpilot	21.6	Stepstone	0.4			TalentManager	1.0	Gojobsite	10.7	Cadresonline	13.4	Job	11.6
Jobat	6.1							TopJobs	4.8	Stepstone	8.6	Jobware	8.0
Lesoir	2.5							Fish4Jobs	1.9				

Source: Adapted from Nielsen/Net Ratings (accessed from Monster.com, October 4, 2001).

Bibliography

"Strategy and the Internet (HBR OnPoint Enhanced Edition)." Porter, Michael E. In ***HBR OnPoint***, Case No. 6358. Published 03/01/2001, **Harvard Business School Publishing,** (21 pages).

"The Real New Economy (HBR OnPoint Enhanced Edition)." Farrell, Diana. In ***HBR OnPoint***, Case No. 5127. Published 10/01/2003, **Harvard Business School Publishing,** (12 pages).

"Chapter 2. The Big Picture: IT and Business." Paul Gray. In ***Manager's Guide to Making Decisions about Information Systems***, pp. 15–36. Published 2006, **John Wiley and Sons, Inc.** (22 pages).

"The Worldwide Web and Internet Technology, Technology Note." Austin, Robert D.; Rodd, Thomas. Case No. 9–198–020. Published 10/08/1997, Revised 02/13/2003. **Harvard Business School Publishing,** (10 pages).

"Web and IT Hosting Facilities, Technology Note." Austin, Robert D. Case No. 9–601–134. Published 04/10/2001, Revised 03/04/2003. **Harvard Business School Publishing,** (11 pages).

"Digital Certificates and Signatures: Microsoft Corp." Farhoomand, Ali F.; Ho, Mary. Case No. HKU203. Published 7/12/2002, **University of Hong Kong,** (3 pages).

"The iPremier Co.: Denial of Service Attack (A)." Austin, Robert D.; Leibrock, Larry; Murray, Alan. Case No. 9–601–114. Published 02/13/2001, Revised 10/17/2003. **Harvard Business School Publishing,** (12 pages).

"Your Next IT Strategy." Hagel, John, III; Brown, John Seely. In ***Harvard Business Review***, Case No. R0109G. Published 10/01/2001, **Harvard Business School Publishing,** (9 pages).

"Cisco Systems Architecture: ERP and Web–enabled IT." Nolan, Richard L.; Porter, Kelley; Akers, Christina. Case No. 9–301–099. Published 03/24/2001, Revised 10/15/2001. **Harvard Business School Publishing,** (23 pages).

"Chapter 4. Enterprise Requirements Planning." Paul Gray. In ***Manager's Guide to Making Decisions about Information Systems***, pp. 58–73. Published 2006, **John Wiley and Sons, Inc.** (16 pages).

"Chapter 11. IS in Managing Business Operations: The Supply Chain." Paul Gray. In ***Manager's Guide to Making Decisions about Information Systems***, pp. 200–215. Published 2006, **John Wiley and Sons, Inc.** (16 pages).

"Quantum Corp.: eSupplyChain Group." McAfee, Andrew; Bounds, Gregory. Case No. 9–601–099. Published 01/23/2001, Revised 03/31/2003. **Harvard Business School Publishing,** (20 pages).

"Monster.com: Success Beyond the Bubble." Hallowell, Roger; Reavis, Cate. Case No. 9–802–024. Published 11/15/2001, Revised 1/7/2002. **Harvard Business School Publishing,** (21 pages).